AGAINST THE ODDS:
THE MEANING OF SCHOOL AND
RELATIONSHIPS IN THE LIVES OF SIX
YOUNG AFRICAN-AMERICAN MEN

Issues in Curriculum Theory, Policy, and Research
Ian Westbury and Margery Osborne, Series Editors

AGAINST THE ODDS:
THE MEANING OF SCHOOL AND RELATIONSHIPS IN THE LIVES OF SIX YOUNG AFRICAN-AMERICAN MEN

Jeremy N. Price

ABLEX PUBLISHING
Westport, Connecticut • London

Printed in the United States of America

Library of Congress Cataloging-in-Publication Data

Price, Jeremy Nicholas.
      Against the odds: the meaning of school and relationships in the lives of six young African-American men / by Jeremy Nicholas Price.
         p.   cm. — (Issues in curriculum theory, policy, and research)
      Includes bibliographical references and index.
      ISBN 1-56750496-5 (cloth)—ISBN 1-56750-497-3 (pbk.)
      1. Afro-American   young   men—Education   (Secondary)—Social aspects—Case studies.   2. Afro-American students—Psychology—Case studies.   3.   Motivation   in   education—United   States—Case   studies. I. Title. II. Series.
  LC2779.P75   2000
  373.1829′96′073—dc21   99-053991
                                                        CIP

Ablex Publishing, 88 Post Road West, Westport, CT 06881
An imprint of Greenwood Publishing Group, Inc.
www.ablexbooks.com

10 9 8 7 6 5 4 3 2

Contents

Acknowledgments

I am deeply indebted to the six young African-American men who shared part of their lives with me, for without these young men, there would have been no study. They are all truly remarkable young men and taught me not only about their lives, but also about my own. There is no doubt in my mind that they each have enriched my life.

I have received support from many people as I have engaged in this study and written this book. My mentors at Michigan State University have supported me in extraordinary ways. In particular, I owe deep gratitude to Lynn Paine and Deborah Ball for the considerable intellectual, emotional, and professional support they have provided me. In addition, a core group of friends across the country and here at the University of Maryland at College Park has been with me in the dark and lonely moments of struggle, frustration, and exhilaration. They have helped me craft this body of work and flourish in the process. Finding the words that capture my gratitude to these people is not easy. They were *always* there for me. There are many who supported me, but I would especially like to thank Margery, Jim, Deb, Perry, and Michelle. A special thanks to my remarkable South African friends who taught me much about the political orientations that shape this work.

Finally, I would like to thank my parents who have taught me so much. They have always believed in me, even when I have been unsure of myself. I am very privileged to have such parents.

List of Tables

1

Introduction

Like when you grow up in the ghetto, they are like slums, basically set up for to keep a black person down. And when you grow up in that, you see things like that, and you be around it, it's just like you're going to be into it. 'Cause the steps already stand up so high, that you know, you ain't gonna get no black male in inner city, crime city, like Detroit where I'm from, he's not going to make it. No. And that's how it is. You know you are going to start getting in trouble, hanging out with the fellas, smoking bud, 'cause it's set up to hold us black people down.

—Dwayne Reynolds

I've got to uphold an image, with myself, my mom and people in Cedarville . . . disproving something. That not all black kids are just a bunch of dumb kids that like to play sports. And what I'm trying to do is, if I can play sports, have fun, and get good grades at the same time, maybe somebody else will try to do the same thing.

—Rashaud Dupont

One of the reasons I go to school, I just want that diploma. Because basically to me, they ain't there to teach, they're just there to get their paycheck at the end of the week. They ain't teaching you nothin'. 'Cause if they was teaching you something, they would be teaching you something about your black African culture, instead of teaching you white is superior. Because that is all they are teaching you, white is so superior, they dominate everything.

—Marcus Williams

These three perspectives represent the heart of this book: Three young African-American men, committed to attending school, develop similar yet different meanings of their school experiences and their lives beyond school. A common thread among these young men is their experiences of racism in the United States; in their own way, each had explanations and understandings of the impact of racism on what they could do and what their possibilities might be. At the same time, each statement suggests that their experiences of the economic world might differ. Significant in these meanings are the relationships with their family, friends, and teachers. Such meanings and relationships do not exist in a social vacuum; they are forged in social, political, economic, and cultural arenas. Within such arenas, access to power and privilege and their encounters of inequality and with some institutions see these young men developing different kinds of choices, different kinds of futures for themselves, and different meanings of success.

The perspectives of these three young men point to the importance of understanding the ways in which race and social class and gender might play out in their lives. Their accounts of their experiences reflect their notions of opportunity, their relationships to school, and their experiences as black men in relation to others in society. Although in part their views might seem quite different, there are threads in their lives that connect the young men's experiences. This book provides an opportunity to understand the threads that bind and separate the lives of six school-going African-American young men by exploring the meanings of their experiences in school, the different relationships they forged in and out of school, and their hopes and dreams for life beyond school.

Over the past 10 years there has been considerable growth in writing and research about African-American men and their experiences in school and society. A somber and depressing picture has been painted about the plight of black men in the United States. Writers such as Gibbs (1988), Madhubuti (1990), and Staples (1987) have documented the complexity of their lives. Part of the story is commonly framed through the numerous statistics about African-American men. And these are significant statistics, for they reflect complex power arrangements in United States society. For example, Gibbs (1988) and Franklin (1991), among others, have noted that African-American men, although accounting for 6 percent of the population in the United States, constitute almost 50 percent of the male prison population; between 1973 and 1987 the real earnings of black men aged 20 to 29 declined by 27.7 percent; 51 percent of black men living in metropolitan areas have been arrested, compared to only 14 percent of white men. Notwithstanding these haunting numbers about African-American men, Duneier (1992) noted that such statistics may tell us "most of what we know about what it means to be a black man in America, but they tell far too little about the black man's inner strength—his resolve, his pride, and his sincerity" (p. 26).

Our understanding of the lives of the six young men in my study needs to be situated in a cultural context that produces, on the one hand, pervasive unidimensional representations and images of black men, and on the other, increasing contributions that have documented the complexity of the lives of black men through intersecting and overlapping lenses of race, class, and gender. Notwithstanding the dominance of images and representations of African-American young men in the popular press and academic literature, there is little written about the texture and the complexity of the lives of young African American men who decide to stay in school. In particular, there is little empirical work that examines the range of school experiences. Through examining the meanings and experiences of these six young men, I hope to expand understandings of the complexities of the lives of African-American men and simultaneously challenge seemingly unidimensional images of black men. In particular, I examine the experiences of these six young men, who come from varying social class locations and attended four different schools. I explain and unravel the meanings they constructed of the high school diploma, their experiences in classrooms, and their relationships with family members and peers. I came to see relationships with family members and relationships with peers inside and outside of school as significant to the meanings they constructed of schooling. These meanings were also integral to their emerging social identities—their classed, racialized, and gendered identities (Collins, 1990; Connell, 1987; Dill & Baca Zinn, 1990; Harding, 1987; Kimmel & Messner, 1992; Smith, 1987; Weis, 1988).

SCHOOLING, POLITICS, AND CHANGE

As *all* children go to school, I live with the hope that they can achieve their potential and successfully participate in the economic, political, and social world on their own terms and in ways that serve their own interests. But such goals are not vividly represented in most educational systems throughout the world, and are the focus of many of the struggles for social change. My own experiences alongside others in the struggle for liberation in South African taught me about the importance of unity, strength, and action in challenging domination and oppression. Through this experience, I was forced to challenge my own privilege as a white, middle-class man and to challenge my conceptions of my role as a teacher in a so-called Colored high school. In working with others committed to fundamental social change in South Africa, I learned about the racism, sexism, and exploitation interwoven through the texture and structure of South African society. I learned about the Sharpeville Massacre of 1960; the Soweto uprising of 1976; the banning, detention, and imprisonment of many activists; and the death in detention of leaders such as Steve Biko and Neil Aggett. Leaders such as Biko inspired me. In his state trial he provided a framework for understanding racism in South Africa:

> The existence in our society of white racism . . . has been institutionalized, and also cushioned with the backing of the majority of whites. In other words, a white child does not have to choose whether or not he wants to live with the system. He is born

into it. He is brought up within white schools and institutions, and the whole process of racism is somehow with him at all levels, privileges that they hold, and they monopolize these away from black society. (Steve Biko, quoted in Woods, 1978, p. 184)

Through my readings and experiences I began to critique the forms of curriculum and pedagogy that pervaded many classrooms and that saw students coming to know and understand in ways that neglected or invariably silenced their biographies and histories—individually and collectively. United around a common thread of caring for human life and dignity, I also learned about the importance of connecting action for change in classrooms to other struggles through work with students, colleagues, parents, and members of the larger community. But the struggle in South Africa for a more democratic and just society and educational system is not idiosyncratic to the South African context. It is connected to other struggles for and about education around the world where educational systems are often seen as representing the interests and experiences of dominant groups in society. But schooling is more complex than this in that schools also have the potential to be a site of emancipation for all students.

As in South Africa, the history of the educational system in the United States can be seen as a struggle to develop and promote a more just and democratic educational experience, particularly by subordinated and oppressed groups. Education is about politics; thus, within this context of struggle, young African-American men attending school today continue to face incredible challenges. Over the past 40 years, numerous actions, programs, and policies have attempted to address the needs of African-American men, with many reforms not being successful in meeting their needs or interests. Further, as many writers have noted, sadly missing from discussions about change in education are issues about power relations, about the overarching dominance of Eurocentric, capitalist, and masculinist ideologies. Key to any programs or policies focused on African-American men are questions such as these: On whose terms? To whose benefit? At what cost? To continue to think and respond to these questions, through developing programs, policies, curriculum, and pedagogy aimed at meeting the needs of African-Americans, in part requires a close scrutiny of the lives and daily experiences of African-Americans in and out of school. We need to understand what and how African-American men make sense of their schooling experiences in the 1990s.

At the time the six young men in this study went to school, there were numerous attacks and assaults against the educational system from both the left and the right. Demands for an educational system that was more inclusive, which suggested alternative pedagogy or curriculum, were often met with school reforms that had been diluted into strategies that "add on" multicultural literature and textbooks. (Sleeter & Grant, 1987, and Sleeter, 1991, provide an excellent discussion of the different versions of multiculturalism that have taken root in the United States.)

In the end, many of these approaches for change have failed to challenge the fundamental structures of the educational system. Few approaches fundamentally challenge the definitions of school knowledge from the multiple perspectives and identities of raced, gendered, and economically oppressed and exploited groups. As Grant (1988) argued, "The relationship of race (with the exception of the white race) to power, economics and *culture* has never been a part of the core curriculum in schools, and schools are slow to accept multicultural education or make needed changes" (p. 567). Approaches influenced by critical theory have also been criticized for their inadequate analysis of race in the United States. Currents of critical theory (see Giroux, 1983; McLaren, 1989) may view schools as a site for the struggle for power and authority, yet as Ladson-Billings (1994) noted, "The failure of these theorists to examine adequately the special historical, social, economic, and political role that race plays in the United States makes their arguments less than complete for improving the educational lives of African Americans" (p. 16). At the same time, writers such as Bloom (1987) and Hirsch (1987) have contributed to the reaffirmation of Eurocentricism in debates over the school curriculum and educational reform. In addition, while debates about representation in schooling abound, few approaches consider the interlocking systems of race, class and gender in critical analyses of schooling.

Further, Apple (1994) suggested that the current wave of "conservative restoration" in the United States is hallmarked by its "unremitting attack on education." He argues that:

> National curricula and assessment, greater opportunities for 'parental choice,' tighter accountability and control, the marketization and privatization of education—all of these proposals may be internally contradictory as a set of 'reforms,' but all are part of a conservative package that have been formed by the neo-liberal and neo-conservative wings of this movement. Some of [the] criticisms leveled by conservatives are partly correct. But, the political and educational response of the Right leads in exactly the wrong direction . . . for the majority of people in this society. (p. 3)

And the litany of the attacks on education continues. At the time of this study, groups in California sought the passing of Proposition 187 and the exclusion of "illegal immigrants" from social services, including schooling. And, more recently, the reform pendulum in some states has swung to an insistence on a "back-to-basics" curriculum. Amidst the often-turbulent currents of various political agendas, however, many students continue to attend school. And those students who are "allowed" or who manage to sustain themselves to complete and succeed in schools do so in contexts where curriculum, pedagogy, and social relationships, in the main, serve to foster privilege for some and penalty for others through a structure and culture of class, gender, and race domination. For African-American students, absent from many of their educational experiences are the voices and images of African-Americans past and present that are integral to any story about the United States, its culture, and its people. Also absent are opportunities to know and understand the world on their own terms.

Building an educational system that meets the demands, interests, and potentials of subordinate groups is one of the enduring struggles that has faced teachers, students, and parents for the past 100 years. The reality facing many students of color in the United States is that they will attend a school where their interests are not represented, where their voices are not heard, and where the likelihood of fulfilling their potential is diminished. However, despite the attacks on the educational system, the struggles for emancipatory curricula and pedagogies (Freire, 1994; hooks, 1994; Shor, 1992; Weiler, 1988) continue. And amidst these debates and struggles many students continue to go to school. Why is it that students who are excluded and marginalized, in the face of so much adversity, continue to go to school? Do they wholeheartedly embrace meritocratic ideology? Do they hanker after material wealth and prosperity? Or is it more complex than that? What meanings do they develop of their schooling experiences? What barriers or penalties may they encounter as they pursue the high school diploma? This study examines these questions through exploring the perspectives of six young men who have decided to stay in school—who in the face of many obstacles get up each day and go to school, attend classes, and attempt to acquire a high school diploma.

YOUNG AFRICAN-AMERICAN MEN, SCHOOLING, AND SOCIETY

Young African-American men attending school today face incredible challenges. It has been well documented how schools have historically ill served African Americans (Lomotey, 1990; Patton, 1981). From the desegregation era of the 1960s to the present day, schools remain and are seen as Eurocentric institutions that require people of color to engage in the process of schooling on white terms (Ogbu, 1988). Though there have been dramatic changes in the access and opportunities afforded African-Americans attending school, little in reality seems to have changed (Grant, 1988). Although there has been a steady decline over the past 30 years in the number of African-American youth dropping out of school, more than one out of five black youth in the 18 to 21 age group do not have the necessary skills for entry-level jobs, apprenticeship programs, or post-secondary education (Gibbs, 1988, p. 6). At the same time, as Mickelson and Smith (1992) noted, while differences in educational attainment may have narrowed somewhat among racial groups, people of color earn on average "significantly less than their white males with comparable educational credentials" (p. 367). Such comparative outcomes tell us about African-American youth and the racial inequities that seem persistent in the labor market. However, what these statistics do not tell us about are the textured experiences of African-Americans in school. These statistics do not tell us the stories of the young men of color who possess the "comparable education credentials," nor do they unravel the complicated picture of their acquisition of such credentials. But it is not just their individual stories that I am interested in. I am also interested in understanding larger questions about access to power and privilege, and the penalties and barriers that may lie in the paths of young African-American men in pursuit of the high school credential.

Responses to Schooling

Those who remain in school remain tied to an institution in which the interaction of structure and social practice contributes to the reproduction and production of race, class, and gender relations of domination in society. But the educational system does not do this alone. It is connected to other institutions that also reflect the interests and activities of the dominating groups. I am in agreement with Mac an Ghaill (1993), who argues that, "The education system is part of a wider system of constraints which, often unwittingly, help to maintain blacks in a position of structural subordination. The major problem in the schooling of black youth is not that of their culture but of racism" (p. 3).

Recent work about the lives of black male students' relationship with school has primarily focused on issues of race and social class. Mac an Ghaill's (1988) study in England, MacLeod's (1995) study in the United States, and Solomon's (1992) study in Canada each attempted to blend stories of black men's relationship with school with larger issues of inequality and oppression. An additional significant contribution has been Weis's (1985) *Between Two Worlds,* in which she provides a powerful ethnographic account for understanding the culture that black community college students construct. In the following pages, I briefly examine each of these works and consider their contributions toward understanding the school experiences of young black men.

A significant study that provides a well-documented account of the formation of an oppositional subcultural group in school is Solomon's (1992) study, *Black Resistance in High School,* about West Indian immigrants in Canada. He focuses on a group of young black working-class men, the "Jocks," and highlights the institutional and broader societal factors that give rise to the oppositional nature of the relationship between the students' subculture and the authority structure of a high school. Solomon suggests that the Jocks' culture of resistance is linked to "a history of white superiority and black inferiority in the slave culture followed by a black exclusion from full participation in the economic, social, and political life [which] nurtured the development of a black oppositional identity" (p. 106). Thus, these students arrived at school with a "predisposition to oppose the dominant-culture institutions they perceive as biased" (p. 107). He argues that the Jocks were able to resist the forms of schooling they detested and simultaneously maintain their commitment to achievement ideology. But their response to school, that of rejecting the dominant culture of schooling, saw them forming an oppositional culture which is not rewarded in the ways that dominant cultural practices are rewarded. The study is significant on one level because it links social responses to school to factors both inside and outside of the school, and on another because it addresses the ways in which race and social class play out in the lives of these young men.

Another significant study that examines the resistance of black males is Mac an Ghaill's (1988) *Young, Gifted and Black*. Here, he examines teacher ideologies and practices and black male and female students' responses and resistances at two inner-city schools in England. He focuses on how racism is mediated through the institutional framework of the schooling process and students' responses to racist practices in school. The black young men and women in his study experience a "different reality" from the white population at school and in the larger society. Their responses to their experiences, can be seen as "involving creative strategies of survival" (p. 155). Through focusing on the ways in which class location informed different students' experiences, Mac an Ghaill argues that "class location informed the students' experience of and response to the dominant social relations of the school and the wider society and, through these relations, their experience and response to racism" (p. 138).

Mac an Ghaill's exploration of the responses of black working-class young women, the "Black Sisters," reveals that they responded to their schooling through a strategy of "resistance within accommodation" where they simultaneously rejected "the racist curriculum" and highly valued "the acquisition of academic qualifications" (1988, p. 11). They valued the academic qualification because it had meaning beyond a vehicle for economic survival via a job. Acquiring the credential was also seen "as a means of social psychological and political development" (p. 35). The black males' responses to schooling— reflected in an Afro-Caribbean group, the "Rasta Heads," and an Asian group, the "Warriors"—suggest different patterns of resistance between the two groups and to the black young women. The two male groups adopted particular kinds of strategies of resistance as a result of how they were perceived by their teachers. The Rasta Heads were perceived by teachers as "rebellious." These students managed and perceived this racism through adopting a response "that was expected of them, and overtly challenged the authority of the school" (p. 85). At the same time, the Warriors were perceived as passive by the teachers who imposed middle-class values upon all the Asian males, which helped to make the forms of responses in school seem "invisible" compared to the visible forms of resistance adopted by the Rasta Heads. Thus, both groups rejected formal schooling, but adopted different strategies. Together with the Black Sisters, they all viewed racism as a major problem in their schooling. But their differing experiences saw the strategies of resistance of the young black men contrast with the Black Sisters' response, a strategy of being pro-education but anti-school.

Mac an Ghaill's (1988) intimate portrait of the young black students' experiences of school provides a significant contribution toward understanding different responses to school. His analysis suggests that different strategies reflect various patterns of gender, race, and social class interwoven through students' lives. Mac an Ghaill's study is one of the most comprehensive works to explore the interplay of raced, classed, and gendered structures and cultural practices in the lives of different groups within the black community that see different responses and resistance to school emerging.

Another significant study that focuses on race and class in the lives of students is MacLeod's (1995) study, *Ain't No Makin' It*. MacLeod explores the lives and orientations toward school of two groups of working-class young men, an African-American group, the "Brothers," and a white group, the "Hallway Hangers." These young men attended the same school and lived in the same housing project, yet they responded to their circumstances differently. MacLeod explored the relationship between schooling and achievement ideology in the lives of these two groups of young men and argues that the Brothers embraced schooling because they believed the era of civil rights had created possibilities for equality of opportunity. At the same time, the Hallway Hangers did not embrace school. In fact, they rejected schooling because they saw their parents struggling to get ahead with little success and saw no hope for themselves. The study is impressive because it focused on differences in family, social class, and attainment that led to the Brothers accepting achievement ideology and the Hallway Hangers rejecting such beliefs. MacLeod develops a fine-grained analysis of the interplay of social class and race in the lives of school-going students.

These studies are significant because they explain the ways in which race and social class experiences interact in the lives of young black men in school. They also suggest that patterns of resistance may take different forms depending on the historical and situated circumstances of race-class groups in particular national contexts. These studies not only focus on the lives of young black men inside school, but also examine their lives outside of the context of school, in their families and in peer group networks. Together with the autobiographical accounts of Ladd (1994), McCall (1994), and Staples (1994), these works help us understand the complex circumstances and experiences of African-American men in U.S. society.

Having discussed these works, it is important to note that there are relatively few accounts of young African-American men's relationship with school, particularly from those who decide to stay in school. In fact, there is a dearth of studies that reflect the experiences of a *range* of young African-American men and their relationship with school. Those studies that focus on African-American men's experiences in or out of school, in the main, tend to focus on inner-city experiences. In saying this, I do not want to minimize the importance of documenting the complex circumstances and devastating consequences over time of the life experiences of young black men in the inner city. Rather, I am arguing that there are few accounts that reflect a range of experiences about young African-American men's relationships with schooling. Notably, many of these studies do not explain the multiple emerging identities of black men through a race, class, and gender lens. The relatively small number of accounts that represent the range of interests and struggles of African-American men and their relations with schools is no accident. West (1993a) notes that:

> The modern black diaspora problematic of invisibility and namelessness can be understood as the condition of *relative lack of black power to represent themselves to themselves and others as complex human beings, and thereby to contest the bombardment of negative, degrading stereotypes put forward by white-supremacist ideologies.* (p. 16)

In noting the paucity of studies about African-American young men's experiences in school, I am suggesting that there are few that focus on schooling through a race, class, and gender matrix. Further, there are very few studies (see Benyon, 1990; Lesko, 2000; Mac an Ghaill, 1994b; Measor, 1983; Thorne, 1993) that have considered the social construction of masculinities and taken gender as a central axis of domination for understanding the gendered lives of boys and young men attending school, let alone focus on race, gender, and class interconnections.

Within educational discourse, Sleeter and Grant (1988), among others, have argued for the "need to build a theory that integrates racism and sexism with class relations, and that does not treat two of these as subsidiary to the third" (p. 149). Similarly, McCarthy and Apple (1988) and McCarthy (1994) draw our attention to "contradiction" and "nonsyncrony" among the dynamics of race, class, and gender. At issue here is that race, class, and gender are not viewed as parallel dynamics, but in fact may interact in ways that they may contradict each other. Race, social class, and gender intermingle in the lives of individuals and groups and have contradictory effects even in similar institutional settings. In this way, understanding race, class, and gender means not only considering the ways in which these dimensions of social circumstance play out in the young men's lives, but also understanding the ways in which these dimensions play out differently in their lives.

Such an analysis requires an investigation not only of the complexity of the interconnections of race, class and gender, but of each dimension of the dynamic. As Ng (1994) argued, race, class, and gender are not simply categories reflecting different and separate spheres of social life, rather they are *"relations* that organize our productive and reproductive activities, located in time and space . . . they are concrete social relations that are discoverable in the everyday world of experiences" (p. 50). Such arguments speak to the complexity of understanding the interconnections and interrelationships of race, class, and gender in the lives of individuals and groups.

INTERCONNECTING SYSTEMS OF CLASS, RACE, AND GENDER

In the social sciences more broadly, there have been tremendous advances and contributions, particularly from critical and feminist scholars, to the debates about our understanding of our social world and the identities we construct and live out. Some of the most challenging contributions have been advanced by feminist scholars of color who have questioned the orientations and theories of many feminists' works and who have further questioned explanations for the continued domination and oppression of people of color (Anderson & Collins, 1992; Anthias & Yuval-Davis, 1992; Baca Zinn & Dill, 1994; Collins, 1990). In particular, they have challenged the domination of Eurocentric constructs about gendered experiences that have infiltrated many of the images, concepts, and ideas that inform the meanings many of us construct in our daily lives. In addition, these scholars have challenged explanations for the ways race, class, and gender are conceptualized and viewed in relation to one another.

Axes of Domination and Oppression

As I noted earlier, these various contributions have helped me develop an understanding of systems of gender, race, and class oppression and domination as interconnecting and overlapping. Connell, Ashenden, Kessler, and Dowsett (1982) suggest that class and gender, and I would add here race (see Omi & Winant, 1986), are "structures of power":

> They involve control by some people over others, and the ability of some groups to organize social life to their own advantage. As power is exercised and contested, social relations are organized, and come to be in some degree a system . . . both class and gender are *historical* systems . . . indeed it may be better to think about them as *structuring processes* rather than 'systems', that is, ways in which social life is constantly being organized (and ruptured and disorganized) through time (Connell et al., 1982, p. 180).

Viewing race, class, and gender as involving control, and the "ability of some groups to organize social life to their own advantage," allows us to see race, gender, and class as processes of exclusion and subordination that involve differential access to resources. These forms of social division emerge historically, which suggests that these relationships may change, as Connell argued, "as power is examined and contested." Within these relations of domination and oppression, on a functional level, there are some that control, and there are others who are controlled. However, the relation is complex in that this relation is not simply reproduced in institutions such as school, the media, or the legal system. Rather culture, social identity, and social relations are produced through a dynamic of structure and agency. Here, it is important to note that relations are produced through the creation and negotiation of meaning and culture in contexts that are dynamically shaped by structures of power relations.

The idea of hegemony is important in understanding the notion of control and the meanings these young men give to their experiences as they construct their social identity. Hegemony can be seen as a form of social control based on consent. Femia (1981) suggests that schooling, in tandem with other institutions, "shape[s], directly or indirectly, the cognitive and affective structures whereby men perceive and evaluate problems and social reality" (p. 24). In essence, hegemony acknowledges the tensions between groups and *how* these groups are formed. The depth of social consensus about meanings, images, and relationships is important to sustain the relationship between groups. This does not mean that there are individuals and groups of individuals who do not recognize and challenge their domination. Rather, "It is a question of how particular groups of men inhabit positions of power and wealth, and how they legitimate and reproduce social relations that generate their dominance" (Carrigan et al, 1985, p. 92).

Race as an Axis of Social Organization

Also significant to my understanding of a matrix of race, class, and gender domination and oppression (Collins, 1990) has been the challenging work about conceptions of race articulated by Omi and Winant (1986). They give theoretical primacy to race as "the fundamental axis of social organization in the United States." They argued that

> The meaning of race is defined and contested through a society, in both collective action and personal practice. In the process, racial categories themselves are formed, transformed, destroyed and re-formed. We use the term *racial formation* to refer to the process by which social, economic and political forces determine the content and importance of racial meanings, and by which they are in turn shaped by racial meanings. (Omi & Winant, 1986, p. 61)

Their work is helpful in conceptualizing race, particularly the process by which the meaning of race is "defined and contested" in a society. Rather than arguing that race reflects "cultural differences," they argue that race is built into the structure of society. As Baca Zinn and Dill (1994) argued, the problem with the cultural difference approach as a central explanation of inequality "is the tendency to marginalize each cultural group, to view as unique, and to imply that each differs from some presumed standard. This often leads to blaming a people's cultural values and practice for their subordination" (p. 4). Through focusing on race at the levels of institutions and social practice, they argue that racial categories can be seen as always in the making, as "race both shapes the individual psyche and 'colors' relationships among individuals on the one hand, and furnishes an irreducible component of collective identities and social structures on the other" (Winant, 1994, p. 59). Important in understanding racial formation is recognizing that the meaning of racial categories may differ from one national context to another. For instance, under the apartheid regime in South Africa, "Black" was used as a social category to define people who spoke indigenous African languages that included Xhosa, Sotho and Zulu, and was a separate racial category from "Colored" (of mixed race).

Understanding race as a social construct and as a component of social structures and practices becomes relevant in explaining the experiences of these young men as they went to school and made sense of the world. For example, while in some ways these six young men may be seen as benefiting from a gender order, race and social class intersect with their gendered experiences in ways that they may be privileged because of their gender but penalized because of their race, and possibly social class, depending on their location within a system of class relations. To grasp the ways in which these young men are privileged or penalized through systems of race, class, and gender, we need to understand the ways in which race, class, and gender play out in their lives. Collins (1990) argued that people resist and experience race, class, and gender domination on three levels, namely the level of personal biography, the group level of the cultural context, and the level of social institutions.

Within this overlapping and interconnected framework for understanding domination and oppression, conceptualizing the identities of these young men required understanding their experiences among these various levels. For instance, at the level of their personal biography it seemed that they each reflected a uniqueness that was textured by their "experiences, values, motivations, and emotions" (Collins, 1990, p. 227). By the same token, these young African-American men's individual biographies are rooted in a variety of overlapping cultural contexts, where groups are defined by race, class, gender, and sexual orientation as they inhabit institutions such as schools and churches or watch television and read magazines and newspapers.

The Significance of Social Class

Integral to discussions about opportunity, power relations, and the role of the culture and structure of institutions in the making of social identities is an understanding of social class. Issues of social class and inequalities in society have continually been the subject of debate. The debate about social class gained a heightened significance in the 1980s with the provocative contribution of William Julius Wilson's (1987) *The Truly Disadvantaged*. This work highlighted the significance of an "underclass" as a distinct historically marginalized group. Wilson eloquently made a case for the existence of an "underclass" in the United States as a way of understanding contemporary U.S. poverty. He provides a structural explanation as the cause of concentrated poverty, increased joblessness, and social

~~isolation in urban black communities.~~ He argues that such a group includes "individuals who lack training and skills and either experience long-term employment or are not members of the labor force who are engaged in street crime and other forms of aberrant behavior, and families that experience long-term spells of poverty and/or welfare dependency" (p. 41). Although Wilson later recommended the abandonment of the term, his contributions provoked fierce debate. For example, Dill (1989) suggests that his proposal failed in a large measure to demonstrate that the ghetto communities are a logical outgrowth of the US economic system. In the same vein, authors from Katz's (1993) volume *The "Underclass" Debate* object to the word "underclass" as inappropriate in capturing the historical conditions such as poverty or homelessness. Instead, they argue that the notion of underclass should rather be viewed as a metaphor of social transformation. Through the discussion the authors from Katz's volume show the complicated shifting relations among historical issues such as family, ecology, institutions, culture, and policy and their interaction with race and gender. The contributing authors make the case against reifying concepts of poverty, underclass, race, culture, and family as fixed entities and rather present them as "history, which is to say as relational, shifting in meaning and content, to be interpreted in terms of time and place" (Katz, 1993, p. 23).

These debates about underclass, and current contributions from social theorists about the relevance of social class, reveal that social class clearly is an important lens through which to understand social circumstance. For example, Apple argues that:

> Just because class is called now (through what I think is a misreading of history) a "grand narrative," one that takes a reductive form, this doesn't mean that class has gone away . . . Too often the idea that class analysis was "reductive" has meant that people feel free to ignore it. This is disastrous theoretically and politically. To purge class does a disservice to the women and men whose shoulders we all stand on, not just to their theory but even more importantly to their lived struggles (qtd. in Torres, 1998, p. 25).

Apple's point is significant when considering the six young men in my study and their differing access to material and cultural resources that significantly influenced how they saw the world and the opportunities and barriers they encountered as they went to school that cannot be explained solely through a single lens of gender or race. As noted, it is when we consider the constellation of race, class, and gender practices that a fuller account of lived experiences can be developed.

Within a race, class, and gender matrix, the dimension of social class can be seen as a relation of economic exploitation and domination that denotes "shared structural positions with regard to ownership of the means of production, level of degree of autonomy in the workplace, or the performance of mental or manual labor" (Higginbotham, 1994, p. 114). As Andersen and Collins (1992) note, "the class system differentially structures group access to material resources, including economic, political, and social resources" (p. 50). Understanding social class formation, however, cannot be accomplished without understanding the ways in which gender and race are interwoven into material relations. Anthias and Yuval-Davis (1992) rightly note that class formation is the "product not only of the processes endemic within the sphere of production, for it is historically constructed in relation to the history of race and of gender. Therefore an investigation of concrete class processes finds them intermeshed with those social relations defined more broadly" (p. 112).

Beyond a "Natural" Differences Approach

Both race and gender rest on meanings, images, and representations about apparent "natural" differences among certain race groups, and between men and women. Gender and race formations reflect the social construction, representation, and organization of gender and race differences. However, the representations and practice around gender for example, "are themselves not the product of this difference but originate in social relations that include those of class and race and ethnicity" (Anthias & Yuval-Davis, 1992, p. 112). In this way, the racialized representations these young men make of schooling may also be simultaneously shaped by classed and gendered interests.

One way of understanding gender in society is through an analysis of a "gender order" that socially ranks and rewards men and women. Connell (1987) suggests that a gender order reflects three major structures, focusing on the division of labor, power relations between men and women, and sexuality. As we interact with others in our lives, we learn about gendered statuses and identities through how we act and respond to others, and thus "simultaneously construct and maintain a gender order" (Lorber, 1994, p. 32). I am in agreement with Flax (1987) who argues that gender both as "an analytic category and a social process is relational . . . constituted by and through interrelated parts . . . each part can have no meaning or existence without the other" (p. 628). Gender and race are given meaning in relation to each other, for example, white/black, male/female. But there is not one meaning of woman or man. As we think about race-gender connections, constructs of African-American men are "being constantly constituted" (Marshall, 1994, p. 91) in relation to, for example, white men, and African-American women. Thus, I would argue that there are various versions of African-American social identities within our class-based and race-formed social order.

Debates about explaining gender as an analytic category and as a social process are not simply about critiquing past arguments and discussions about gender. Much of the debate is focused on the interconnections of race, class, and gender that challenge many of the additive models of oppression and patriarchal and class forms of domination. It is when we look at race, gender, and social class as interconnected that we learn how the relations of domination and oppression often lead to the marginalization of some groups and provide "unacknowledged benefits for those who are at the top of these hierarchies—Whites, members of the upper classes, and males. The privileges of those at the top are dependent on the exploitation of those at the bottom" (Baca Zinn & Dill, 1994, p. 5).

Many of the studies about schools as gendering contexts have focused more extensively on girls than on boys. Among the studies that focus on girls and young women in schooling, only a few studies, notably, those of Brah and Minhas (1988), Fuller (1980), and Grant (1992, 1994), have focused on race-gender connections, and there are others that have focused on gender-social class connections (see Anyon, 1983). In the main, studies about gendered identities have been guided by "sex role" theory, a position that argued that particular behaviors, attitudes, and attributes were associated and seen as appropriate for men and others for women, and thereby "continued to mask questions of power and material wealth" (Carrigan et al., 1985, p. 72). More recent analyses challenge sex role theory which "directs attention away from larger structures and focuses explanation of inequality on what's going on in the heads of the subordinate groups" (Kessler, Ashenden, Connell, & Dowsett, 1985, p. 35). As West and Zimmerman (1991) point out, we are *always* doing gender. They suggest that although it is individuals who "do gender," "rather than a property of individuals, we conceive of gender as an emergent feature of social situations: as both an outcome of and a rationale for various social arrangements and as a means of legitimating one of the most fundamental divisions in society" (p. 14).

Emerging from these discussions has been research (Carrigan et al., 1985; Connell, 1987; Hearn, 1987; Kimmel, 1987) of men and masculinity that argues there are multiple masculinities where "the meaning of masculinity is neither transhistorical nor culturally universal, but rather varies from culture to culture and within any one culture over time" (Kimmel & Messner, 1992, p. 9). These advances together with significant contributions from feminist scholars have dramatically influenced notions of gender and masculinity. "Studying masculinity transformed the question of sexual difference from asking how women are different from men, to investigating how men are constituted by gender" (Baron, 1994, p. 150). For example, in the case of the six young African-American men in my study, their versions of masculinities may be considered as forms of subordinated masculinities. Such forms of masculinities in part come into being through, for instance, responses to the institutionalized structure of schooling that seem to strongly shape the construction of racialized masculinities (Mac an Ghaill, 1994a). However, such a process is not smooth. Hearn and Collinson (1994) noted the complexity of the masculinity formation process and argued that "masculinities may simultaneously be an *assertion* of a social location and a form of resistance of one social location to another" (p. 110). Hearn and Collinson (1994) point to an important issue in debates around the social construction of social identities, namely that of the complexity in the shaping of masculine identities.

MULTIDIMENSIONALITY OF SOCIAL EXPERIENCE

My discussion thus far has pointed to the complexity of race, class, and gender and their interconnections. Furthermore, I have argued that there has been little attention afforded to understanding the complexity and multidimensional nature of the lives of African-American men. Important contributions that address this concern have been advanced by Franklin (1991), Hunter and Davis (1994), and Majors and Billson (1992), who, among others, point to the contradictory nature of the emergence of black masculinity, whereby African-American men are seen simultaneously as agents and victims of their destruction. McCall (1994) writes about the hardships facing some African-American men:

> Sometimes I get mad at the brothers, especially those hanging idly on street corners, thinking they were bad. At the same time, I understand why they were having such a hard time getting it together. I know why many young brothers, and black people in general, were losing their minds. They look up and see that they're catching hell from the cradle to the grave, and that the whole fucking country is pointing fingers at them and saying it's black people's own fault that they're catching hell. They're beating the pavement, trying to find work, and nobody will hire them, and white folks cite them as examples of people who are trifling and don't want to work. And those blacks who have jobs are catching hell, trying to move up the ladder, like everybody else, and the same white folks who hold them back accuse them of being lazy and unambitious. Times for brothers were getting rougher when it seemed things couldn't get any worse. When I think of all that the brothers have to go through in this country. I am reminded of something I once heard someone say: "If we ain't in hell, we sure see it from here." (p. 362)

This poignant image painted by McCall (1994) reflects the complex circumstance of African-American men in the inner city. In essence, McCall's (1994) autobiographical account challenges the unidimensional images of African American men dominating the popular press and society at large. Often cited are the exaggerated and self-destructive aspects of some African-American men. But these accounts need to be seen as related to African-American men's responses to economic and social inequalities, historically shaped by institutional and cultural forces of racism that promote high rates of unemployment, crime and poverty among the African-American community (Staples, 1987). Further, as Roberts (1994) has articulated, "Rarely, if ever, is the issue raised concerning the possibility of healthy and constructive relationships among African-American boys and young men" (p. 381). In this light, Franklin (1991) and Staples (1986) note that African-American men are visible figures in the United States yet their lives and everyday experiences are little understood. In particular, Staples (1987) argues that dominant ideas about African-American men as "deviant," "socially disorganized," and "sexual" seem to disregard the systemic racism most African-American men confront daily. Duneier (1992) also argues that "Black men are badly misunderstood, probably no less because of the well-meaning liberal media's constant barrage of images showing how bad things have become than to Republican advertisements indicating that liberals have placed killers like Willie Horton back on the streets" (p. 25).

African-American men are placed at risk in society (Gibbs, 1988; Madhubuti, 1990; Staples, 1987) not only because of structural factors such as racism, unemployment, and poverty (Glasgow, 1980; West, 1993a; 1993c; Wilson, 1987), but also because of cultural factors (Franklin, 1984; Oliver, 1988; Staples, 1982; 1986), such as the expressive rage of the African-American men which is often portrayed as "hypermasculinity." But these accounts often represent only *some* of the visible strands of *one version* of black masculinity, and tend not to represent the *array* of masculinities that exist not only within urban areas, but within the larger African-American community itself. Westwood (1990) argues that accounts that focus on role provide a limited view of masculinity, one that reduces gendered relations and identity to role. Such accounts serve:

> to pathologize and stereotype black men noting the difficulties they have in assuming the male role due to the forms of socialization, the black family structure etc. It is an account which feeds on and feeds racist assumptions about black men, and while racism is crucial the problem also relates to the insistence of 'the male role' against which all men must be measured. (p. 58)

Further, hooks (1992) argues that much of the writing about black men "does not attempt to deconstruct normative thinking" and laments "that black men have not had full access to patriarchal phallocentricism" (p. 97). Alternative conceptualizations of masculinity are important in understanding and explaining the identities of black men of varying experiences. Such conceptualizations also seem important in understanding young African-American men's relationships with schooling. Masculinity "must be seen as an active process of construction, occurring in a field of power relations that are often tense and contradictory, and often involving negotiation of alternative ways of being masculine" (Connell, 1993b, p. 193). Such an approach seems to demand an alternative conception of gender relations, as well as an understanding of gendered identities within a matrix of race, class, and gender domination and oppression.

The stories I share about these young men's experiences in schools, with their families, and in peer relationships are not intended to reify images of African-American men. My intention is to provide glimpses into the complexity of individual circumstance that allows us to consider these circumstances dynamically in relation to larger social and political contexts. Therefore, this study aims to build upon studies such as those by MacLeod (1995) and Mac an Ghaill (1988) through attempting to explore the meanings and experiences that six African-American young men developed in relation to schooling. In addition to examining their different and similar day-to-day experiences in school, I also explore their relationships with family members and friends inside and outside of school.

To conclude, the book has a number of aims: first, to explore the range of meanings these young men gave to schooling and their relationships in and out of school; second, to explore the multidimensional nature and the complexity of their individual experiences; third, to understand the relational nature of social identities and the meanings of symbols, interests, images, and relationships with others in the context of institutional and social practices that the young men develop; and finally, to examine the ways in which the structures and social practices of race, class, and gender interplay in these men's daily experiences.

FRAMING MEANING OF SCHOOLING AND RELATIONSHIPS

Unraveling the interconnected strands of these young men's identities as represented in their meanings, images, symbols, relationships, and experiences is no easy task. One of the reasons for this complexity is that social identities are not constructed in a vacuum. They are multilayered and complex, constructed through interactions among social actors within social institutions. Viewing social identities as in the process of becoming, I believe, allows room for explaining not only how identities come into being, but also how identities change over time. At the same time, the approach is helpful in explaining how identities and the interests that flow from them become gendered, raced, and classed.

The following chapters will unravel and explain the meanings the young men develop of schooling and their relationships with family members and peers. Although my study was initially framed through a central research question, "Why do young African-American men stay in school?" I realized, as I began to have conversations with the young men and during the post-field analysis, that my study increasingly became one about identity construction and the connections among the institutions they inhabited. Part of this emerging focus was influenced by the content of the young men's narratives. The focus also changed because my understanding about the connections between social experiences and social identity changed. I began to realize how complex it is to unravel and understand their various experiences and try to explain these experiences in the context of their social identities in the making.

Although a race/class/gender matrix is important to my analysis, dimensions of the matrix are explored unevenly in this work. For example, this study provides little exploration of young men's sexualities and their sexual relationships with others. I point this out because understanding sexuality is integral to understanding these young men's locations in a gendered order and thus a social order. One of the reasons for this omission is linked to the broad range of issues and topics we covered; some topics or issues naturally were less focal than others. Studies such as this are extremely time consuming and required not only my time, but also the valuable time of the participants, and not all topics could be discussed in equal depth. Another reason, I believe, was that discussing their sexuality with a person who was almost a stranger may have been troubling for them, and thus they steered away from naturally introducing such issues into the conversation. Consequently, our limited discussions about their sexuality suggest that the images, meanings, and interpretations I present here are partial and incomplete.

As I sketch the content of the following chapters, there are a few points that I want to make. First, these chapters are shaped, on one level, by what these young men chose to tell me given my questions, at a particular point in time. Second, there was certainly a social distance between us, given that I was an outsider to their cultural and social lives, and an outsider carrying certain status and privilege because of my age, race, and social class. Third, their identities were continually unfolding as they engaged in different experiences in different contexts over time. I present much of what they said in the past tense, as this representation suggests the narratives are situated in time and place, the meanings of which may be told differently today. In some of their narratives I am able to show how their relation to schooling or with friends changed over time.

Most importantly, the stories I present provide particular glimpses of their emerging identities. A thread that dominated their discussions was the attention to racialized meanings and the emergence of their racial identities. This means that my analysis does not fully capture explanations of the dimensions of gender and class in their lives. Consequently, for the purposes of analysis, I conceptually separate the dynamics of race, class, and gender, and examine the ways in which, for example, the dimension of social class interacts with race, or race with gender. Thus, many of the stories on their own represent only partial interpretations of a race/class/gender dynamic. Toward the end of this work, however, I begin more systematically to explore race, class, and gender connections. This analytic approach reflects the complexity in unraveling the multilayered and interconnected themes that were interwoven through their lives, and by no means is intended to suggest that the dimension of race is more significant than gender or social class in understanding their experiences in school.

Chapter 2 provides the reader with an introduction to the six young men in the study. I share glimpses of how I met the young men, and note some of the important issues that seemed to dominate their lives. In Chapter 3 I discuss the complexities and challenges I faced as I conducted this study. In particular I focus on the politics of a white man conducting a study about young African-American men's experiences. Chapter 4 explores the various meanings these young men developed about the high school diploma. I examine these meanings by connecting their experiences inside and outside of school to the ways they made sense of the high school diploma and schooling. The chapter gives central importance to the racialized and classed identities of the meanings they developed.

In Chapter 5, I explore the kinds of relationships with and experiences of curriculum, pedagogy, and relationships with teachers these students experienced in their various classrooms. This chapter is dominated by their discussions of the racial images and meanings they encountered in classrooms. At the same time, I contrast the social class experiences of the young men. Thus the stories predominately are shaped by understanding their racial and social class experiences in school. Although gender is not necessarily part of their conversation, it is very much part of the subtext of their identities in the making. Thus this chapter tries to untangle race, social class, and gender in an attempt to show how their masculinities are shaped by race and class relations.

In Chapter 6, I examine their relationships with others in and out of school and connect these relationships to their gendered and racialized identities in the making. In particular, I examine these young men's relationships with family members, considering the ways in which schooling and work play out in the making of their relationships in families. I also explore their relationships with friends, examining the peer groups they formed and consider their relationships with others in formal and informal organizations and networks in and out of school.

In Chapter 7, I explore the various racialized and gendered images of others that they talked about. This chapter explores the relational and oppositional images of themselves and others. The chapter unravels their conceptions of "acting white" and examines the sexualized images of young women in the context of the making of their racialized gendered images.

In the final chapter, entitled "Power, Privilege, and Inequality," I focus on two central and complex themes interwoven through this study. First, I examine the complexity of the range of meanings the young men gave to schooling. This discussion is informed through considering the interconnection of the social institutions they inhabited daily in the making of meanings of schooling. Second, I discuss the conceptual challenges I encountered as I tried to unravel the social worlds of these six young men through a matrix of race, class, and gender domination and oppression.

2

The Six Young Men

In this chapter I introduce the reader to each of the young men. These biographical sketches provides a glimpse of the young men's social experiences as they went to school. Each of the young men lived within the metropolitan area of Allerton in Michigan. Allerton's economic base reflects both public and private sector employment, with many of the private sector jobs being located in the service and manufacturing industries. Like many large metropolitan regions in the United States, the area has been plagued with unemployment, thereby swelling the number of people who live below the poverty level in the city. Local newspapers and the Children's Defense Fund have reported that one out of four families live in poverty. At the same time, the larger metropolitan area of Allerton has considerably affluent neighborhoods. Consequently, school students living just a few miles from each other may find themselves living in very different conditions, and experience a very different education. The metropolitan area has a diverse racial and ethnic community, with a sizable African-American population.

Of the six young men, three attended school in two of the large urban high schools in Allerton. Two of the young men lived in Cedarville, a neighboring town to Allerton. Cedarville is considered part of the larger Allerton metropolitan area. One young man attended a private Christian school in Allerton. All of the participants were in Grades 10 or 11 at the time of the study. Common among the participants was that they all had decided to stay in school, were all African-American, and were all young men. Table 1 provides an overview of aspects of the young men's backgrounds.

TABLE 1.   Background information on participants

Name	Age	Participants' Social Class	Grade	School	Percentage of African-American Students in School
Shawn Braxton	17	Middle class	11	Cedarville H.S.	6
Jeff Davidson	17	Working class	10	Allerton Christian School	3
Rashaud Dupont	15	Middle class	10	Cedarville H.S.	6
Dwayne Reynolds	16	Underclass	11	Central H.S.	46
Zakeev Washington	16	Working class	10	Western H.S.	30
Marcus Williams	17	Working class	10	Central H.S.	46

Table 1 reveals that their ages ranged from 15 to 17 years old, and that they attended four different schools where the percentages of African-Americans attending ranged from 3 to 46 percent. Of great significance is their differing social class locations. Not reflected in the table but also significant to their stories is that they lived in household units of different structures. (In Chapter 6, I more fully discuss the idea of household units and their conceptions of family). Some had more friends than others; one had fathered a child; two had had recent encounters with the criminal justice system; some seemed more engaged in school than others.

EXPLORING SOCIAL CLASS

Unraveling the social class location of these six young men has been difficult. In the previous chapter, I noted that understanding patterns of hierarchy, domination, and oppression are integral to understanding social class. But part of the problem in using certain social class categories of students, as Mac an Ghaill (1994b) noted, is that they are not fixed unitary categories, and selecting the categories is essentially a heuristic device to highlight a range of experiences. Having noted this, I began to think about these young men's access to material and cultural resources as a way of thinking about their social class location. Thinking about these young men's class position, I turned to the work of Langston (1992), Messner (1992), and Connell, Ashenden, Kessler, and Dowsett (1982). Langston argued that important elements in understanding social class locations are the ways in which people live their lives, the kinds of options they have and use, and the kinds of priorities they place for themselves. Messner, in his study about sport and the social construction of masculinity, considered the kind of parents' work, living conditions, and the kind of schools the participants attended to develop social class locations. In understanding social class location, Connell and colleagues argued it is what people "*do* with their resources and their relationships that is central" (p. 33). Bearing these points in mind, the social class categories in this study are developed through considering the *kind* of work their parents did; they are also based on my inferences about their living conditions, how they spent their recreation time, the kind of schools they went to, and their experiences at school. I thus began to consider a number of dimensions of their lives in order to get a sense of their social class location.

Dwayne Reynolds had spent most of his life in Detroit up until the beginning of the 1992–1993 school year, when he moved to a foster home with a working-class family. He seemed to have lived in poverty for much of his life, and at an early age began to attend school infrequently. His involvement with drugs resulted in his arrest at the age of 13; he then spent 3 years in a juvenile home before moving to Allerton. It is through such considerations that I came to think of Dwayne's social class location as underclass. Although I acknowledge that *underclass* is a contested category, there seems a vast distinction between Dwayne's access to resources and that of the other five young men. And, having noted this distance between Dwayne and the other five men, there also seemed a distinction in the access and opportunities available to Marcus Williams and Zakeev Washington, on the one hand, and Rashaud Dupont and Shawn Braxton on the other. Marcus's and Zakeev's parents performed blue-collar or pink-collar work, and lived in a seemingly predominantly working-class neighborhood. Although they attended multiclassed schools, their schooling in a sense represented the distinctions that Anyon (1981) made about various students from different class positions. In the main, Marcus's and Zakeev's experiences in school reflected a teacher-controlled curriculum, and a teacher-centered pedagogy, wherein much of their time in classrooms involved completing assignments and worksheets that emphasized memorization and seemed to demand minimal student engagement. Noting this and other information they shared with me, I suggest that they occupy working-class locations.

Marcus's and Zakeev's experiences dramatically contrasted with the schooling experiences of Rashaud and Shawn, who attended a predominantly white middle-class high school. For example, Rashaud and Shawn talked about the centrality of discussion in their classrooms, the use of multiple resources in their learning, and the limited use of textbooks. Further, their parents performed college-educated professional jobs and they lived in a professional community. Through considering these dimensions of their lives, I argue they occupy middle-class positions.

It was most difficult to determine a social class location for Jeff Davidson. I began to hesitate a little about his class location because he moved from attending the same school as Marcus and Dwayne, having almost dropped out of school, to attending a private Christian school. His parents both worked in the manufacturing industry and he lived in a working-class neighborhood—the same neighborhood as Marcus. These experiences may reveal him as having both working-class and middle-class experiences. However, weighing all the information, I decided that he seemed to be located within the working class because at the time I met him he had recently enrolled in the private school, and most of his experiences and circumstances seemed similar to those of Marcus and Zakeev.

I raise the issue of the complexity of capturing the social class location of the young men because I want to acknowledge that categories are complex and reflect a fluidity in their social class locations. Although I have outlined some elements that may be used to characterize class differences, the structural and cultural aspects of these young men's lives clearly reveal that each class fraction is far from a heterogeneous and neat category. Structural racism, the racial and gendered division of labor, and the gendering of institutions and social practices also dynamically shape their access to options and privileges. Nevertheless, social class seemed to be a powerful explainer, in part, for some of their different and similar experiences and opportunities, and the barriers or privileges they encountered. In the end, I came to think about the social class categories for each of the young men through taking into account the differences in their access to economic and cultural resources. With this glimpse of the social class backgrounds of the six young men, I now turn to a brief introduction of each of them.

MARCUS WILLIAMS

My first conversation with a participant in this study was with Marcus Williams. My first face-to-face conversation with Marcus occurred after numerous telephone conversations. Marcus worked almost every day in two different jobs at two different fast food restaurants. Thus, it was difficult for him to make time to see me in a face-to-face interview. I met him in a neighborhood MacDonald's restaurant, about 150 meters from his house. Arranging this first interview was not easy. At this time, Marcus was not living at home with his parents, and he spent much of his time outside of school working to pay for his living expenses. This first meeting lasted almost 3 hours. I had a few issues that I wanted to talk about, but it became apparent that many of the questions I wanted to talk about were not always focal in our conversations. Marcus wanted to talk politics and he wanted to talk about the conflict between him and his parents. Marcus was a member of a study group that read the work of Farrakhan and other Africanist black leaders. Marcus was also very proud of his knowledge of and commitment to the lives of African-Americans. He was particularly committed to generating unity among members of the African-American community and talked constantly about the centrality and strength of the African-American woman in binding the African-American community. These were important topics for Marcus, and it is through these topics that I was able to bring up some of the issues and concerns that I thought important.

Marcus's relationship with his parents was complicated. He seemed emotionally attached to his mother, but had a very strained relationship with his father. He resented his stepfather of 6 years, and yearned for greater contact with his biological father. At the same time, his mother constantly ridiculed and criticized Marcus' biological father. But this did not weaken Marcus's ties with his biological father. In fact, he would try to see his biological father as many times as possible, even though his father lived more than 100 miles away.

Marcus was a very independent and self-sufficient person, despite his age. In fact, my struggle as to what to call this group of African-Americans was influenced particularly by people such as Marcus, Dwayne, and Jeff. These "young men," as I decided to represent them, as opposed to "boys," had experienced hardships, problems, and difficulties that many people of their age would never experience in a lifetime. Their lives were difficult and complicated, yet they still had the fortitude to continue, not blindly, but balancing between realism and hope.

Most striking about Marcus was the disparaging way in which he spoke about the educational system. In particular, he spoke of the racism infiltrating and dominating his schooling experiences. But his critique of racism was not confined to schooling. He also talked about racist images that dominate the commercial media and racism at his place of work. After graduating from school, he hoped to work in a restaurant because he loved to cook. His dream would be to open a black-owned business that he said would more than likely be a restaurant because he liked cooking, and most significantly because he argued "we need black-owned businesses." Throughout the ensuing chapters, the reader will increasingly become aware of the various layers and facets of Marcus's life, a world that reflects a complex and contradictory arena of discontent, hope, critique, and acceptance.

ZAKEEV WASHINGTON

I spoke with Zakeev Washington and his mother a couple of times on the phone before our first meeting at his home. After this first meeting, we met and talked in a local fast-food restaurant. As time passed, it became apparent that Zakeev had few friends outside of school and really enjoyed the companionship generated through our discussions. He was an energetic talker and loved to tell me about his life in school.

Zakeev was born in a manufacturing town in northern Illinois and moved to Allerton in early grade school. Zakeev had attended a several schools—five elementary schools, one middle school, and two high schools. He did not like the fact that he moved around a lot as he said it was difficult to make friends. Unlike the other young men I came to know, he did not have a network of friends that he spoke with on the phone daily, nor did he have a group of friends that he would hang out with after school.

Zakeev lived with his younger brother and his mother. His mother had been divorced for several years; while working full time as a sales representative, she struggled to support her family. His 19-year-old sister attended a university in Ohio, and his 22-year-old brother was in jail. His father lived in Detroit, with a partner and their child. He occasionally saw his father, but not very often.

Zakeev was an avid reader, and spent much of his time reading novels or informational books from the local public library. Occasionally, he played basketball after school, but other than that, there were few friends with whom he interacted in his recreational time after school. He was a regular churchgoer and attended church every Sunday with his brother and mother. In the course of the year, he joined a black male youth group connected with the church that would meet sporadically on a Saturday. Coincidentally, I was able to briefly observe one of these meetings that met in a conference room at a local airport. At this breakfast meeting, which Zakeev attended with his brother, I noticed that Zakeev and his brother sat to the side of the main group, seemingly interacting little with the other members of the 20-member group.

Despite the apparent ease with which he spoke with me, he was very wary at times. Some things he refused to talk about. For example, he would not discuss why his older brother was in jail. But on other topics he was extremely forthcoming. He lamented how difficult it was to make friends at school, and talked about how he was trying to figure out what he was doing "wrong" at school. He was also open about his feelings about school. He resented much of the content at school and did not always speak highly of the pedagogy or the connections teachers developed with him.

In many ways, Zakeev seemed a loner, proud of his African-American heritage, and critical of aspects of schooling, yet he believed going to school provided him better options than dropping out. He seemed very aware and articulate about the racism in the labor market that he believed privileged white people over black people. Not getting the high school diploma and dropping out from school to him meant that he would be unemployed and living in poverty. And while skeptical about the likelihood of getting a job after high school, he had ambitions to be an orthodontist.

DWAYNE REYNOLDS

I first met Dwayne Reynolds at the house of Latasha Butler, a 10th-grade school friend of Marcus. I was visiting her because she had asked two other young men, Kevin and Nico, to visit me that evening at her house as she thought they might be interested in the study. In the end, they decided not to participate in the study.

Dwayne and his foster brother also visited Latasha that evening. Latasha began to tell Dwayne about my study and how it was important for him to participate. He told me that he really wanted to talk with me. I asked him to think it over. A few days later I spoke with his foster mother and foster father and they each were interested in the study and said Dwayne could participate if he really wanted to.

My first meeting with Dwayne was a little tense, not just because I was almost a stranger to him but because of the venue in which we met. We met in his neighborhood's MacDonald's and he was a little late for our arranged meeting because he had fallen off his bike along the way. He was *so* apologetic that he was late. But that was not the only reason I ascribe to the apparent tenseness. He seemed to be very wary of the people, especially the youngsters of his age, who frequented the restaurant.

At this first encounter, after buying something to eat, we began to settle into a fascinating conversation about his life in Detroit. As we talked, however, I found him continually fidgeting and turning around in his seat. It was hard to sustain a conversation with him. He was intent on observing just about every person who frequented the restaurant that evening. He was also concerned about his bicycle, which he had propped up against an outside wall of the restaurant. About a half hour into our conversation, he jumped up without warning and ran outside. A few minutes later, he returned, explaining that he had thought someone had stolen his bicycle, but that it was still there.

This first meeting lasted almost 2 hours. At times the pace was slow. One of the reasons for this slowness was because Dwayne was trying to understand my accent and I was trying to understand his. Another reason was that initially he was not very forthcoming in the conversations. So, as we talked I began to reveal aspects of my life and my experiences in South Africa. School did not really seem to be a topic that enthralled him. Nonetheless, he did talk about school and his friends. I began to learn just what a complex and frustrating life he had lived. Dwayne's family seemed virtually to have been destroyed by life in inner city Detroit. His mother was on welfare. He described her as a regular drug user. His younger brother and sister lived with his mother, as did his uncle and grandmother. Two other brothers were in foster homes. His father, who did not live in the family home, had been laid off from Chrysler about eight years previously and had not worked since. His older sister was still looking for a job and did not stay at home. Dwayne said he had been taking drugs since he was about 12 years old. He said he took them mainly to escape from the world in which he lived, and as a way to connect with his "boys" in the neighborhood. He also said it was a way to make money. For the past 3 years, since he was 13, he had been in juvenile centers.

Dwayne's relationship with school was erratic. He had attended several schools before Central High School, and for a period of time he did not attend school as he ran away from the placement center. He did not seem particularly interested in school, and talked little about what he did in school. This is not to say that he was not committed to going to school, just that there seemed little in the classroom that excited him.

A central strand of Dwayne's view of the world was that "the odds" were against him. He believed that being African-American would hinder him as he tried to "make it" in the world of work. At one time he said, "Yeah, it's still slavery going on right now, but it is an illusion, it still goes on. ... You will never see a black man getting paid more than a white man in a job. You got some white man who'll get a job before a black man." Despite all the barriers and constraints, Dwayne seemed to generate a sense of hope about life ahead of him. He had hope that he would acquire the high school diploma, that he would no longer be a statistic, and that he would get a job that would provide him with an income to support his family.

RASHAUD DUPONT

I met Rashaud Dupont through Latasha Butler, the same friend of Marcus who introduced me to Dwayne. I had asked her if she knew anyone from Cedarville, knowing that it was a predominantly middle-class area, and as it happened she knew Rashaud from a social organization they both belonged to. I met Rashaud at Latasha's house, and after a while we were joined by Dwayne and two other young men who came to visit Latasha. As it happened, this first conversation with Rashaud was extremely interesting, because it was one of the few conversations I was able to conduct with a number of youngsters simultaneously. The other conversations I had with Rashaud, at his house or over the phone, were one on one.

Through our conversations, I learned he had lived and attended school his whole life in Cedarville. Cedarville is a decidedly middle-class neighborhood with a very small number of people of color. He was an only child and lived with his mother in a double-story house. He had lived in the house for much of his life. In fact, I learned that out of the six young men, Rashaud was the only one who was born in the greater Allerton area. Four of the others came to Allerton in the early years of elementary school, and the fifth arrived in the ninth grade.

Rashaud Dupont, like Zakeev, also struck me as a very lonely person. He said that he really only had one friend, an 11th grader whom he had befriended during his 10th-grade year. Any recreational time he spent with friends invariably was spent with this friend, Siko, whose parents were from Africa. Occasionally, he went to see a ballgame, or to the movies or a party. But on the whole, Rashaud had few people he called friends. In order to maintain ties with other members of the African-American community, Rashaud's mother belonged to the *Jack and Jill* club, an organization established for black mothers and their children. Latasha also belonged to this club, and that is how she came to meet Rashaud. The club met generally on a Sunday, with activities aimed at entertaining and educating the children. It was also an opportunity for the mothers to get together. They also organized trips, for example going to Toronto. Most, although not all, the families who were members lived in the more affluent neighborhoods in the greater Allerton area.

Rashaud spent much of his time after school completing homework and engaging in class projects. He seemed to spend much more time than any of the other participants doing homework. He seemed to like school and complained little about the work in classrooms. He seemed firmly located in a college-bound track at school, and unquestionably assumed he would be going to a four-year college. He was an honors student at school. Although uncertain in some ways about his future career, he seemed driven by a desire to accumulate material wealth.

SHAWN BRAXTON

Shawn Braxton also lived in Cedarville and was in Grade 11 at the same school as Rashaud. He had lived in Cedarville for over 2 years when I first met him. He moved from a suburb of Detroit because his father accepted a job transfer. Shawn lived in a relatively affluent neighborhood in a double-story house. He lived there with his brother, who was a year older than him, and his father. His mother, who had remarried, lived in a Detroit suburb with his younger brothers and sisters. While Shawn lived with his father and his brother in Cedarville, he remained close to his mother and his other two brothers and a sister. He attended church almost weekly in Detroit, attempting to maintain ties with his former community and friends. His older sister attended a major university on the East Coast.

Most striking about Shawn was how quiet he was. He seemed the quietest of all the young men. In fact he described himself as a "quiet" person. Even though we had spent a number of times chatting over the phone before first meeting, it was really difficult to generate a conversation with him face to face—more difficult than with any of the other participants. Most of his responses or statements appeared to be matter of fact, with seemingly little complexity or insight. But Shawn was much more complex than he seemed. This will become more evident as I explore his stories in subsequent chapters. I struggled as I wrote about him because I wanted to ensure that his voice was present among those of the other young men.

Shawn had lived for most of his life in a suburb of Detroit and attended schools dominated mostly by African-American students. Although he had been living in Cedarville for over 2 years, he felt that he was still struggling to get used to the school and the neighborhood. Shawn admitted that he did not have many friends, and he spent most of his time with a couple of friends from school who were on the wrestling team with him, and his brother who was in 12th grade at the school. Shawn did have friends in Allerton, and in fact spent much of his social time with people from Allerton. He was a member of a brotherhood that had an almost exclusively African-American membership. He felt that this organization was important to him because it allowed him to keep in contact with other African-Americans.

He also belonged to his school's wrestling team. His coach had indicated that he might be in line to receive a wrestling scholarship to attend college. But regardless of whether he received the scholarship or not, Shawn was adamant that he would go to college. He hoped to be a histologist and possibly work in a local hospital. Shawn's career plans seemed mapped out, a striking contrast to Dwayne, who was also in Grade 11 and had little idea of what he intended to do beyond acquiring the high school diploma.

JEFF DAVIDSON

I first heard about Jeff Davidson from both Marcus and Latasha during two separate interviews. He was someone they talked about a lot. They each knew Jeff's girlfriend, Sharon Dixon. Latasha said Sharon was "good" friends with her for a few years. They talked not only about the way Jeff treated Sharon, but also about the fact that he had fathered a child yet continued to go out with other women. Given that I did want to capture many different kinds of experiences among young African-American men going to school, I decided that I would explore whether Jeff would be interested in being a participant in this study. I did not want to interview him so that I could say "this is how teen fathers see the world"; rather, I wanted to understand his relationship with his girlfriend, and how he felt about fatherhood and going to school in the context of *his* experiences as a young African-American man.

During our first telephone conversation, I learned that Jeff was very keen to speak with me. He seemed to have no hesitancy at all. In our first conversation, I learned he had moved to Allerton from an industrial city in mid-Michigan when he was 8 years old. He attended one elementary school, a middle school, and then Western High School followed by Central High School (the same school as Dwayne and Marcus) before transferring to Allerton Christian School. How and why he came to attend a private school is very significant for understanding Jeff's experiences.

Jeff had recently, during November 1992, spent a month in a juvenile detention center. He was charged with armed robbery and assisting in the theft of a vehicle, a crime that he decided to plead guilty to, although he argued he did not commit the crime. He said he was in the wrong place at the wrong time. As we talked, I learned how his embroilment with the criminal justice system had shaken the foundations of Jeff's life. Before the encounter, he had all but dropped out of school, attending school very infrequently. Yet after the encounter, he not only returned to school, but at his mother's insistence attended a private Christian school.

Jeff did not hold back on telling me about his life and his time in the criminal justice system. That experience and his new school were the two main things he talked about besides his girlfriend, Sharon. Sharon was important to Jeff, as was his daughter, Cheranne. During the course of our conversations, I learned that Sharon was white. Her racial identity becomes significant in subsequent analyses.

Jeff's narratives became the most complex to unravel and explain. Each time we met he reflected a nervousness about who frequented the restaurants we visited. Jeff claimed that a gang member who had threatened to kill him lived nearby. However, I was never sure about his reasons for the apparent uneasiness. Despite his complicated life, there seemed no doubt that Jeff wanted the contact with me and that he enjoyed talking with me. Threads of his sentiments about fatherhood, the dramatic change in his view of schooling, and his embroilment with the criminal justice system all seemed at play as he talked about his life.

3

The Politics of a White Researcher Learning About Young African-American Men's Experiences of School

Within social science, and particularly qualitative research, increasing attention has been given to the study of race, class, and gender and the lives of people of color. There have also been discussions about the influence of Eurocentric and masculinist perspectives in relation to research about racial–ethnic communities (Andersen, 1993; Mac an Ghaill, 1994b). Little has been written, however, about the complex set of power arrangements that are reflected in and endemic to the relationship between the researcher and study participants, particularly in studies conducted by white, male middle-class researchers in their work about racial–ethnic communities. Such discussions are important not only to understand interpretations of researchers, but also to position and locate ethnographic texts in relation to one another. This chapter focuses on a number of methodological, ethical, and political issues that I, as a white, middle-class man, both brought to and emerged with from my study of six young African-American men.

The layers and strands of politics that are interwoven through any kind of research have been well documented (Andersen, 1993; Burawoy, 1991; Frankenberg, 1993; Gitlin, 1994; Lather, 1991; Mac an Ghaill, 1991). Here, I understand the political dimensions of research endeavors to include the relationships of the researcher to the participants, the social location of the researcher in relation to the production of knowledge, and the social location of the researcher in relation to other researchers and institutions. The political dimensions of my work also included the ways I went about collecting and analyzing data and the ways I made connections between my political view of the world and the data and theories that informed and emerged from my study.

Given that my research tool was the ethnographic interview, I began my conversations with the six young African-American men in my study by asking them to "tell me what happened at school today." But having such open-ended questions that allowed room for the participants to shape the direction of conversations did not resolve the unequal power relations that lay between the researcher and study participants. In fact, like all research, our relationships generated their own set of contradictions and controversies. Such contradictions, however, did not emerge solely from the kinds of questions that were pursued in my study. The contradictions emerged from a much larger set of issues relating to the production of research, texts, and knowledge, and the role I played in that process.

This chapter, then, through a discussion about my study of the meanings and experiences of six African-American men who stayed in school, intends to explore these multiple layers: the political dimensions of relationships, the research process, and knowledge production. I argue that in order to understand the lives of the six young men who participated in my study, I needed not only to develop a stance as a researcher that allowed for fluidity and change of my research focus, but also to critically examine my own social location in relation to the young men and in relation to their lives in school. I further argue that as a consequence of my stance of wanting to get to know the participants on their terms, the study continually was evolving and was shaped by and through our interactions.

DEVELOPING A RESEARCH AGENDA

As a teacher and teacher educator I have been intrigued by certain themes and issues; in particular, understanding the experiences of historically marginalized groups and their relationships with school. But my focus has gone far beyond schools and schooling in that much of my reading in sociology, history, philosophy, and gender studies has had me exploring issues of identity construction; power, privilege, and inequality; as well as emancipatory curriculum and pedagogy. These interests did not emerge in a vacuum; they are deeply connected to my sense of activism in schools and in the larger community. In this way, my attempt to understand and explain the day-to-day experiences of marginalized people such as these young men represents what Fine (1994) described a "troubling but delicious stew of theory, politics, research, and activism" (p. 31).

I did not reach this stance by chance; it emerged from my experiences in and out of classrooms in South Africa and the United States. My own history and experiences in South Africa and my experiences of teacher education in the United States became opportunities for me to live out and develop my stances as a teacher educator, a teacher, and an activist. In South Africa, through my experiences in grassroots organizations and as a high school teacher in a so-called Colored school, I was able to learn about the brutality of racism, exploitation, and oppression. And it was through these experiences that I learned about the intermingling of politics in every aspect of human endeavor and experience. This work was foundational in my research and teaching agendas in the United States. While located in a teacher education department, I have continually been committed to and interested in making connections between broader issues of power, knowledge, and teaching and the lives of teachers and students in urban classrooms. In particular, I have been interested in the lives of historically disenfranchised students, and their experiences in schools. Many analyses of students tend to present broad universal images of school students, and it was my intention to better understand the complexity of historically disenfranchised students' lives, and particularly African-American students.

THE POLITICS OF DATA COLLECTION AND ANALYSIS

Primarily, I view my study as an interpretive study that interweaves critical, anti-racist, and feminist perspectives (see Carspecken, 1996; Connell, Ashenden, Kessler, & Dowsett, 1982; Fine, 1991; Gillborn, 1995; Harding, 1987; Lather, 1991; Mac an Ghaill, 1988; Weis, 1990). Like critical ethnography, my approach is one that is influenced by debates in research that emerged from a dissatisfaction with social accounts of "structures" that dehumanize social actors, and a dissatisfaction with cultural accounts of human actors that neglect broad structural constraints such as class exploitation and oppression, patriarchy, and racism (Anderson, 1989). I wanted to explore the daily experiences of these six young African-American men as a window for understanding the institutional and social processes that are interwoven through their lived experiences. As Burawoy (1991) noted: "We are interested not only in learning *about* a specific social situation, which is the concern of the participant, but in also learning *from* that social situation" (p. 5). Narrating what we learn about and from a social situation is no easy task because it is complicated by the complex, contradictory, and multilayered aspects of these experiences.

In order to develop understandings of the young men's meanings of school, I conducted numerous informal interviews in which I was searching for the events and meanings that seemed significant in their lives as they went to school. I interviewed each of the young men between two and seven times (a more detailed account of the interviews is provided later in this chapter). I decided to use unstructured interviews as a vehicle to learn about the young men because I wanted to understand their perspectives on schooling, family, friends, and their social identities, not to observe *how* they went about constructing these meanings.

This method, however, does not define my methodological and epistemological stance as a researcher. As Harding (1987) notes, "a research *method* is a technique for (or a way of proceeding in) gathering evidence" (p. 2), whereas "*methodology* is a theory and analysis of how research does or should proceed," and an epistemology is a "theory of knowledge" (p. 3). Her distinctions are important because the "method" did not define my study; it reflected how I gathered evidence for the assertions I developed. The way I gathered evidence, how I analyzed the evidence, how I developed texts to represent the lives of these six young men, and how I position myself in relation to their narratives all reflected critical and feminist influences, and hence the methodological and epistemological forms that emerged from and through this study.

In order to consider the methodological and epistemological dimensions of my study, and to illustrate the political dimensions of this work, I now turn to critical strands that reflect these aspects of my study.

Entering the Field

At the beginning, I intended to select a group of young men attending the same high school in Allerton. I was hoping to include between five and eight young men who were in Grade 10, and in different tracks within the school. In the United States, Grade 10 seems to represent a significant point in the schooling of subordinated groups, a point at which they decide to drop out or continue to attend school (Fine, 1991). Through focusing on Grade 10 students, I wanted to explore the similar and different experiences of young African-Americans within the same school. This plan did not hold for very long.

At one time, during the preliminary stages of crafting the study, I thought I would work with a classroom teacher and with a group of young men from that classroom. As I thought further about this approach, the strategy caused me much anxiety. Foremost in my mind was that I, as a white, middle-class man, did not want to be associated with the institution of school, particularly the authority structure of schooling, as I thought it would hinder my opportunities to be open with the young men, and their ability to connect with me. Consequently, I decided not to formally begin my study in the institution of schooling. This was not an easy decision. I am sure that my study and access to participants would have gone more smoothly had I decided to begin my study through direct access to a high school.

Mac an Ghaill (1991) reflected on a similar conflict in his study, *Young, Gifted and Black* (1988): "I found that while observing and participating with both the Kilby School teachers and the anti-school students created tensions of identifying and being assumed to be identifying with groups who were hostile to each other, it was productive for understanding what was really going on in the classroom" (p. 116). With Mac an Ghaill's focus, it seemed that involvement in school was appropriate. In contrast, my study was not about the perspectives of teachers, nor was I seeking their approval or the sanction of other groups. My study was about the lives of young African-American men and therefore it was their approval and trust I sought. A key factor, however, that led me to decide to interview the young men outside of school was the social distance that lay between us, given my social identity as a white man and theirs as African-American men. My priority was to gain the acceptance and trust of the study's participants. Hence, I decided to interview the participants outside of the institution of school, in their 'own' territories and in places they felt most comfortable in their neighborhoods. Inevitably this also meant *not* interviewing them in their homes. In fact, they wanted an excuse to be away from home. They also wanted an opportunity to talk freely without their mothers, brothers, or sisters prying or eavesdropping. They took this study seriously. Over time I learned that while they did see me as a white person, they did not quite always see me as an "American." For example, Marcus, on introducing me to a group of friends after a basketball game, referred to me as "my friend from Africa." This seemed to be to my advantage in that I was seen an outsider to the United States and as somewhat of a stranger to U.S. culture. Even though I note that the young men may not have quite seen me as a white American, there still remained a social distance between us.[1] Certainly, interviewing the students outside of school, and my being a foreigner, might have lessened the social distance between us; however, we were certainly not equal partners in this study in that our differences in age, social class, and race all were at play in the making of our relationships.

The central criterion I used to select the six young men was their willingness to participate in this study. An equally significant criterion was the contrast each of their experiences provided in relation to one another. Marcus and Zakeev were the first two to agree to participate in the study. I asked a teacher at a high school in Allerton to describe my study to her class and ask for volunteers to participate in the study. Out of this request, Marcus and Zakeev were the ones who finally agreed to participate. Through Marcus, I met a friend of his, Latasha Butler. She was perhaps the most helpful in suggesting participants for this study. Through her various networks of friends, I met Rashaud and Dwayne. I decided to select these four because each of their experiences potentially provided contrast. I then met Jeff through Latasha and included him because his experiences seemed different from those of the other four young men. Shawn was the last participant to be selected in this study. I chose him because he attended a middle-class school and was in the same grade as Dwayne. As I met with each of the young men, I asked then if they knew of anyone else who might be interested in participating. Although they suggested names, they did not follow up. Notwithstanding, before I knew it, 6 months had passed since my initial contact with Marcus in August

1992 and there were six young men in the study. However, these six young men were not all in Grade 10; thus, while grade level was significant in selecting the young men, more influential was the range of their experiences in relation to one another.

As I began my conversations with the young men, I wanted them to get a sense of who I was. In particular, I wanted to share with them stories of my experiences in South Africa. I learned that they wanted to have conversations about South Africa too. Among the six young men I came to include in this study—namely, Shawn Braxton, Jeff Davidson, Rashaud Dupont, Dwayne Reynolds, Zakeev Washington, and Marcus Williams—South Africa was of particular interest to four of the young men—Dwayne, Marcus, Rashaud, and Zakeev. In fact, as previously noted, when Marcus introduced me to his friends, he described me as his "friend from Africa." I came to believe that these four young men were interested in the study not only because they wanted to talk to me about their experiences in school and their broader social life, but also because they were intrigued with me as a person from Africa. This is not to say that they did not see me as a white person, but they did not always see me quite in the same light as a white American.

During an initial conversation, Dwayne asked me about why I came to the United States.

Dwayne:	Did you just come here for the experience?
JP:	Yes, and to learn from Americans.
Dwayne:	Were you born in South Africa?
JP:	No, I was born in England. I went to South Africa as a teenager, and then was a high school teacher there. One of the things I wanted to do was learn from the U.S., issues about black and white people's experiences. And I want to learn that from you. Instead of reading in a book, I want to go to people and find out.
Dwayne:	Yes, 'cause the books don't tell you the whole truth.

It was in such conversations that I was able to tell them that although British-born, I spent 15 years living in South Africa prior to coming to the United States. Presenting myself in this way was not only an issue of honesty, and one of trying to establish myself in relation to each of these young men, it was intended to let the participants know about me because I did not want to portray myself "as an invisible, anonymous voice of authority, but as a real, historical individual with concrete, specific desires and interests" (Harding, 1987, p. 9).

I told them how in 1980 I became involved in grassroots antiapartheid activities at the student, community, and national levels in South Africa. On leaving the university setting, my commitment to transformation in South Africa led me to work in a number of different organizations: broad-based community action groups, youth, groups, and education organizations. For 3 years I taught at Bethelsdorp High School, a "Colored" high school, in the city of Port Elizabeth. My classroom teaching and work provided an opportunity for me to further develop my ideas about schools and classrooms as sites for social change. Out of my commitment, I worked on campaigns relating to education, youth, workers, and women. During the mid-1980s in South Africa, teachers, parents, and students in black schools through their individual and broad-based organizations played an important role in the struggle against the practices and institutions of apartheid. After the imposition of the 1987 state of emergency, many of our teacher, student, and community organizations were considered banned organizations and prevented from operating. A number of our school's teachers, parents, and our school principal were also detained. Despite these obstacles, we were able to continue our work, albeit under very stressful conditions.

These experiences at my school, in the community, and in organizations were foundational to the development of my ideas and practices about the role of schools in society and the nature of social change. My involvement in student and community politics became a catalyst to challenge my own thinking and actions and certainly were influential in the shaping of this study.

I shared these reflections about my life in South Africa over a period of time. Sharing these experiences, was one of the ways in which I hoped I would be able to put the young men at ease. Although the study was not shaped by my stories of my life in South Africa, it was shaped by a set of guiding questions which, in part, were shaped by my experiences and understandings of race, class, gender, and education in apartheid South Africa.

Guiding Research Questions

At the beginning of this study, I entered the conversations with a set of issues that I felt it was important to explore. These issues were informed particularly by various theoretical and empirical considerations. The literature seemed to give very little attention to the connections between African-American men's identity and their experiences in and out of school. In particular, few studies focus on the perspectives of young African-American men attending school. At the same time, I wanted to explore the experiences of these young men beyond school, because the students inhabited these institutions for only a part of their day. I wanted to learn about their experiences outside of school and learn about how school experiences are constructed not just within the schooling process— through direct experience within school—but through interactions with others in what they said, or how they related to school, or how they viewed the role of schools and education. Further, I wanted to better understand relationships in their lives, particularly relationships in their family and peer networks. Thus, the interview questions were in part shaped by the following original research questions:

Why Do African-American Men Go to School?
(a) What does school mean to young African-American men?

(b) What is the role of family in the lives of this group of young African-American men?

(c) What is the role of peer relationships in the lives of this group of young African-American men?

(d) What do masculinity and femininity mean to these young African-American men?

(e) According to these six young African-American men, what does it mean to be African-American, Latino, and white?

These questions in a sense framed the territory of our many conversations and framed many of the questions I came to ask the young men, although, admittedly, many of our conversations went beyond these questions. The first three questions were about uncovering the experiences of students in the school, in their family, and with their peers. The fourth and fifth questions attempted to connect the gendered and racial identity of these students in these institutions and their raced and gendered experiences to interactions in school, with family, and with peers.

Although these questions framed the territory of the conversations, they were just a beginning. Many of our conversations were focused on accounts of incidents in school, or with family members or friends. Over time, however, the focus of this study shifted because of the kinds of conversations that emerged and my evolving understanding of the significance of production of meaning and the relationship of the production of meaning to social identity construction. Thus, the study developed into questions about the meanings, images, and experiences of schooling, family, and peer relationships. It was no longer just about the "role" of these social institutions in their lives. It was about how they came to understand and give meaning to these institutions. I began to think about this study as being shaped by the research question: What meanings and experiences of schooling become significant to young African-American men in their lives in and out of school? This research question represents a number of subsidiary research questions. For instance, as I was learning more about these young men's experiences of schooling, and asking questions about family and friends, I began to realize how interconnected were their various social relationships. Hence, while this study started off primarily as one about schooling, the subsidiary interests of family and peer relationships became integral to the study. Further, as I began to have conversations with the young men, and to analyze the accounts they provided of their experiences, I realized the significance of understanding the construction of their social identities in relation to the meanings and experiences they talked about.

The Interviews

The interviews were both situational and situated within the context of the experiences that I brought to the conversations and the larger study, and the kinds of experiences they chose to share with me in response to questions I asked or comments I made. The interviews included informal conversations and more formal, though relatively unstructured, interviews. Conversational and relatively unstructured interviews were also conducted with some of the family members of the young men in their homes. These conversations were difficult to arrange because of the various family, work, and community commitments of the family members. All interviews were tape-recorded with the consent of the young men and their parents.

I began most conversations with an introduction about my background, my interest in the lives of African-Americans, and why I thought a study about young African-American men was important. From there I launched into what I considered a "safe" request, that being "tell me about your school day." I began with this request, because I felt as though it provided the participant an opportunity to talk at his own pace, with few questions from me. I learned a lot from this inquiry, and the responses provided me with opportunities to pursue themes that I saw as significant. It also allowed me to understand what activities or interactions the young men gave importance to in their school day. In subsequent conversations, I began with questions such as, "How have things been going at school?" or statements such as "Tell me what happened at school today." Once again these open-ended inquiries, while framing the conversation, provided opportunities for the participant to shape somewhat the direction of the discussion. However, sometimes these second questions were not always fruitful. For instance, Dwayne, once responded "its alright" and said little else. Thus, I turned to questions about his friends at school and out of school. In this way, the starting point of the interviews may have been similar across the participants; however, we ended up pursing questions in very different ways.

Over time I learned that it was important for some of the young men to have someone to talk with, not only about their experiences more generally, but about their day-to-day encounters. This was of particular significance to Zakeev and Marcus, whom I interviewed more than any other people in the study. From the beginning, Marcus wanted to talk about more than school, as the following interaction reveals:

> JP: Has there been anything interesting that's happened since I saw you last week that's been going on? In your job, or at school?
>
> Marcus: Something happened, I just kind of got mad because someone was kind of saying that I wasn't doing my job, 'cause the busses that I work with, they are white anyway, and they went and complained to the manager trying to say I wasn't doing my job. But, I was the only one on the floor bussing tables.
>
> JP: Was it the woman manager who made you angry last week?
>
> Marcus: They're all there, 'cause on Sunday's all the managers are there.
>
> JP: How long do you work on Sunday?
>
> Marcus: Long time, seven o'clock till two thirty.
>
> JP: Seven in the morning?

Marcus: Yeah. To me that's a rip off, 'cause you don't make no kind of money, Like seven hours, that's too long, plus you don't get paid that well, and they be trying to work you to death. So worn out from the last day, you don't have enough energy to work again.

JP: Tell me about your work schedule. So, you work every Sunday?

Marcus: Yeah, I always work the weekends, I just now started working on Saturday. Take these off in the summertime. Fridays and Saturdays I take off in the summertime. Now I've got weekends, I've got the whole weekends and they give me like two days during the week. So, basically, Sundays, I always work on Sundays.

JP: And do you get paid weekly there?

Marcus: No, every two weeks, still don't come out to nothin'. I don't even make a hundred dollars. I may come out, like the comparison, the amount of hours that I'm getting there I should be making around three hundred dollars. I don't even make. . . . I make like ninety something.

In this interaction Marcus talked not only about his job and the amount of hours he worked, but also talked about how he felt underpaid. This interaction, as with many of the interactions among the young men, provides a glimpse of our interactions. I really felt as though they wanted to talk to me, and most of the time, with the exception of Shawn, who described himself as a quiet person, they seemed to have little reluctance to talk about their lives. In fact, Marcus and Zakeev each told me that they looked forward to seeing me. But even Marcus and Zakeev were not consistent in their contact with me. It was difficult to maintain a sustained relationship with these young men. They had responsibilities and preferences in their complicated lives which meant that conversations with me were not always a high priority for them. By the same token, I was a full-time student, with responsibilities as a graduate assistant for teaching and as a researcher in a large study about education policy and practice relations, which saw me having to juggle my time so that I could make the time to meet and talk.

Besides the interviews, which I transcribed within days of the interview, I also kept various sets of field notes. One strand of these field notes described interview situations and environments, the neighborhoods they lived in, and any interactions of the participants I deemed significant. Another strand entailed accounts of telephone conversations and conversations that were not tape-recorded. I also kept a summary journal. In this analytic journal I recorded my personal reactions to conversations and interactions among the subjects, inferences, and emerging questions and assertions. I was also able to highlight important aspects of conversations I had with each of the young men in this journal. The journal was kept separately from any observational field notes I collected. The purpose of this journal was to assist me in keeping track of interesting questions, responses, and ideas that emerged from conversations with individual young men. These notes were helpful to me as it was sometimes weeks, and occasionally a couple of months, from one interview to the next. I used these notes to help me focus and make connections through the episodes and experiences they chose to discuss with me. In this journal, I also kept track of issues and questions that the young men were reluctant to talk about, as well as the questions and issues they seem enthusiastic to talk about.

Collecting Data

I went into the study with open-ended questions in my head, not really knowing how or specifically what I was going to ask, and a little nervous about how I would be received by the young men. The process of meeting the young men, including arranging the times and venues, and striking up the conversations, was much more difficult than I initially anticipated.

I entered the field with the idea that it would take time for me to develop a rapport with the young men, and that we would be able to spend a lot of time talking about various topics and issues. The reality was, however, that we did not spend as much time talking as I had hoped. As I have suggested, these busy young men did not always prioritize talking with me. Not only was the time I spent with the young men different than I envisioned, the entire process of collecting data was vastly different than I had anticipated.

My original strategy for data collection involved two phases. During the first phase, I intended to conduct three in-depth interviews with each young man. These interviews were to be shaped primarily around the first set of questions detailed earlier in this chapter. I was to ask about their experiences with school, their views of schooling, and the kinds of activities they engage in. I anticipated this initial phase of interviewing to begin at the end of August and to be completed by the end of October. The second phase was to be developed by looking at issues common to these young men but also following up on issues particular to each of their lives.

Well, that was my plan; a plan that did not hold for long. While I knew that qualitative research is certainly influenced by constraints outside the control of the researcher, I was unprepared for the length of time it took to contact and negotiate participation in the study. By the end of October, I had met only four of the participants, and conducted one interview with Dwayne and Rashaud, and three each with Marcus and Rashaud. I had not met Shawn or Jeff by this stage. So, it emerged that I would not be able to enter into parallel conversations with each young man, complete that round, and then engage in the next phase of the research, as I had originally anticipated when designing this study. Therefore, I began to develop a research agenda for each young man. This is not to say that I did not pursue the same kinds of topics, questions, and issues with each of them, but that the time in between the various interviews across the six young men differed, as did the number of interviews I conducted with each of them. For instance, I conducted seven more interviews with Marcus yet I was only able to conduct two more interviews each with Shawn and Jeff, with each interview lasting about 2 hours. In each case we had, in addition, between 4 and 12 informal telephone conversations.

Data Analysis

Given that most of my questions were open-ended and that I did not have a formal interview protocol, but rather a set of issues I wanted to interweave into our conversations, the flow of conversations and the prominence of issues within conversations were not always of my making or my choosing. Maybe this is not surprising as I tried to create interview situations that were intended for these young men to "tell their story" as much as was possible given the conditions and our relationships. What this did mean for me was that numerous themes began to emerge. Having such an abundance of data certainly required continual and intensive data analysis. In qualitative methodology, "Data analysis refers to a process which attempts to identify themes suggested by the data" (Weis, 1985, p. 173). Such analysis promotes the development of strands of analyses that are surprises to the researcher and, in fact, may not have been noted by the researcher on framing the study. But allowing room for issues to emerge from the data requires a close reading of data and the variants of the themes emerging.

Data analysis was not something that occurred after data had been collected. It was a continual process of construction of themes and issues, considering multiple alternative interpretations. This process became more focused during the post-fieldwork stage, but actually occurred from the beginning of data collection through the actual writing of descriptions and interpretations. Lather (1991) made a crucial point about the fluidity of propositions and analyses emerging from the data. She argued, "Data must be allowed to generate propositions in a dialectical manner that permits use of *a priori* theoretical frameworks, but which keeps a particular framework from becoming the container into which the data must be poured" (p. 62). Such a stance is difficult yet crucial if one is committed to understanding and explaining the perspectives of the participants. Yet this stance does not negate the fact that we all bring perspectives to the context of our study, and we use these as lenses to understand and explain the world.

Part of generating a dialectical relationship between my frameworks and my data was not only how I framed issues, but also how I allowed for the questions that may initially have framed this study to change along with my interpretations. Let me share a couple of examples of how my questions began to change, as I collected the data, conducted analysis, and wrote about the young men's experiences. These examples relate to the significance of family and peers in their lives.

I began asking the young men questions about their relationships with family members. I learned about how they related to their parents and to their brothers and sisters. Along the way, particularly in the postfield analysis, I discovered an interesting question about the shape and form of families. I began to recognize that many of the young men drew a distinction between family and household units, that the people who counted as family to them were more than the people who lived with them at home. I thus began to explore the different ways in which they conceptualized family.

Another example emerged when I began to explore the patterns of friendships in their lives. They talked about the various friends, the difficulty in maintaining friendships because they trusted few people, and the dimensions of friendship they deemed significant. As I began to unravel their friendship patterns, I began to realize that my initial question, which focused on who they were connected with and what they talked about, was a bit skewed. I wanted to know what they talked about with their friends, but for the young men, an equally important issue was the meaning of friendship in their lives. Further, initially I was so intent on using the institutional connections to shape my analysis that I tended to fragment their relationships with others although these relationships did not seem fragmented to the young men. For instance, they may have had friends at school, but these friendships may have simultaneously developed outside the context of school. And it was only by understanding the patterns of friendships in each of their lives that I was better able to understand their meanings. Therefore, I came to focus more on the actual features of the process of relationships, not solely the institutional contexts in which these relationships were developed. This may not appear to be too different. But what my analysis began to allow for was more fluidity, connections, and disconnections among the relationships in their lives.

Some Critical Reflections

As I looked back on the year I spent collecting the data, I began to recognize just how long it took me to arrange interviews and get to know six young African-American men. And yet, I asked myself, how well did I really get to know them? Maybe what I learned is that I was able to tap into only a small aspect of their lives, that the study on some level was very narrow in conception, despite the wide range of topics we covered.

I have questioned how I could have done things differently, but there is no easy answer to this question. I wanted to study these young men outside of the school environment, not because I had no interest in understanding their experiences of schooling but because I wanted to understand the world from their perspectives, and school may not be as pivotal in the lives of students as many educators would like to assume. Also, I believed that I would have a better chance to gain insights into their perspectives of school by talking with them in environments in which they were comfortable, in places they chose.

There were a number of topics that never arose during the discussions, and it became very difficult for me to ask them about such topics. One of these topics was their sexuality. This tells me something about how close I really was to each of them. It also may reflect the ways in which "discourses of desire" (Fine, 1991) are much more difficult to talk about than discourses of race, which were more readily brought into our conversations. While they all "passed" themselves as heterosexual through the heterosexualized talk about young women, I learned very little about how they thought about their sexuality as young African-American men. Such questions, I believe would only emerge after long contact time, and a more intimate and connected relationship. I felt that these young men were very vulnerable at times, and I tried to respect their situation and their position in relation to me as a white researcher from the university. But there were other topics of a sensitive nature that they spoke about with ease: their troubled relationships with their family and friends, or their racist encounters with teachers. So it seems that there are some topics that were more sensitive than others to them, whereas these topics may appear equally sensitive to the researcher.

The interviews themselves did not always go as planned, and neither did the interactions nor the ensuing relationships. For example, during a discussion with Marcus, about 4 months after I had met him, I began to ask him about his discussions with friends at school. He had told me that he talked about friends and women during some of his conversations, so I asked him what he had discussed. Rather than answering my questions, he began to explain to me the language he used, and implicitly he explained how he took much of it for granted—it remained unexamined:

> *JP:*   What kind of things do you talk about when you talk about women?
> *Marcus:*   Women, yuuu!
> *JP:*   What? "I like her" or "she's going with this guy"?
> *Marcus:*   One we don't use them terms of words.
> *JP:*   What terms don't you use?
> *Marcus:*   We don't say "girl," we say "female." And we don't say "go together," we say "hook up."
> *JP:*   This is maybe American, I'm a foreigner. You know white Americans don't understand all my expressions. I'm learning about African-American culture as well, I don't know much, so you're teaching me stuff. It's important.
> *Marcus:*   *(Laughs).*
> *JP:*   What you're finding funny? The language?
> *Marcus:*   The language! How you ask me what it means. That's basically how we talk. It's just how people say, ghetto language, street talk. There is a difference though in the language. I could talk the language I talk right now and still a lot of people say you switch your language over to a different language to talk to white folks. You know, I need to talk your language, but just don't use so much slang. Like de', he', you know like that kind, because I had that, when I moved up from Port Edward because we cut off all our words. I still got a little bit, not as tight.

This interaction began with my trying to find out about the content of the conversations among his male friends about young women. But our conversation drifted away from that focus, in that Marcus began to talk about our different usage of language. This is a good example of how the participants in the study in a sense shaped the direction of the conversations. The path that Marcus chose seemed an interesting one to pursue further. Incidentally, I had never used the word "girl" in our conversation prior to that point. This was, however, something that he associated with me, given my white racial identity. A further point worthy of mention is that he informed me about his switching his language code because he was talking with me. I found his discussion about language usage very interesting, because in my eyes, he seemed to "cut off" many of his words, and he used a fair amount of slang when he talked. For instance, the way in which he talked contrasted dramatically with how Rashaud or Shawn, the middle-class young men, spoke, yet in his eyes he saw himself as switching codes.

This interaction not only told me about how Marcus gave racial meaning to language usage, but it also reminded me of how he saw me. He may have trusted me, he many have been open with me, but the fact remained, in his eyes, I was a white person associated with the racial power structures of the United States. Understanding what Marcus thought and understood about the meanings he developed is at the heart of understanding how he saw himself in the world.

How I went about collecting data, that is, by interviewing the young men, allowed the young men to shape the stories I chose to tell. Part of this method involved acknowledging not only my social identity as a researcher but also some of the political, personal, and professional experiences that were integral to this project. An equally important issue that confronted me was the nature and form of the relationships in relation to my stance as a white, middle-class researcher, which certainly brought some thorny ethical issues to the fore.

CROSSING DIVIDES: RESEARCH AS AN OUTSIDER

Engaging in research that found me, a white, middle-class male, studying African-American men of varying social class locations created some uneasy tensions as I collected the data and continue to write about their lives. A critical concern that continued to surface as I progressed with this study was the nature of my relationship with the young men. I felt that this work brought about for me a degree of hypocrisy, both before and during data collection. I was an outsider to their community, trying to understand their social world, and these young men were providing honest, heartfelt stories and accounts of their lives. Yet, what was I providing in return? I was, on one level, a passive listener, a taker. Although I shared with the young men glimpses of my life, they did not really get to know me in reciprocal ways. At the same time, I recognized that I was not going to be part of these young men's lives for a lengthy period, as I would soon be moving from the area. Consequently, I presented myself to the young men as a researcher wanting to tell their stories about school and their experiences as young African-American men in and out of school. In presenting myself, I felt it only ethical for me to be as honest as

I could about why this study was important to me. I was conducting a study to complete the requirements of my Ph.D. degree at Michigan State University, but I was not pursuing the topic merely for the sake of the degree. This study has a political importance to me because it provided me contact with and opportunity to learn from a group of people that I not only care about but am committed to politically, socially, and culturally.

Revealing myself and my intentions and trying to be open with the young men was but a first step in building a relationship. It was not enough by itself. As I evaluated the situation, it still seemed that I was attempting to clear my conscience about the purpose of the study and that talking with them about my research intentions would somehow strengthen our relationship. Maybe it was a good starting point. But there was so much that lay between us: The fact that I was a white man, middle class, albeit from another country, in some ways left me continually and unsteadily walking a fine tightrope with me feeling that they trusted me but they were also wary of me.

The social distance that lies between the participants and researcher in a study is one of the enduring questions that pervades research such as mine. Andersen (1993) raised some important questions in this regard. She asked: "How can white scholars elicit an understanding of race relations as experienced by racial minorities? How can white scholars study those who have been historically subordinated without further producing sociological accounts distorted by the political economy of race, class, and gender?" (p. 41). Responses to these questions, in part, require me not only to acknowledge my social identity, but also to situate myself and my view of the world in relation to these young men's lives.

Andersen's (1993) questions are important ones that are central to research about racial minority communities conducted by white researchers. While I may argue that it is important to generate multiple perspectives of the life experiences of racial minority communities, at the same time, there are significant ethical and political imperatives that seem to pervade work such as mine. An important question I continually asked myself was: Whose interests does this work really serve? I was entering their worlds, and in some ways I provided support for some of the young men as they went about their activities and relationships; but the fact remained, I was an intruder to and outsider in their world.

Granted, there was distance between us and, to a certain degree, the distance lessened, depending on the particular individual, their need, their trust, and the number of times and the ways in which we met. Although I was keenly aware of the intrusive role that I played in these young men's lives, the conversations themselves were not entirely framed by my questions. In fact, the participants initiated much of the interaction. For instance, I learned about the various kinds of friendships they had, and I learned about whom they were friendly with at school. Such conversations emerged from comments they made, which I followed up on. As noted, sometimes I asked open-ended questions, such as, "how do you spend your time after school?" Although, the question may have shaped the territory of the particular interaction, it did not limit what they talked about.

Notwithstanding, I still carry with me an overwhelming sense of intrusion into their lives. I was entering their worlds and they really did not enter mine. They were telling me all, but what was I *really* providing in return? There is no way to truly know the answer to that question. The question in itself does, however, raise some central ethical issues and questions that need to be examined as we continue to develop research and explore issues and ideas in the lives of people around us.

The question about whose interests this study serves was raised by some of the young men. Some of them raised the topic of my intentions, and my rewards, especially material rewards reaped from conducting this study. One of the young men, Jeff Davidson, was particularly critical of this kind of study. His mother refused to be interviewed. Her rationale, he told me, was that there are many white people who conduct studies of African American people, write a book, and "make lots of money." Whether this is a reality or not, for the vast majority of researchers engaging in studies similar to mine, there is no doubt that the researcher has something to gain and the researched, little.

A central theme in this discussion about the ethical and political dimensions of my study has focused on the social distance that pervaded my relationships with the young men. An additional, equally significant question concerns how a white researcher can generate an understanding of social relations as experienced by people of color. These questions are fundamentally questions about the political context of relationships in research and how knowledge production is, in essence, political work.

Unquestionably, the relationships between the young men and me were unequal, given that as a researcher I would be able to build an academic career through this work. Baca Zinn (1979), a Chicana sociologist, noted the thorny methodological problems she faced when conducting research about Chicano families. She argued that:

> Gestures of reciprocity do not, by themselves, alter the unequal nature of research relationships. Nor is having research conducted by insiders sufficient to alter the inequality that has characterized past research. Field research conducted by minority scholars may provide a corrective truth to past empirical distortions in that we are able to get at some truths. However, our minority identity and commitment to be accountable to the people we study may also pose unique problems. (p. 218)

Conducting research in racial ethnic communities undoubtedly poses methodological and ethical problems for *all* researchers. However, there are critical questions that need to be raised and discussed in relation to white researchers conducting research in racial-ethnic communities. There is no doubt, as Andersen (1993) argued, that "minority group members have insights about and interpretations of their experiences that are likely different from those of white scholars"

(p. 43). Maybe the most central questions become ones about which interpretations should be considered as the most authoritative (hooks, 1989), or whether one interpretation should be considered as more authoritative than another.

Responding to these questions does not resolve the uneasy tensions that plague research such as mine. But they certainly do force me to address the central political and ethical dimensions that pervade my research. From these questions, I argue that my interpretations as a white, middle-class man represent one of an array of potential interpretations and that my interpretation should not be considered as *the* interpretation of these young men's lives. Such a stance requires me to acknowledge that my understandings of these young men's lives will be partial and incomplete and requires a continual investigation of my own privilege as a white male researcher. My interpretations are intended to be considered as a contribution to various questions and issues in the hope that our collective questions may help us explain and understand the lives of these young men as well as broader questions about race, class, and gender relations of privilege and power.

In this chapter, I have focused on some of the methodological issues that emerged during and after data collection. I have argued that the study and my interpretations were continually evolving and shifting: my relationships with the young men; the kinds of data I was able to collect; and the relationship of data to theory. Another strand of my discussion is the inherent political nature of research which reminds me not only about my political responsibility, but also about the intellectual and ethical integrity that is demanded in crafting the work. I noted that the making of this study was continually changing and shifting and that the process of collecting and analyzing data is in itself a political act. My interpretations and the ways in which I wanted the study to challenge my own and others ideas were shaped by my view of the world and my view of research as contributions to understanding and changing the world. All studies have political dimensions. The challenge for us as researchers, particularly researchers who benefit from access to privileges and options in our society, is to acknowledge the political dimensions of our work and our experiences and their concomitant and shifting location in an interconnected web of power relations. This means not only understanding the social distance of the researcher and study participants, but also examining how conversations are constructed and interpreted, and it also means overtly positioning the study in relation to others, given the political dimensions of research relationships, the research process, and knowledge production. Finally, acknowledging the political dimensions of research means acknowledging, critiquing, and challenging the power of a text as a tool to examine *and* transform relations of power.

4

Situated Meanings of the High School Diploma

This chapter explores the various meanings of the high school diploma to the six young African-American men. As I asked them why they stayed in school, the diploma emerged as one of the most consistently talked about topics. It seemed to represent a bridge between their present lives and their hopes and aspirations beyond high school. For some, it also represented a symbol of achievement in its own right.

In this chapter I argue that the high school diploma did not represent the same symbol, value, or interest for these young men. Although there were similarities in some of the ways in which they thought about the diploma, these young men did seem to hold different meanings about school, the high school diploma, and aspirations beyond school. In part, the meanings they constructed of the high school diploma seemed to be connected to their social identity, which in turn seemed to be shaped by and to shape the meanings they constructed. The different meanings they constructed can be explained through considering their social location and experiences of race, class, and gender power relations. Here, meanings and ideas were constructed through daily interactions that shape and are shaped by the structure and culture of the social institutions they inhabited as African-Americans, as young men, and as classed individuals.

Although these young men embraced dominant meanings of the high school diploma as a ticket for social mobility, or as a ticket for entrance to higher levels in the education system (Collins, 1979), they were not the only meanings they constructed. For example, two of the young men explicitly saw the high school diploma as a symbol of personal achievement. It is the purpose of this chapter, then, to explain the ways in which these young men came to see the high school diploma, examining both the similarities and differences in the meanings they constructed. This chapter first examines the individual meanings these young men developed of the high school diploma. Toward the end of the chapter, I more thoroughly compare and contrast their differing and similar meanings, and also consider the extent to which they seemed to accept achievement ideology.

JEFF DAVIDSON: "IT'S KIND OF LIKE A REWARD"

Jeff Davidson was 16 years old[2] and attended two schools during the 1992–1993 school year. He attended the 10th grade of Central High School until November 1992. Then, from January through June 1993, he attended Allerton Christian School (ACS), a K–12 private Christian school. Central High School was a large high school of 1,500 students with an African-American student population of approximately 46 percent, and a white student population of approximately 42 percent. ACS had a smaller student enrollment than Central and had considerably fewer African-American students. ACS was a predominantly white school of approximately 500 students with an African-American student population of approximately 3 percent. Jeff's decision to move to ACS was strongly encouraged by his parents. The move represented a serious commitment to go to school regularly and a concerted attempt to acquire the high school diploma. The school itself represented the possibility of going to school in a "better environment" in comparison to Jeff's previous school, Central High School.

After his release from the juvenile detention center, Jeff seemed to develop an enthusiasm to attend school regularly and established a quest to attain the high school diploma. This represented a dramatic shift in Jeff's relationship with school. Previously his school attendance was sporadic, because of the disengaging pedagogy and curriculum at Central and the bitter quarrels with his parents that resulted in his leaving home. Jeff's new turn seemed to be fundamentally driven by the hope of acquiring the high school diploma.

> JP: Is graduating from high school, is that by the way, something in the long run?
>
> Jeff: Oooh, no, that's the main thing.
>
> JP: Why do you want to graduate though, what will that do for you?
>
> Jeff: First of all it will get me out of school. Second of all, it's kind of like a reward to me, by graduating, I win. Through my years of school I earned it.

Acquiring the high school diploma seemed to become the major incentive, "the main thing," for Jeff to go to school every day. Given the centrality of the diploma in his rationale for attending school, going to school itself seemed to become a rite of passage that he had to endure. "[I]t will get me out of school," he said, as though he had to acquire the high school diploma before leaving school. For Jeff, the diploma was seen as a "reward" and as something he "earned" for staying in school. While the high school diploma represented a reward, it also represented a possibility of going to college. After his transfer to ACS, it seemed that Jeff took a dramatic turn and embraced the possibility of acquiring the high school diploma. This current meaning of the high school diploma that Jeff constructed needs to be located within the context of his experiences outside and inside of school and in the context of his hopes and ambitions beyond high school graduation.

Before attending ACS, Jeff was not committed to going to college and was unsure as to whether he would acquire the high school diploma. However, his move to ACS seemed to symbolically represent new possibilities: possibilities of acquiring the high school diploma, of getting "good" grades, of establishing an academic record that would enable him to meet college entrance requirements, and of going to college. At one point he said that,

> Allerton Christian would be a whole lot better environment for me, then I got to start thinking about college. Get a few years at a good school, get good grades, grades I can stand behind, start looking at colleges, and they start looking at me.

Jeff believed that ACS "is a whole lot better environment," in comparison to his previous school, Central. What Jeff did not like about Central was its "reputation." To Jeff, Central's reputation was one of "drugs . . . gangs. And em, you know, a lot of shootings and stuff, fights, crazy stuff." It was Central's reputation that Jeff wanted to disassociate himself from. Consequently, he changed schools to get out "of that situation where you know, getting a chance to get back into that group. Well hey, he goes to Central, and maybe he does do such and such." But Jeff's concern about the reputation of Central became significant *after* his embroilment with the criminal justice system. Further, Jeff's mother believed moving from Central might force him to disassociate himself from some of the students at Central and thus be less likely to be in a position of committing a criminal offense. It was only after his arrest and conviction, however, that she became concerned about his friends at Central. Thus, Jeff's move to ACS was a reaction to his arrest, a month in a juvenile detention center, and a conviction of charges on robbery and assisting in the theft of a vehicle.

Jeff's encounter with the criminal justice system became a catalyst for a dramatic change in how he viewed school. Jeff was so badly shaken by the experience that he tried to dramatically alter the direction of his life. He was scared by the ordeal, and even more scared by the thought of actually receiving a prison sentence. Jeff told me that he did not commit the crimes for which he pleaded guilty.

He described how he made the decision to plead guilty to the charges of armed robbery and assisting in the theft of a vehicle:

> I got on armed robbery, assisted stolen car. 'Cause they said well here's the deal, well my lawyer told me, "you can agree that you did such and such, and you assisted in a stolen car and everything, and you can walk out today as a free man. Or you can go to juvenile, you know, keep going to court, keep going to court till they figure whether you are guilty or not. And then, that is not to say if you keep going to court that they are going to figure that you are not guilty. 'Cause you are still facing the chance, if they figure you are guilty, then you still go to prison."

Jeff was charged as a minor, because he was arrested by the police two days before his 17th birthday, and he was sent to a juvenile detention center. He spent a month in the center. The center held about 30 minors—15 boys and 15 girls, with 27 of the 30 youngsters being people of color, and the majority being African-American.

Jeff recounted the night on which he was arrested and explained the judge's response to his charges:

> You know, to cut it all down, I was in this car; some people had got into trouble, so I went to jail also. Somebody else did, and they try to blame it on me. . . . I guess the police officers, 'cause the guy that I got caught with, he was Mexican, and I guess the police officer said we probably know it was the black guy you know, if you tell us such and such, he probably, you know. I was just riding and stuff, and all this other stuff. . . . What it was, they had robbed somebody and stolen a car. So, when I went to court, the judge was like confused, 'cause I don't have no record. . . . That's another thing the judge said. He said "either it's the case, or my age, but I'm confused. Young man you went seventeen years, no trouble nothing bad or anything, and something as serious as this." 'Cause the things I was tried for I could have got life in prison. . . . [T]hen they put it on my juvenile record. He said, "when you walk out of this court room, you are an adult now and anytime you get into any more trouble, you are going straight to jail. And if it is anything serious, you are going to prison." He said, "Merry Christmas," and I was like Merry Christmas to you too.

The incident shook the foundations of Jeff's existence and deepened his sense that the criminal justice system does not seem serve the interests of African-Americans. "We probably know it is the black guy," he surmised the police officers concluded. Such a statement provides a glimpse of how Jeff as an African-American man may attach racial meanings to societal institutions, and the extent to which police enforcement and the criminal justice system can work in opposition to the interests and rights of African-Americans.

As Jeff concluded the preceding account to me, he revealed how jubilant he was to be out of the juvenile center. Once he returned home, his parents encouraged him to enroll at the local Christian school. Even though the move represented a financial burden for them, they said they were prepared to make the sacrifice. School thus suddenly began to play a central role in Jeff's life:

> *JP:* What kind of role does the school play in your life really? Is it a big part, or is it something you have to do?
>
> *Jeff:* It's a big part now.
>
> *JP:* It wasn't before though?
>
> *Jeff:* No, 'cause you know you get the attitude that [the teachers] don't care, they are just in it for the money. . . . What made me take that turn was juvenile. Like I was telling Mr. Chisholm [a teacher] today, you go for so many years, not worried about getting locked up or anything, being the goodest guy I could, one hundred percent American, and then you know, just recently, everything starts running down, get locked up. There goes my freedom right there. And for me, if you wanna hurt me, take away my freedom.

Although Jeff claimed that teachers "don't care," school became more central in his life as a consequence of his experience of the "hurt" emerging from his encounter with the criminal justice system, an encounter which he believed he did not deserve, given his stance as an "American." This seems ironic. Jeff was disconnected from school, considered himself law-abiding, yet it was school that he turned to and embraced in opposition to the criminal justice system. Going to school symbolically represented a desperate attempt to retain his "freedom" and seemed to become a counterpoint to going to jail, which viciously stripped him of his freedom. However, Jeff did not turn to any school. He elected to move to a private school with a good "reputation" and dominated by white, middle-class students rather than return to his old school. School thus emerged as playing a contradictory role in his life. For a time he felt disconnected from school, yet it was a predominantly white and middle-class school that emerged as his salvation in attempting to build his dignity and pride.

I will now turn to an examination of Jeff's relationship with school prior to his conviction. As previously noted, Jeff's relationship with school before his move to ACS was very tenuous. He sporadically attended school, and when he attended he found his work disengaging. Across the 1991–1992 school year, he had skipped so many classes that he did not receive the necessary credits from courses to be considered a junior at Central. Consequently, his return to Central High School in the 1992-1993 academic year saw him recategorized as a sophomore and repeating many of the courses for which he was enrolled the previous year at the school. Jeff provided two reasons for his disengagement and poor attendance at Central. First, he felt that his teachers did not care, and second, he was experiencing "family problems." Jeff linked his disengagement from Central to both internal processes within the school and to the difficulties he was experiencing outside of school. Outside of school, he was having altercations with his parents that affected his desire to go to school:

. . . from my behalf, when I was having confusion with my Mom and everything, getting out of the house. I was like what was the point of going to school. You know you cannot wear the same clothes to school every day and stuff.

Jeff's disputes with his parents often resulted in his parents evicting him from his home or him leaving voluntarily. During the 1992 year, he left his home approximately five times.

In the midst of his disengagement with school and quarrels with his parents, Jeff also fathered a baby girl, Cheranne, who was born in August 1992. Sharon, the mother of the baby girl and Jeff's current girlfriend, was 15 years old and an honors student at Central High School. During her pregnancy and after the birth of Cheranne, her attendance at Central also became sporadic. "She got pregnant and everything, and I was happy and everything, we was trying to keep it undercover." In their attempt to keep Sharon's pregnancy "undercover," Jeff and Sharon spent a lot of time away from school at Sharon's home. Sharon's mother was unaware of this because she worked during the daytime. Thus, Jeff stayed away from school not only as a consequence of the altercations with his family but also because of his desire to be with his girlfriend during her pregnancy. After Cheranne was born, Jeff continued to attend school sporadically.

Jeff began to think differently about the consequence of the birth of Cheranne following his catastrophic encounter with the criminal justice system. Cheranne became a meaningful reason to attend school, seek the high school credential, and seek entrance to a college.

[Cheranne] kind of helps me, because she makes me want her to be proud of me and pass something. "My Dad went to such and such school such and such college." I wanna give her a good life. I wanna have something in my past that she can be proud of.

Jeff cited the birth of his daughter as a reason to want to finish school; he wanted to accomplish something that Cheranne would be proud of. Although Cheranne was born in August 1992, it was only in December 1992, after his experience in the juvenile detention center, that the high school diploma became important to him in relation to his young daughter. "Basically right now I'm concerned about my work. Getting a nice job and taking care of my daughter," he said. Previously, Cheranne was a reason to stay away from school; she then became one of the reasons to stay in school. Most important about his experience with the criminal justice system was that the encounter saw him developing a different relationship with school, which simultaneously saw him reconsidering other spheres of his life. He moved from almost rejecting school to zealously embracing school.

Consequently, the move to ACS in itself represented his new relationship with school. It not only represented the potential of acquiring a symbol of achievement but the possibility of attending college as an option after high school graduation. Though Jeff talked about a goal of attending college, he had not acquired the resources nor the access to resources that would enable him to develop a sense of life beyond the high school diploma. In essence, the diploma represented a reward, not for just staying at school, but for staying out of jail. It seems that acquiring the high school diploma became the most available symbol to develop his pride, reflect his potential to succeed, and seek social recognition. It was through attending a school that was comprised almost exclusively of white, middle-class students, and not staying at Central, that he felt he could reach a position that others could be "proud" of because he would graduate from high school.

Jeff struggled as a young African-American man to gain the diploma, which not only represented potential economic and social mobility, but more profoundly the accomplishment of a personal goal. Paradoxically school, an institution he almost rejected, became the very source and symbol of his current aspirations. Jeff's changed relationship with school needs to be located within the context of his experiences as an African-American man. He felt victimized as an African American man, and jolted by his reverberating experience with the criminal justice system. The diploma represented an acceptable accomplishment, in opposition to what incarceration may represent. To gain recognition and redemption, he embraced not only a dominant symbol of success, the high school diploma, in opposition to the criminal justice system, but embraced a white, middle-class private school as a vehicle for such recognition.

DWAYNE REYNOLDS: "BE NO STATISTIC"

Dwayne Reynolds was a 16-year-old who spent most of his early years living in inner-city Detroit. When he was 13 years old, Dwayne became a ward of the court. Since then he had lived in various juvenile placement centers and foster homes outside of his familiar Detroit neighborhood.

> I'm recently from Detroit. . . . I was on the run from a placement there . . . [it's] like a facility for boys that get in trouble. I ran from there, so I had a warrant out for my arrest. . . . I got picked up with drugs and AWOL from the placement. So then I went to the youth home, then I went to a holding facility, then I went to placement, then I came here. That adds up to two years or somethin'.

During the 1992–1993 school year he moved to Allerton to stay with new foster parents and enrolled as a junior at Central High School in Allerton. The move to Allerton was not easy for Dwayne. Although he lived in Allerton, he still considered Detroit his home and a place where he would rather be.

At the beginning of our first conversation Dwayne adamantly announced, "you know, I just want to make it through school." Not making it through school, he claimed, might result in him being a "statistic." Dwayne wanted to go to school, because going to school and acquiring the high school diploma symbolized being successful as opposed to being a statistic. Dwayne did not receive high grades, but this did not appear to concern him. A deeper concern was maintaining the courage to stay in school. So, success seemed more about making it through school than scoring high grades in the process. At one point he said he went to school:

> so I can be someone successful. 'Cause the odds are already against me, statistics. Plus, the things that I've been through and the people I hung around with, selling drugs and all that, getting into, other people and stuff. It's on my record, so I want to be someone successful in, you know, I want to be no statistic or whatever. You already know all the statistics out there, high crime areas in inner cities.

Dwayne's primary reason for attending school was to acquire the high school diploma. On one level, his desire to graduate from high school represented actualizing economic security. On another, it represented a symbol of achievement in his fight against "the odds." For Dwayne the odds against him included his record for selling drugs and also represented the hardships faced by African-American men from the inner city. "A lot of things I did was wrong, some of the time I didn't understand some of the things I did was wrong . . . that time there was no way out," he said.

Acquiring the diploma represented a fight against the constraints he encountered as an African-American male growing up in Detroit—a context that limits the life chances of African-Americans. Dwayne saw the high school diploma as a ticket to success; a particular form of success. Success did not primarily mean economic and social mobility. Rather, most fundamentally it meant *not* being characterized as a victim of crime and poverty. Being a statistic meant being unacknowledged by others and viewed as a nameless person. "That's what society label you, just like they label you like nothing but a damn number. We ain't nothin' but a number, out here in the streets you ain't nothin' but a number," he stated with intense anger and resentment. The odds were not merely statistical accounts of Dwayne's experiences; they were *lived* experiences he encountered as he grew up in Detroit. He described these experiences in Detroit as a manifestation of racial injustice.

> It's not right to treat a person 'cause of the color of their skin. If they was in our shoes, and we was like had control of the country was over to us, then see how it feels. But then I guess they do us as niggers. We low down, we this, we that, and all of the things they're saying around. Out there and suffer. But we living through war, every day we living in hell, taking a chance at getting shot, taking a chance, and they want to blame the drugs.

Dwayne talked articulately about his life in inner city Detroit before moving to Allerton. He spoke with anger about the stranglehold that life in the "ghetto" had upon him and how people in the inner city were "living through war, every day we living in hell, taking a chance at getting shot." He painted a somber and depressing picture of his life growing up in inner city Detroit, and talked about how the inner city is "set up" so the "black male" from Detroit is "not going to make it."

> Like when you grow up in the ghetto, they are like slums, basically set up for to keep a black person down. And when you grow up in that, you see things like that, and you be around it, it's just like you're going to be into it. 'Cause the steps already stand up so high, that you know, you ain't gonna get no black male in inner city, crime city, like Detroit where I'm from, he's not going to make it. No. And that's how it is. You know you are going to start getting in trouble, hanging out with the fellas, smoking bud, 'cause it's set up to hold us black people down.

To Dwayne, believing he might not "make it" as a consequence of living in inner-city Detroit, the move to Allerton represented a chance to acquire the diploma. He described the multiple problems he encountered when living in Detroit.

> You know why I got involved in that stuff, 'cause I had problems and things. It was difficult to deal with them in the environment, the situation I was born into. You know, people I was hangin' around with, the neighborhood I was in, like when I was at home in Detroit with the guys. Plus, I had family problems; it was hard to deal with, so I took that route. And basically I used that I guess as a scapegoat, and I started doing what I wanted to do, hanging out, smoking weed, drinking beer and all that.

Dwayne acknowledged he became involved in crime and drugs because of family problems that forced him out of his home. His friends were also his connection to drugs and alcohol. These friends were very important to Dwayne. The friendships he formed in his neighborhoods were Dwayne's solace: "My boys, they be like my brothers, NFL, Niggers For Life. When we do this and that, we go down together. . . .They gave me love, they were there for me." So moving to Allerton became an opportunity to be away from the problems he encountered in Detroit. But by moving away from the problems, Dwayne also moved away from his family and friends, particularly friends he cared about and who cared about him. Although he attempted to embrace life in Allerton and acquire the high school diploma, he yearned to be around his friends in Detroit. Despite wanting to avoid the problems in Detroit, Dwayne felt more connected to Detroit and to the friends he had been "hangin' around with" than to people in Allerton. He did not trust people in Allerton. The pull of Detroit saw Dwayne run away from his foster home in March 1993 and return to Detroit. From March onward, he continued to stay in Detroit despite his foster parents' attempts to persuade him to return.

The conflict between being in Allerton and wanting to live in Detroit was at the heart of many of my conversations with Dwayne. Notwithstanding, Dwayne continually argued that he wanted to complete high school in Allerton. But this was not an easy commitment for him to live by. On the immediate level, moving to

Allerton meant that he had to choose between his way of being in inner-city Detroit and his new ways of being in Allerton. By attending school in Allerton, he believed that he could acquire the high school diploma and thereby provide economic support for his family. He felt a responsibility to support his younger brothers and sisters and his drug-dependent mother, who at the time was a welfare recipient.

Dwayne talked about the high school credential in two ways: first, as being "something to show," and also as being a vehicle to college study. But it was the first meaning that Dwayne constantly talked about, not the second meaning. Without the diploma, Dwayne believed that he would have little chance of gaining employment, as he shared with me during the following interaction:

JP:	Have you ever thought about leaving school?
Dwayne:	Not really.
JP:	Why not?
Dwayne:	Ain't gonna make it.
JP:	So by graduating from high school, how's that going to help you?
Dwayne:	Help you going to college, have something to show, all them things.

While acquiring the high school diploma represented access to college for Dwayne, he never talked about attending college himself. As noted, his responses seemed almost rehearsed with little indication that he had knowledge of how to pursue such a path.

Essentially, without the high school diploma Dwayne believed he "ain't gonna make it." Making it for Dwayne appeared to mean having a certain degree of financial security. The diploma became a potential vehicle to such ends, but a vehicle to a job that did not necessarily require a college credential. In part, the diploma represented a connection to employment.

Another significance of the high school diploma was that it represented a symbol of achievement. With limited access to dominant symbols of recognition, Dwayne's focus on the high school diploma as a form of achievement is noteworthy. The high school diploma seemed to be an avenue for acquiring such recognition. Thus, the high school diploma emerged not only as an opportunity to potentially acquire economic security for himself and for his immediate family, but was also as a way of receiving an acceptable form of social recognition, "something to show."

Dwayne's quest to acquire the high school diploma was not easy for him to live out. This was reflected in an internal struggle he waged; a struggle that he said entailed working on being a "better person." While in his "placement," "[T]hey had me grow them ways," he said. He talked with anguish about his struggle to develop new values and beliefs.

Dwayne:	But since I'm at the placement, they had me grow them ways or whatever. You know, I still have those same things, you know, streets, because that's

> what I was born into. At home, I be with the fellas and it helped me to slow down, think more whatever, and try to make better decisions. It's hard, it ain't easy, I know that what I'm saying. But I just try to make it. There is still things I need to work on.
>
> JP: What would you like to work on?
> Dwayne: (Pause) I'd like to work on being a better person or whatever.
> JP: What does it mean to be a better person?
> Dwayne: I guess, you know, change some of the values I have.

Dwayne tried to take on new values and beliefs dynamically shaped by a different set of rewards and symbols of achievement than those he previously valued. While these values seem to represent middle-class values of success and achievement in school, it is difficult to unravel the new ways and values he struggled to acquire. He was encouraged to "make better decisions." But he did not embrace such a set of values with ease, nor with total commitment.[3] His anger about his experiences was most apparent in the following comments: "It's hard, once that's what you know, you growin' up in a placement, going to jail, it's not teaching you nothin'. That's punishment. That just makes you madder." For Dwayne, the high school diploma represented a desire to live a different kind of life. The high school diploma also represented an achievement that he believed his brothers and sisters might follow:

> Successful in my mind is to finish school to go to college. Be something up here [points to his head]. Passing on to my little sons and daughters, and be a role model for them and passing on. I don't want my little brothers and sisters, I don't want them to be bad.

Although Dwayne was not an active student at school, acquiring the high school diploma became a symbol that represented his attempt to develop new ways of being; ways of being that previously did not include a wholehearted commitment to staying in school and hence acquiring the diploma. But on one level staying out of jail was a victory, providing a sense of success to Dwayne. He told me that he wanted to be successful, "'Cause I got fear. They know I might take the wrong move or the wrong step, but I try to not let that bother me. I try to keep goin'. That's what I hope I do." The diploma became a symbol to "show" that he can be successful, that he kept "goin'," and it represented the possibility of having a good paying job. "I want to be successful, have a nice paying job, playing basketball, have a nice family." Despite the image of success Dwayne painted, he was scathing about the African-American middle class:

> . . . guess some of them forget where they came from. If I ever made it rich, you've always got to remember where you came from, how you grew up. That's how you grew up man. That's the lifestyle. They've got money into their head, they think they are better than us.

Dwayne, like Jeff, was vague about his intentions for college study, and even more vague about the entrance requirements for attending college. He had not spoken to a school counselor about his future job prospects after acquiring the high school diploma, let alone talked with someone about study at a tertiary educational institution. He did not know of anyone attending college and was unaware of how to access such information. Dwayne told me that he wanted to be an engineer or own his own business on completing high school, and that he would learn about either of these options "by going to school, finishing school, and college." While the acquisition of the high school diploma seemed to represent a job generally, rather than a particular career path or occupation, Dwayne had little knowledge of these paths. And with a low grade point average he seemed unlikely to gain admission to college.

Over the past few years, Dwayne's relationship with school had been unstable. During his years in middle school, he said he "used to skip and stuff." I asked him why he used to skip, and he told me, "I was stupid, tied to other things." At one time, he could not attend school because there was a warrant out for his arrest. Of late, staying in school was a way of staying out of trouble with the police. But this did not mean that he found school attractive or that there was something to entice him into school. In our conversations Dwayne talked very little about what he learned or did in school. At one point he said, "Sometimes, I got short patience anyhow, it just be getting on my nerves and stuff. I just don't like it." Of his previous teachers he said, "A lot of them, attention might not gonna be right. . . ." This comment might suggest that he did not receive the kind of attention he sought in schools. Dwayne was adamant, though, that it was not just his encounters in school that were influential in his truancy: there were other explanations as well:

> . . . don't know if they all got to do so much at school, like some things happened in the family, maybe affecting you in school, and like getting locked up and stuff like that. It affects you and a lot of things on your mind.

Dwayne's attempts to shape his material and social world were in part embodied in the symbolism of the high school diploma. The process of acquiring the diploma, and the actual acquisition of the diploma, represented his attempt to live a life away from crime, away from gangs, and to be employed in a job. But Dwayne did not embrace such a world with ease and instead constantly battled to live a life away from his experiences in Detroit. At the same time, however, he wanted to be connected to the people from his world in Detroit. His will to run away from his foster home in Allerton and return to Detroit, in a sense saw him rejecting the possibility of acquiring the high school diploma, a symbol of achievement that he seemingly wanted. I later learned that Dwayne was arrested in August 1993 for selling drugs and was awaiting trial.

For Dwayne, his world *was* the people in Detroit, people whom he knew and cared about. The struggle to acquire the high school credential then seemed to leave him having to choose between living an alienating life in Allerton and acquiring the high school diploma, or living in inner-city Detroit with his friends and family but with little chance of making it. As Dwayne said, African-American men from Detroit are not going to make it: " 'Cause the steps already stand up so high, that you know, you ain't gonna get no black male in inner city, crime city, like Detroit where I'm from, he's not going to make it. No. And that's how it is." Ironically, even though he wanted to stay in Allerton, he was uncertain about where the diploma would take him. But this choice potentially seemed to provide a greater opportunity for him than if he stayed in Detroit. Dwayne seemed faced with an impossible choice. In the end, the separation from his friends in Detroit combined with the degree of alienation he felt in Allerton saw him returning to Detroit, never to return to Allerton or to a high school.

RASHAUD DUPONT: "A GUARANTEED FUTURE"

Dwayne starkly contrasted with Rashaud Dupont, who attended Cedarville High School, located in a middle-class neighborhood. Although these two young men were similar in age, Rashaud being 15 and Dwayne 16 years old, and both were African-American men, Rashaud's life experiences greatly differed from Dwayne's encounters in the world. These differences include the neighborhoods they had lived in, their home environments, the curriculum and pedagogy encountered at the schools they attended, the hopes and ambitions they pursued, and the forms of cultural capital they could access. Rashaud had lived in Cedarville since he was 6 years old. His mother moved to Allerton from Mississippi in her early twenties, and then moved to Cedarville where Rashaud attended elementary, middle, and high school. Cedarville was a decidedly affluent area with a predominantly stable, white, middle-class population. At one point Rashaud described Cedarville High School as a school with "rich white kids." "It's like 90210 with a little bit of color," he laughed, as he described his school as similar to the weekly television drama about the lives of wealthy teenagers living in Beverly Hills. "They try to make it deep and interesting, I mean how deep and how many social problems can you have, when you have a white girl who has had a nose job, and drives a BMW?" he commented.

Despite Rashaud's scathing critique of Cedarville High School, he admitted that he would not want to attend another school: "I don't like it but I wouldn't want to go anywhere else," he said. What he didn't like about the school was the "social environment," but he did like the "learning environment." For Rashaud, part of the social environment he detested was being put on a "pedestal" by white people at the school. "Whatever you do is considered special," he said. At the same time, he talked about the cliques of groups at the school.

At Cedarville, the cliques dominate so much that nobody really knows somebody. I know a lot of people by name, I can tell you just about everybody's name at Cedarville High School. It seems like the cliques are so tight that no one from somewhere else can get into one. The reason why I hang out where I hang out is anybody can talk to anybody.

Rashaud told me that he spent his social time at school in an area frequented by most of the African-American students and some Latino students attending the school. Thus, despite the apparent acceptance and respect of African-American people in the school there was still strict segregation between the white and African-American students. It was this aspect of school that Rashaud did not like. Rashaud's peer group was almost exclusively African-American because he "can talk to anybody" in this group. While this seemed a choice to Rashaud, it seems as though the choice was constructed in reaction to the ways of being of the white students at school. Rashaud admitted, however, he would not want to go to school anywhere else. It is within the context of simultaneously criticizing and embracing Cedarville High School that I want to situate Rashaud's meanings of the high school diploma.

Rashaud had few people at school he would call friends. He did not intimately socialize outside of school with many of the students from Cedarville High. While he criticized many of the students who attended the school, mostly the wealthy white students, he simultaneously shared the career and material aspirations of most of his peers. Given that 85 percent of Cedarville High students went to college, it is not surprising that he constructed ideas and ambitions that seemed in keeping with the ideas, beliefs, and values that dominated experiences at school and aspirations beyond school. Notwithstanding the shared values, beliefs, and aspirations of life in and beyond school, Rashaud was marginalized from the dominant student culture at school and found it difficult to connect with most of the students.

Despite the apparent segregation of African-American students from white students, Rashaud shared with the white, middle-class students access to ideas and information that enabled him to develop particular goals. For instance, he had considerable information about the requirements to pursue college-level study and indicated that grades were a significant indicator of the college he would attend. Entrance depended on "how my test scores and grades come out, that probably will tell me where I would like to go and where they would accept me." Further, Rashaud interestingly drew a distinction between getting out of high school and getting into college.

To get into college, you have to take the PACT or ACT. Those are the ones to get in. To get out of high school, you have to take three years of science, I think four years of mathematics, two years of history or world studies, fine arts, two years of physical education, one semester of swimming.

Rashaud shared with me a folder that his school distributed to all the students. The folder contained documents that carefully outlined requirements to acquire a high school diploma. He was considering a career in the sciences, possibly as a chemical engineer. "Engineering, or sciences, or something like that, I kind of excel in sciences," he suggested. He was adamant that he would attend the University of Michigan and not other institutions in Michigan such as Eastern Michigan University, Wayne State, or Michigan State University. Rashaud nevertheless was cautious about his future, and suggested that entrance to the University of Michigan was dependent upon his grades and test scores. Other young men in the study, besides Shawn, had not developed such a firm knowledge of the credential accumulation path as Rashaud.

Rashaud, like Jeff and Dwayne, wanted the high school diploma. The diploma for Jeff and Dwayne represented the accomplishment of a personal goal and potential employment. For Rashaud it seemed much more than an end in itself; it seemed a springboard to a future career plan based on the acquisition of a college level credential. To Rashaud, the diploma represented social and economic mobility reflected in the job and the money he might earn. Rashaud wanted to enter a profession that would make him wealthy, "make money, make lots of money." The high school diploma represented, "Getting paid, a job to me, or a future, a guaranteed future just about. Not money back, but a 90 day guarantee." The consequence of getting a high school diploma was centered on his belief that the high school diploma would lead to a well-paid job. "[T]o me it's the dollar, the better I do, the better I will do later on in life." Intertwined with Rashaud's quest to acquire the high school diploma was a goal of accumulation of wealth for personal gain. He linked accumulation of money to personal power. "I think money is power. So, the more money that I have, the more power that I have."

Rashaud said that grades were the biggest challenge that he faced in his quest for the diploma. "Grades, that's what's on my mind, the biggest. I don't give a rip about anything else," he said. And Rashaud worked hard to achieve his high grades. On average he spent 3 hours a day completing his homework.

It helps to spend a couple of hours, maybe three hours every day. It seems like with me, I don't know why, the part of my day where I do homework, I can't remember. It's just like I hope I did it. And you come back and get your 95 or 100%, whatever on it. You've been programmed for so long to come home and then do your homework or whatever.

In fact, Rashaud canceled a number of meetings we had arranged due to his commitment to work on a school project or some homework. Many of his after-school activities centered on completing homework tasks. He talked about homework more than any other young man that I interviewed. Intrigued with his strong determination and his response to my question about the biggest challenge he faced, I asked him why grades were important to him. "For me it's an ego thing, I like doing well. I always like doing well. When I do well, I like to show off a lot," he told me.

Rashaud saw himself as a "role model" to other African-Americans. In particular, he wanted to be seen as a "role model" for younger members of his mother's extended family. The idea of being a good role model developed from observing his uncles and his grandfather in Mississippi. Rashaud spent most of his summers in Mississippi with members of his mother's family. He said family members served as his "good" role models and "I think that is how I should behave." Following their example, he believed he should serve as a "role model" for the younger members of his extended family, believing his cousins would be able to match his accomplishments. Rashaud seemed to operate within a paradigm where all students have the same opportunity to succeed. He did not indicate that he thought he had a better chance than other African-Americans to achieve his goals.

> Myself, I think what I do comes first. And seeing that I have to be an example, that's the right outlook. I think I should look at myself first, and what am I going to do. If I'm going to be able to do anything, I think anybody should be able to do it. If I am going to get all A's, I think that just about anybody should be able to do it, that's how I feel. 'Cause if I do it then I think that everyone else should do it. That's why I don't drink, because if I do it, then I think that everyone else might do it. I think of myself more as a role model.

Rashaud appeared to have great confidence in himself and his achievements. The above-mentioned comments not only reveal his sense of duty to his family as a "role model," but also his sense of his connection to the African-American community.

On another occasion he told me grades were one of the most important aspects of school to him.

> Basically 'cause I've got to uphold an image, with myself, my mom and people in Cedarville . . . disproving something. That not all black kids are just a bunch of dumb kids that like to play sports. And what I'm trying to do is, if I can play sports, have fun, and get good grades at the same time, maybe somebody else will try to do the same thing.

Rashaud's goal of achieving good grades and upholding "an image," was not just an image to be imitated by his immediate family or peers, but also by the broader African-American community. He constructed an identity and used the grading system not only to "show off," but also to challenge stereotypes that exist about African-American achievement and abilities. His audience was both the African-American community, where he wanted to be a role model, and the white community, where he wanted to challenge stereotypes about African-Americans.

Rashaud received high grades for all his classes and deemed these high grades important to gaining access to college. During his senior year, he hoped to attend classes in math or science at a nearby university, because "it helps you get your foot in the door to get into college."

Rashaud presented himself as a self-assured, goal-oriented person. Whereas Jeff and Dwayne talked about their goals, they did not speak with the same knowledge as Rashaud of what it would take to achieve the goal of acquiring a "guaranteed future." He did not see any barriers that would prevent him from achieving his goal. When asked whether he saw any particular barriers that could hinder African-Americans in their access to opportunities, he replied, "Outside of academics, there may be some that I haven't encountered yet. Inside the Cedarville public school system, and where I choose to go to college, there shouldn't be any problems for me." Rashaud's experiences and encounters as a young African American man in Cedarville, while somewhat alienating for him, helped him develop views about mobility and advancement that seemed unattainable for someone like Dwayne from Detroit. Rashaud did not acknowledge such differential access. His experiences of racism and classism seemed different from those of Dwayne and Jeff. Therefore, he seemed to hold different ideas of the barriers that could temper his ambitions and goals beyond high school.

Rashaud's encounters in the world and his experiences in the Cedarville public school system convinced him that he would be able to achieve the goal of going to college without much hindrance. Given that 85 percent of the students went on to college, and that Rashaud had a track record of high attainment in his advanced placement courses, it seemed probable that he would go on to a four-year college. Rashaud was firmly located in middle-class life through his experiences in his neighborhood and school. His mother was enrolled in a Ph.D. program and worked as an educational professional for a statewide organization. Rashaud made seemingly smooth connections between the diploma and his long-term aspirations, because of his academic achievements and his immersion in a middle-class school and neighborhood. The experiences saw him constructing a picture of the world whereby he predicted his success story becoming inspirational for others. He viewed himself as serving as a role model. His notions were based on his experiences and his encounters. They ignored differences across race and race–class boundaries. Rashaud's attempt to hold himself up as a role model, however, failed to take into account the personal cost of attempting to achieve in a predominantly white, middle-class neighborhood and school. His image of success and becoming successful was constructed through using a lens of middle-class success and social mobility to define a path of success for the rest of the African-American community.

Rashaud painted a complex picture of his relationship with school. He argued that he would not want to attend another school, despite feeling disconnected from the dominant social life at the school. Rashaud's strong commitment to acquiring the high school diploma and his aspirations for economic and social mobility were central to the significant role that school played in his life. He seemed prepared to tolerate alienating interpersonal relationships and was compensated by a hope of attaining his social and economic goals.

SHAWN BRAXTON: "IT'S MORE LIKE A START NOW"

Shawn Braxton, like Rashaud Dupont, attended Cedarville High School and lived in Cedarville. Shawn was an 11th grade student at the high school, having transferred during his ninth-grade year from a predominantly African-American school located in the outskirts of Detroit. Like Rashaud, Shawn was aware of the social class composition of the students who attended his school. He suggested "a lot of other schools have recognized us as a bunch of snotty-nosed kids." Shawn, like Rashaud, was committed toward a particular career path. Unlike Rashaud, Shawn had been living in the Cedarville area for only two years. His parents were divorced, and he lived with his older brother and his father in Cedarville. Shawn told me that he found it difficult to adapt to the environment in Cedarville. His father encouraged him to move to Cedarville because the school was "better" than his previous high school and would provide him better opportunities to pursue his goals beyond high school. His father, an education professional, moved to Cedarville because of a job transfer.

In essence, Shawn's move to Cedarville, encouraged by his mother and father, represented the belief that a diploma from Cedarville would carry more social and economic weight than a diploma from his previous school. He was one of the few young men to acknowledge that not all diplomas carry equal weight. Shawn did not talk about the high school diploma as a symbol of success or achievement; rather, he viewed the high school diploma as a vehicle to employment via a college credential. The high school diploma seemed to serve a functional role in his life as a springboard to acquiring a tertiary-level credential. "I realize that it's that they are hiring the person with the most experiences, the most education learned," he reflected. He felt that he would get a better education at Cedarville High School than he did in Detroit, and that after graduation,

> . . . in Detroit, it would be probably be harder to find a job . . . one of the reasons is that there are less jobs. I'm thinking about the level of education there. . . .I think employers will look at it, you know the person coming out of Cedarville first than he would coming from Detroit.

Shawn, like Rashaud, anticipated going to college after graduating from high school. In fact, he had already considered several options and was convinced that he would study histology. He talked about the prospect of getting a wrestling scholarship to go to college. Shawn's wrestling coach at school indicated that he had a strong possibility of receiving a scholarship. The prospect of receiving a scholarship, however, was not the sole determinant of whether Shawn would go to college. "I plan to [go] with or without a scholarship," Shawn asserted. During his 11th grade year, his grade point average was about 2.5. Nevertheless, Shawn believed he had a good chance of gaining acceptance to a local college. He did not indicate that his grade point average would be problematic in gaining access to a college, although that may be the case when considering current college entrance requirements.

Unlike Dwayne and Jeff, Shawn did not see the high school diploma as a significant achievement in its own right. For Shawn, the high school diploma was "more like a start now." Most of my conversations with Shawn were about the various options at the college level that he had considered pursuing once he graduated from high school. He seemed convinced he would go to college whether or not he received a scholarship. This stance suggests that the employment he sought required a college-level credential.

His ambitions also were firmly rooted in and connected to his family's orientation toward education. He openly admitted that "I think if I didn't have my Dad making me, I probably wouldn't go" to school. Yielding to this pressure from his father, Shawn went to school and also actively surveyed the many resources at school that would inform him of requirements and possibilities for high school graduation and college entrance. Also, Shawn received support and information and ideas from the career center he attended daily. During the year of the study, he spoke to counselors and to various speakers who came into his school to talk about a range of career options. All the options Shawn listed involved going to college. At the time of this study, he was interested in becoming a histologist "because that was the highest paying." Shawn had a great interest in the sciences, receiving B grades at school in both math and science; he openly admitted that he did not like English and history, for which he routinely received a C and a B, respectively.

Shawn attended a local career center where he spent each morning in classes, before returning to Cedarville High School in the afternoon. The career center was located about 10 miles away from his high school. Shawn believed his involvement in the program at the career center allowed him to gain skills that would serve as a foundation for a future program at the college level: "It was designed for people who weren't planning to go to college. Wanted to learn a trade, get a job after high school. The program I'm in is a great start to get into college."

While many of Shawn's peers did not intend to go to college after high school and viewed the opportunities at the career center as a vehicle to employment, Shawn saw the opportunities differently. He saw the skills he learned at the career center as providing an opportunity to take a job after high school graduation that would enable him to support himself while he studied at a college. Thus, if he did not receive a wrestling scholarship, his alternative would be to work as a laboratory technician at a local hospital, most likely Allerton General Hospital, while studying part time at a local college.

Through viewing the high school diploma as a "start now," Shawn made a direct connection between the high school credential and the acquisition of another credential. To Shawn, the high school diploma "just means that to me I've just fin- ished high school, it wouldn't be a big achievement that I would cherish or anything, I'm done." The high school diploma thus becomes a vehicle to reach further levels in the credentialing process whereby the higher the level of creden- tial attained, the better will be the social and economic status of one's job. His view of the high school diploma as representing "more like a start now" suggests that he did not see the diploma as a significant achievement. Shawn said the high school diploma "could say that this person is smart or whatever," but he did not sound convinced that this was the case, because, as noted earlier, he commented that, "I mean, it really can't say too much because a person can graduate through high school with all D's. . . ." So, Shawn suggested the social and economic weight of the diploma varies across institutions and among individuals from the same school.

Shawn talked about school as something he had to do. He did not speak much about his need to achieve good grades, nor did he speak much about enjoying school. His attitude to schoolwork was most evident when he talked with me about his various career options. I asked him whether he had considered going into a medical field. He told me,

> One guy I talked to, he said why don't you go ahead and be a doctor? Because if any- one discovered the cure for AIDS, the doctor would be the one getting all the credit for it. But I don't really like school all that much, and six years of school doesn't seem like me.

For Shawn, acquiring the credential meant gaining access to a well-paid job. It seemed as though it was a given to him that he would receive the diploma.

Shawn's comments suggest that he believed he would be afforded the opportu- nities that would allow him to pursue a credential beyond the high school diploma. He also indicated that not all credentials have the same social and economic weight, and there were differences in the value of credentials acquired within and across schools. Armed with this knowledge, Shawn moved to Cedarville and carved out a path for his future that firmly rested upon his acquisition of the high school diploma and the acquisition of another credential at the college level.

ZAKEEV WASHINGTON: "TICKET TO COLLEGE"

Zakeev Washington attended Western High School in Allerton, which had an African-American student population of approximately 30 percent, and a white student population of approximately 58 percent. Zakeev transferred to Western at the beginning of the school year because his mother decided to move to another neighborhood in Allerton. He previously had attended Central High School, the school that Dwayne Reynolds and Marcus Williams attended, and that Jeff Davidson attended before he transferred to Allerton Christian School. Zakeev preferred aspects of Western to Central but really missed the people of Central. At Western, he preferred the form of pedagogy which he described as "quicker." He ascribed the difference between the pedagogies of the two schools to the high proportion of white students attending Western. He considered the school a "majority white" school.

> *Zakeev:*   I'd rather be at Central. To me, school wise, not the people, Western teaches you more. And the reason I think that, is that it's majority white. That's what I'm saying, it's majority. And they're quick.
> *JP:*   Who, the students or the teachers?
> *Zakeev:*   The teachers, they go through things like that. I'm thinking, see, soon as it's majority white, you start teaching people quicker and putting it in their minds. . . . In my history class, I'm doing a test almost every three days. Like at Central, it would be every other week. It was weird to me, as soon as I got there, it was quick, and teachers were teaching like they were supposed to be teaching. They were teaching at a speed, you know, we were supposed to be at. At Central, they were teaching at sixth grade level, not their teaching but their speed.

Although Zakeev preferred the pedagogy of Western, he often complained of having few friends at Western. He preferred the "social" aspect of Central High School, where he was connected to more people at school. But Zakeev was tied to Western because he lived in the school's catchment area.

Zakeev was strongly committed to acquiring the high school diploma. After high school graduation, Zakeev planned to attend college. He intended first to attend Allerton Community College, followed by the University of Michigan. Zakeev wanted to be "an orthodontist, have lots of money." He decided on the possibility of an orthodontist "because my teeth aren't so good, like I can see. I'd like to work on other people's teeth because mine aren't so great to begin with. And that's the reason I want to work there." Although Zakeev established a goal of acquiring the high school diploma, he ascribed minimal importance to acquiring the credential. He spoke of the acquisition of the high school diploma in ways similar to Shawn. Zakeev saw the high school diploma as a "ticket to college." "I think it's like a ticket. College is really what you need, diploma not really much anyway. Ticket to college," Zakeev told me. Zakeev seemed to place less importance on the actual acquisition of the high school diploma compared to Jeff or Dwayne, and developed a stance similar to Shawn and Rashaud. Zakeev situated the acquisition of the high school credential within the context of acquiring a college credential. He seemed to believe that the acquisition of the diploma was within his reach, and thus the diploma took on a lesser significance in comparison to the college diploma he aspired to attain.

Although Zakeev seemingly crafted a clear vision for himself along a particular credential accumulation path, just like Jeff and Dwayne he admitted he was unsure about the requirements to attend college. However, unlike Jeff and Dwayne he was aware of a difference between meeting requirements to graduate from high school and meeting the requirements to gain college entrance. He criticized the kind of information that school counselors gave him about graduations requirements:

> . . . mostly the counselors are really doing nothin'. What is required to graduate, what is required to graduate? I was like, I'm not interested in that. Like what is required to go to college? . . . They kept telling you what is required to graduate. . . . Graduating ain't nothin' if you ain't going to college. They won't tell you that.

Zakeev wanted to know more about college entrance requirements, but he felt that his school counselors withheld the information from him.

Zakeev's comments suggest that he held particular ideas about how he would utilize the high school credential as a tool for social and economic advancement. Although the diploma did represent a significant achievement in its own right, its central significance was that it symbolized a ticket to higher social and economic status, probably a college-level credential. While Zakeev aspired to gain a college level credential, he did not envision a smooth path in attaining such a goal. He suggested that he might encounter difficulty in securing entrance to a university. For example, one of the barriers that might prevent him from attending a university was his grade point average. At the time, his cumulative grade point average was 2.3. He told me that the implications of getting such a grade point average would mean that "I'd have to go to a community college." For Zakeev, the community college became a springboard to a university and not a terminal degree in itself.

Zakeev's quest to go to college needs to be located within the context of his relationships at home, particularly in the context of his relationship with his mother and his brothers and sister. Zakeev had two brothers and one sister. His sister was a sophomore at a university in Ohio, while his 22-year-old brother was serving a sentence in jail. Zakeev's younger brother attended middle school. Zakeev described his mother as one of the most important people in his life. He said that he tried to get good grades "to prove my Mom. Because when I get bad grades, I just feel so bad, I like to prove to my Mom." My discussion with her also revealed the importance and stress she placed on the acquisition of the high school diploma. His mother held a very strong belief that education is the key to economic security and social advancement. Zakeev likewise embraced such a perspective.

Zakeev, like Shawn, talked about the parental pressure to go to school. Unlike Shawn, however, Zakeev, did not talk about not going to school if his mother did not "make" him go. Interestingly, my question to each of the participants was, "why do you get up and go to school every day?" In part, Shawn's and Zakeev's responses to the question included the word "make," which could mean there was some form of parental authority that each of their parents wielded over their sons. Zakeev situated such parental influence within a context of broader political and economic realities. He constructed the alternatives if he decided not to attend school. For him, the alternative of dropping out of school was to be unemployed and to stay at home. Interestingly, the theme of the law and the criminal justice system also entered his conversation. This particular theme connects to the experiences Dwayne and Jeff spoke about earlier in my discussion. Zakeev told me,

> What makes them go to school is their mothers. . . . She doesn't want me sitting on the corner. What are you goin' to do if you are not in school? What else you got to do? . . . if you can't stay in school, there's nothin', unless you break the law or sit around and be lazy. It's not like you're dropping out to get a job or anything. You're dropping out just to be lazy. And do nothin'.

An interesting aspect of Zakeev's statement is his belief that staying in school potentially represented active participation in social life, the opposite of "doing nothin'." Zakeev had virtually no friends outside of school, so school became a central place for him to form social relationships. It is within the context of his being unconnected to others in his neighborhood that school played a significant role in his life. The high unemployment rate also influenced Zakeev's belief that a diploma might increase his chances of being employed.

Although Zakeev relied upon school to form friendships, constantly moving around Allerton made it difficult for him to develop sustained friendships. Paradoxically, it was the moving around that made him rely upon relationships in school to develop friendships, a place where he admitted he found it difficult to connect with others. Zakeev attended school in numerous settings across the Allerton area that includes two high schools, one middle school, and five elementary schools. His mother had moved many times. For example, during 1992 he lived in three different houses and transferred to Western High School in September of 1992. He claimed that moving around left him with having to constantly make new friends. Hence, for Zakeev, going to school was important, not just because he did not want to be "lazy," but so he could meet people.

Zakeev argued, however, that just because he went to school did not mean that he "likes" everything in school. "I don't like everything. I hate that I have to do these courses that I have nothing to do with, and they show nothing on me." Although Zakeev disliked almost all of his classes, he did look forward to his band class where he played the saxophone. Many times when I visited Zakeev at home, he was practicing his saxophone, and took great joy in performing for me. It was one of the things that he really enjoyed about school. Despite Zakeev being generally unenthusiastic about activities in school, the fact remains that he did go to school regularly and he stayed in school. So the commitment to acquiring the high school diploma represents a paradox for Zakeev as it does for most of these young men; he placed little value on the process of acquiring the high school diploma, yet greatly emphasized the attainment of a high school diploma.

Despite his not liking "everything" in school, Zakeev did not absolutely reject the content of his classes of school. He developed a justification for learning at school that simultaneously dismissed the content and acknowledged that such knowledge had some intrinsic value to him.

> If I want to change something I got to go to school. I got to learn everything I've got to learn. White, black, whatever. I kind of know the dates, that's something. I would rather know the white knowledge than knowing no way at all. And if you don't know it that way, how can you change it?

Zakeev developed a rationale for going to school that included embracing knowledge he described as "white knowledge" and wanting to change "it." He never really clarified what he wanted to change, and never really talked about wanting to change a particular aspect of school per se. Nonetheless, he painted a complex picture of learning a content that "shows nothing on" him, yet he suggested that knowing white knowledge was better than "knowing no way at all." This theme of both embracing and critiquing the content and form of school will be explored in the following chapter. He recalled a conversation with a friend at school:

> I was asking this girl. . . . "You think you will get a good job without diploma?" And she was like, "yeah, you can get a good job without your diploma." I was like, "you get out of high school, you think you can get a good job? There's a lot of folks, how many people do you think are going to make it to Hollywood?"

Zakeev's comment suggests a belief that acquisition of the diploma would lead to employment, and there would be little chance of economic success without the diploma. Failing to acquire the diploma seemed to limit the chances of acquiring a job; the chance of "making it" is diminished. On another occasion, he said he wanted to acquire the high school diploma because "I don't want to be on the welfare line." So acquiring the diploma represented a greater potential to acquire a job than that available without the diploma. Notwithstanding, he argued that it was difficult for an African-American to acquire a job even with the credential in hand. He puzzled about the nature of the credentialing process in the United States:

> What's so strange about America, there are people who have got Master's degree, still can't get a job. You've got to search for jobs. You have to sweat for jobs. . . . There's not very much opportunity in this period now. . . . White people have got a better chance of getting it. Because we have to play their game. And all they have to do is act natural.

Zakeev spoke of the privilege and power that is afforded to white people in the quest to get a job. This view markedly contrasts with the perspectives of Jeff, Rashaud, and Shawn, who did not bring into the conversation the racial barriers that may confront them in the labor market. For Zakeev, acquiring a job was intertwined with learning to play the rules of "their game."

In a sea of complex and seemingly contradictory explanations and justifications for going to school, and setting a goal for acquiring the high school diploma, Zakeev continued to go to school, and remained in school. Zakeev appeared to be perhaps the most socially isolated out of the six young men in this study. School was a place where he could develop friendships, yet he admitted that he had few friends at school. Zakeev was considering going to college after completing high school, yet criticized the fact that he had not been informed about college entrance requirements. He also criticized the racial nature of the school curriculum that "shows nothin' on" him. He developed a position whereby he argued that it was better to know the "white knowledge" than "knowing no way at all." This suggests a tension of both embracing and critiquing the content and form of school. Zakeev's case reveals the complexities involved in going to school as an young African-American man: wanting to acquire the high school diploma, yet resenting what he had to learn to acquire the diploma.

MARCUS WILLIAMS:
"I JUST WANNA MAKE SOMETHIN' OUT OF MYSELF"

Of all the young men in this study, Marcus Williams was perhaps the most critical about the nature of the school. In particular, he was critical about the racist nature of the content of aspects of schooling. For example, he criticized the racist nature of the curriculum and pervasive racism in many student–teacher relationships. Despite such criticism, Marcus went to school daily and was strongly committed to acquiring the high school diploma.

Marcus was 17 years old and attended the 10th grade of Central High School. He often revealed that he felt too old for his grade level and should be graduating in 1993. Marcus had been held back a grade when he arrived in Allerton in Grade 3. He also was found to be dyslexic and retained for a year in sixth grade. As a consequence of his diagnosed dyslexia, Marcus convinced himself that it was difficult for him to recall information he learned at school. Despite the diagnosed dyslexia and feeling older than his peers, Marcus developed the courage to go to school.

He went to school because he felt as though he wanted "to make something out of himself," although he admitted that school was "not a big part of his day." School became almost a ritual that he had to endure.

> Because I don't really acknowledge it really, it just something I have to do. . . . Just to survive, just have to do it, just to survive. Because basically what I feel is this. 'Cause what I've been learning now I'm understanding what they're doing, they're really taking us back. So basically I don't have a feel for school. I won't drop out. . . . I have to do it, I wanna get my education, you know I want to hurry up and get out of here.

He spoke of school in very much the same way as Zakeev Washington. Like Zakeev, going to school and acquiring the high school diploma for Marcus was necessary in order to "survive." His view seemed rooted in his sense of economic survival.

Marcus had lived in Allerton for the past 8 years, having previously lived in Port Edward, a medium-sized town with a predominately African-American and poor population. The town had been badly hit by structural changes in the economy and many residents were unemployed for lengthy periods of time. Marcus's mother moved from Port Edward to Allerton to find a job and because she thought the educational system in Allerton was of a higher standard.

> *Marcus:*   And down there it's real bad. . . . You've got black on black crime, you've got killing one another down there.
> *JP:*   Really, what's going on in their lives?
> *Marcus:*   The major one thing, is that you can get a bunch of money in practically an hour. More than a thousand dollars in practically an hour. And the way white folks got it today, black folks can't get no jobs. And so they get forced into that. And the way I was brought up. I won't touch that with a ten-foot pole. My grandmother made sure. . . . She brought us up not to do that, you know and I consider myself to be a strong brother because the environment I grew up in, I didn't come out like those other people, on drugs, those dope addicts and selling the stuff. That's how my family is, none of us sell drugs.

His quest to achieve the high school diploma was shaped by a number of forces. For instance, life in Port Edward shaped how Marcus viewed the world, particularly his understanding of the impact of unemployment and poverty on the lives of people. Essentially, he wanted a diploma because it represented a potential job. Fundamentally, Marcus' ambition to acquire the high school diploma was not linked to getting a higher level credential. His mother and grandparents, whom he had much respect for, shared his belief in the value of an education as a tool for economic advancement. Also, acquiring the high school diploma was one way of declaring a commitment to not get involved in drug use and trading in drugs.

An aspect of school that was attractive to Marcus was the strong social network of friends attending Central. Notwithstanding friends at school being important to Marcus, his routinized attendance at school was primarily motivated by his wish to acquire the high school diploma.

> One of the reasons I go to school, I just want that diploma. Because basically to me, they ain't there to teach, they're just there to get their paycheck at the end of the week. They ain't teaching you nothin'. 'Cause if they was teaching you something, they would be teaching you something about your black African culture, instead of teaching you white is superior. Because that is all they are teaching you, white is so superior, they dominate everything.

Marcus was scathing about the content of school. He felt as though he was not learning anything of significance to him as an African-American. In particular, Marcus criticized the Eurocentric perspective that dominated the curriculum.

Marcus's desire to acquire the high school diploma appeared contradictory. He dismissed the nature of the school curriculum, yet it was the very curriculum that he had to endure in order to acquire the high school diploma. Numerous African-Americans thinkers, particularly Farrakhan and Malcolm X, influenced his framework for critique of school. Of the six young African-American men in this study, Marcus was perhaps the most vocal about the complexities of being an African-American attending a public school. "Like they have an African-American class at school and I heard there's a white lady teaching the class too. I said how can a white lady tell us about our own culture? She don't know nothin' about us," he argued.

While Marcus focused on acquiring the high school diploma as a ticket to employment, he also talked about going to college, but as something in passing. If he went to college, he would take cooking classes "for real expert cooks." It is perhaps the goal of employment and the value his mother placed on education that were influential forces in Marcus attending school. He attended school, "Because of the way my Mom made us feel [it's] important to go to school. Beat my tail if I don't. I don't mess around with her. I may be bigger than she is, but I'm scared of the woman." But Marcus was even critical of his mother's sense of why he should attend school. He said that his mother told him to go to school because he had "to learn." But Marcus questions this belief: "Learn what? They ain't teaching us nothin'. The stuff I learned, I learned on my own," he disclosed with aggravation.

> They just want, all the teachers there, is to get their paycheck at the end of the week and to be in class to give you that old stuff that you heard before, that's it. Give you a bunch of dittos and papers and all that stuff. They won't sit down and discuss stuff with you and everything.

Marcus suggested that much of the work at school was repetitious, that there was very little interaction among the teachers and students, and that most of the work that they engaged in was through work sheets.

Marcus presented few options for actions he intended to pursue once he acquired the high school diploma. At one time, he considered being a lawyer "but I'd be putting my brothers in jail. Ugh, ugh. Even if they did do something wrong, I'd just feel bad," he argued. His primary commitment after school was to enter the food service industry as a chef. He also said he would like to own his own restaurant.

> I love cooking, that's it, that's my hobby. That's what I want to make a career out of.
> . . . Basically because I'm good at it, and I love doing it. . . . See I want to be my own

chef, so like if, basically like a caterer. So I can raise my own time, do what I want to do. Lord knows we need more black businesses around here.

Marcus's quest to own his own business was motivated by the fact that he thought there needed to be more black-owned businesses.[4] In part this goal was influenced by his experiences at work, which Marcus claimed was fraught with racism. Particularly, he spoke of how the management unfairly treated him compared to his white co-workers and how they were reluctant to hire African-American people to wait tables. At another job Marcus held, he complained of the manager's criteria for hiring and the kinds of jobs each person was allotted. Marcus alleged that race was a significant factor in determining the kinds of jobs each worker was allocated.

> They have no black waitresses. And they will not hire none either. . . . You know, I've got a lot of friends that would like to get into it, that would like to be a waitress. And, they're so scared of black folks, they think were stealing their tip. I said if I was stealing their tips they wouldn't know about it, believe me. . . . [T]hey have all the black folks in the back where you can't be seen, or you're bussing, doing dirty jobs, cleaning off tables for somebody. That's basically what it is. You've got one black host waiter. So, I keep asking for a position change.

Marcus's critique of the racist nature of the hiring practices at work was part of the critique that he developed about his experiences in school with teachers, about the content of school, and about other arenas of social life.

In the same way as his racial critique of hiring practices at work was connected to his views of school, his relationship with his parents had a bearing on how he approached school. Often he engaged in verbal wrangles with his parents, particularly about the control his stepfather attempted to wield over Marcus. From April until October 1993, he left home because felt he could not tolerate the hostility between himself and his stepfather. During this period, he stayed with many friends for about 2 months; thereafter he moved into an apartment with his 21 year-old cousin, who was receiving social assistance and struggling financially to make ends meet. Marcus used his income from his evening and weekend job to pay for a portion of the household expenses. Over this 6-month period, Marcus did not receive any support, emotional or financial, from his parents. In fact, he had only spoken with his mother a couple of times during this period.

Marcus's need to work was intensified when he decided to move out of his parents' home. He was desperate to seize his independence from his parents and was also committed to showing them that he could be successful at staying in school. Realizing his job at the fast-food restaurant provided him with insufficient income to support himself, he tried to get a better-paid job, but was unsuccessful.

> I asked for a different position, they know I've got an apartment. I barely had enough money to pay rent this month. 'Cause my cousin paid for half of it. Luckily

his check came. He ain't got no job neither, so he gettin' unemployment. He had the money, I had a little bit to put down on it. I had only about $70 to put down on.

Despite the difficulties with his parents, and his need to work to pay for his rent and food, Marcus continued to go to school, and attended school every day without fail.

I'm not going there so they can educate me, I educate my own self. I read books for myself. They teach me the wrong thing. . . . [T]hey don't really care about education. To me, because of how they got the system there, they just want you to get grades, and get the hell out of their class. That's what it is. Because they just give you grades. I know because I haven't learned nothing from that, nothing that I ain't heard before, because I've been hearing the same stuff for years and years.

Although Marcus asserted that grades were insignificant, they did play a role in his day-to-day relationships, particularly in his fragile relationships with his parents. Going to school, and getting good grades, was one of the ways Marcus tried to prove himself to his parents. "To me, I'm trying to prove something to my parents that I can come home with a 3.0 and keep it up. And that's one of the reasons why" he went to school. Grades were tied in to Marcus's relationship with his parents, and to his desire to be recognized by his parents. Grades seemed the most available tool to gain such recognition.

He viewed grades as a way of proving to his parents that he could achieve in school despite his not being at home as regularly as he used to be.

Marcus: My parents gonna think I can't do it. They think I gonna slack off because I ain't in the house now. I wasn't slacking off, I used to be so nervous that trying not to do stuff wrong and I always do and they was always on me and I was forever on punishment. I stay on the punishment for the whole year.

JP: Like what is the punishment?

Marcus: I can't go outside or something, I had to stay in the house.

JP: For doing what?

Marcus: Nothin'. It's just stupid stuff, if I didn't clean something. It don't necessary have to be because of my grades. It's because I didn't do something around the house. To me that's stupid. Because I say if I bring home good grades, because one semester I brought home a 3.6. And, I was like four As, a C and a G. And em, you know, I had got in trouble too 'cause I didn't clean up something. I said, yahoo, you be yelling at me about my grades, then when I get some good ones they all act like they're unhappy about them. And they just look at me, and they just yell at me 'bout something else. And I'm like, hey, I'm proud that I got good grades.

Marcus clearly used his grades as a way to seek approval from his parents. In fact, in many conversations he complained of how he did not get much attention from his parents. Attaining good grades was one way in which he could command the attention of his parents. But as he noted, such attempts were not always met with the enthusiasm he anticipated. Thus, despite Marcus not living at home for a while, school, or rather his performance in school, served as a bridge to connect with his mother and to gain her approval.

So, the picture becomes more complex. Marcus did not value the content of school. Yet he did like being able to meet his friends. He did not find the work engaging in classes, yet he tried to get good grades, especially to please his parents. At no time did Marcus talk about the importance of attaining good grades for college entrance. In fact, as I have noted, Marcus did not really talk about a college he wanted to attend. He talked about learning to be a chef, but not about learning in any formal institution.

Marcus developed a contradictory position toward school in his quest to acquire the high school diploma. He was not learning anything of significance to him as an African-American attending school, and he argued that the teachers were disinterested and were teaching him "white is superior." Yet it was grades from his classes that he used to strengthen his tenuous relationship with his parents. All the while he was committed to going to school. Despite these contradictory positions, he mustered the courage to go to school daily, and he really wanted to "make something out of [him]self." Making something out of himself did not mean acquiring a considerable sum of money, or reaching a certain status position. Rather, he wanted to prove his capabilities and independence to his parents through achievement in school. In addition, he wanted to get a job in the food service industry or own a black business so he could support and serve his community. Marcus had a strong commitment to the African-American community. The next chapter explores his critique of school more thoroughly.

SYMBOLS, MEANINGS, AND SUCCESS

The high school diploma emerges as playing a somewhat different role in each of these young men's lives. I am not arguing that the meanings they constructed were solely of their own making. As they each experienced the social world and inhabited different schools and neighborhoods, and encountered different economic, social, and cultural conditions, the significance of the diploma and the ways they came to view the high school diploma varied. For all these young men, the diploma represented a *form* of social and economic mobility. However, they did not all set the same kinds of goals, nor did ideas of social and economic mobility enter the conversation with the same intensity or commitment. Through their experiences they embraced and rejected different elements of their social world.

Connected to such mobility were dominant images and ideas about what it means to be a successful man, with the images and ideas dominant in society reflecting the experiences of white, middle-class men. Also connected to these images are what Connell (1993b) described as buying into "a different construction of masculinity, in which the notion of long-term career is central" with different themes of "rationality and responsibility rather than pride and aggressiveness" (p. 199) interwoven through their career paths.

From their accounts, it appears that the act of making meaning of the high school diploma was constantly in a state of change and never complete. Their accounts revealed underlying beliefs, however, concerning what the diploma can say about them, and what it is a tool of. Their social location influenced how they could use the diploma as a tool for social and economic advancement. Their social location also significantly influenced the ways in which they each came to view and think about the high school diploma. Two themes emerge around the significance of the high school diploma: it was viewed (1) as a symbol of personal achievement; and (2) as a ticket to economic success.

Symbol of Achievement

Dwayne and Jeff were committed to acquiring the high school diploma because they believed that it represented an important personal achievement. For Dwayne, it was "somethin' to show" whereas for Jeff it was "kind of like a reward." This is not to say that they did not tie the diploma to the economic world, but the central significance of the diploma was that it symbolized a form of achievement. For these two young men, the diploma and its significance in their lives took on a particular form in part because of their encounters with the criminal justice system. The diploma became a vehicle to assert their version of masculinity as being successful in the world, but the success they constructed represented images that were more limiting than those of the other young men. Their versions seemed markedly different from Shawn's and Rashaud's versions. Their race, gender, and social class experiences were significant influences on how these choices emerged as important to them.

After Jeff's encounter with the criminal justice system, he drastically altered his relationship with school and turned to embrace it—and not any school, but a white, middle-class school. Going to school became one way of redeeming himself, in the eyes of his parents, and of others in the community. His entanglement with the criminal justice system stripped him of the potential to develop an acceptable form of masculinist success, which attending school now seemed to provide him. The high school diploma then became a reward to Jeff, a reward for completing schoo—regardless of what his experiences in school were.

Similarly, Dwayne's experience with the criminal justice system, combined with the harsh life experiences he encountered in inner city Detroit, saw him using the acquisition of the high school diploma as a tool for recognition. With little access to dominant symbols of success, the high school diploma became an available tool to prove that he was not a statistic of the inner city. He saw the high school diploma not solely as a vehicle for potential economic security and advancement, but as a tool to show he was not a victim of poverty and crime from the inner city.

These two young men, suffering the wrath of a society that penalizes young black men, tried to craft images of success through the diploma. They rejected hegemonic ideas about black men and embraced the diploma as a vehicle to success. Interestingly, the diploma can be seen as supporting privilege in that it is part of a credential accumulating path where in white, middle-class men are most rewarded[5] and many African-American men such as these two are not similarly rewarded. Though their stances may be similar, there were differences in how they embraced and rejected versions of subordinated masculinities—versions of African-American masculinities—with Jeff "acting white" in opposition to these images and ways of being, whereas Dwayne deeply valued the ways of being of his male African-American peers in Detroit.

Ticket to Economic Success

Jeff's and Dwayne's view contrasts with that of Marcus, Rashaud, Shawn, and Zakeev, who primarily argued that the diploma by itself had limited social or economic value. For these four young men, the diploma became a tool for economic and social advancement through the acquisition of a college credential. It became a vehicle for them to assert pride in their racial identities, but was also an image that reflected masculinist success and social class mobility through the material rewards and status the credential could reap. Granted, to some degree, the diploma also represented economic advancement to Jeff and Dwayne. Further, Marcus, Rashaud, Shawn, and Zakeev each talked about plans to go to college. Marcus was more hesitant about going to college, however, than Rashaud, Shawn, and Zakeev. For these three, the diploma was a tool for the acquisition of a college-level credential. College was the next step in the credential-acquiring process. Acquiring the high school credential became a strategy these three young men adopted to ensure their successful admittance to a college. They seemed to embrace meritocratic ideology, which rests on individualism and competition. However, it was only the two middle-class young men, Rashaud and Shawn, and not the four other young men who were working class and underclass—who had information about what it took to gain entrance into college.

At the same time, the high school diploma represented a level and form of achievement valued by their immediate family members. Through acquiring the diploma they would embark on a path that for many young men symbolized success and status. However, the intermingling of class and race privileges or penalties in their lives may hinder their goals and opportunities. For instance, although Zakeev talked about going to school and getting good grades to go to college, there was little evidence in my conversations with him that he had thought about a particular path he wanted to pursue beyond college, nor was he provided with information about how to gain access to college. Recall his outrage, as noted earlier in this chapter; he said, "they kept telling you what is required to graduate. . . . Graduating ain't nothin' if you ain't going to college. They won't tell you that." This raises questions about his opportunities to learn about requirements for college admission, and about his schooling experiences, which saw him receiving a 2.3 grade point average.

Although these young men all talked about the diploma as a vehicle to economic success, it was only Marcus and Zakeev who also explicitly talked about the *process* of acquiring the high school diploma. They were perhaps the most open about how they viewed school and the content of school. They each pointed to the racist nature of the curriculum and criticized student–teacher relations and the pedagogy of their experience at school. This is not to say that these themes were not in some way prevalent in the minds of the other participants in this study. Rather, it is that these two talked specifically about this feature of schooling. These were the issues they brought to the fore in our conversations. For Marcus and Zakeev, acquiring the high school diploma became a contradictory goal. They rejected the content of schooling but engaged in the process of acquiring grades, completing tasks in order to acquire the credential. They did not value the process of acquiring diploma, but they valued the diploma as a tool for social and economic advancement. I will discuss the contradictory nature of their views of schooling and the high school diploma in the following chapter.

Most of the young men, to varying degrees, had witnessed and felt the onslaught against black men in U.S. society. Their differing experiences of racism, classism, and sexism emerged from the different neighborhoods they lived in, the different schools they each attended, and the kinds of interactions they experienced with different groups at school, out of school in their community, and in their family. Therefore, acquiring the college diploma signified different levels of economic security and economic success to them. The diploma took on different meanings according to their relative privilege and access to resources. Economic security for some of the young men was essentially defined as bringing in enough income to support themselves. For others, it represented a firm location in middle class life and status.

Achievement Ideology

Each of the young men implicitly or explicitly suggested that if he did well and worked hard in school, he would receive the high school diploma which, in turn, would lead to a well-paying job. The extent to which these young men embraced meritocratic ideology, however, varied. This variation was manifest in each of their lives, in what they said about going to school and in how they talked about their future career ambitions upon finishing school. This is an important point. Many authors have recognized the importance that achievement ideology plays in the lives of school-going students. In the main, this ideology has been represented as serving to reinforce social inequalities among groups in society. Some authors have focused on the differential ways in which the ideology plays out in schooling across students' relative track positions in school (Oakes, 1985), or on comparing social classes (Bowles & Gintis, 1976) or race–class groups (MacLeod, 1995). Others have compared students who stay in schools with those who drop out (Fine, 1991). However, few writers have focused on looking within and across social class–race groups in relation to young African-American men committed to attending and completing school.

An exception has been MacLeod's (1995) study, which focused on the ways in which two groups of students, the African-American "Brothers" and the white "Hallway Hangers," respectively embraced and rejected achievement ideology. MacLeod asserted that the Hallway Hangers rejected achievement ideology whereas the Brothers accepted achievement ideology. He claimed that the Brothers embraced achievement ideology because "poor blacks have racial discrimination which they can point to as a cause of their family's poverty" (p. 129). On the other hand, the Hallway Hangers believed that accepting "the achievement ideology is to admit that their parents are lazy or stupid" (p. 130). MacLeod suggested that the Brothers believed the "achievement ideology to be an accurate depiction of the opportunity structure as it exists in the United States today because they perceive the racial situation to be substantially different for them than it was for their parents" (p. 130). The stance of the Brothers toward achievement ideology contrasts with the views of the six young men in my study.

Although all six of the young men seemed to accept achievement ideology, at the same time, they did not all believe that the ideology accurately depicted the opportunity structure. Granted, the ideology was deeply embedded in their sense of the value of the high school diploma in their lives, and the significance of the high school diploma in the eyes of many of the important people in each of their lives. The achievement ideology did underlie much of what they said about the significance of going to school, their approaches to school and to school learning, and their hopes and ambitions beyond acquiring the high school diploma. At the same time, however, Dwayne, Marcus, and Zakeev were weary of the racial barriers that lay in their way as they attempted to enter the world of work. This did not seem to be the case for the two middle-class young men, or for Jeff, of the working class.

Dwayne, from the underclass, was the most hesitant about his future in that he thought "the odds" were against him, given his upbringing and experiences in Detroit. And Marcus talked about racism generally in society and in his workplace at the fast-food restaurant. Also, as noted, Zakeev commented that "there's not very much opportunity in this period now. . . . White people have got a better chance of getting it [a job]." For these three young men, their view of achievement ideology was also tainted with beliefs about how their racial location might hinder their advancement. Their views differed markedly from those of Jeff, Shawn, and Rashaud, who did not hint at the possibility of barriers that might lie in their way as they attempted to accomplish their goals beyond school.

Achievement ideology and the ways in which these young men rejected and embraced dominant ideas and processes about success, achievement, and mobility can been seen as significant in the making of social class differences. However, as noted, meritocratic ideology seems to benefit white, middle-class men more than any other group in ways that not only are maintained through racial and social class orders, but also through gender relations. And though the ideology can be rooted in class-based versions of success, the ideology simultaneously seems to reflect masculinist versions of success and achievement that involve intense competition and individualism. The ways in which these young men responded to and were involved in the process of schooling as African-American men could be considered as an important strand of their masculinities—the ways in which they "did" gender as African-American men in relation to schooling. While masculinist ideology may seem to serve all these young men, their racialized experiences and, in some cases, their social class experiences, might serve to situate these young men in subordinate locations within a gender order; an order in which working-class and middle-class African-American masculinities may reap considerably less privilege than white middle-class masculinities. Thus, while meritocratic ideology may be deeply rooted in masculinist ideology, the interaction of social practice and institutional barriers finds these young men potentially denied the privileges that are accessible to many middle-class white men. Hence, while Rashaud may be afforded more access to privileges and options than Dwayne, it is open to question whether he was afforded the same privileges and options as many white male students at his school.

Explaining the Similarities and Differences

From the discussion thus far, it is clear there were patterns of similarity and difference in how these young men came to talk about and view the high school diploma in their lives. In a sea of complex relationships with others, they developed different sets of meanings about the high school diploma. As noted, there were also differences within social class groups. This is an important point, and although it may be an obvious one, it speaks to how meanings of the diploma are socially constructed and how these meanings emerge from their differing class and gender experiences, and also their experiences in a racial hierarchy. At the same time, their meanings shape these experiences. For example, if we compare what Dwayne and Rashaud wanted to accomplish with the diploma, their images of success through acquiring the symbol of the diploma were different. To Dwayne, of the underclass, acquiring the diploma represented a form of success, whereas to Rashaud, a middle-class young African-American man, it seemed a trivial accomplishment and merely a stepping stone to his college degree. Not only did they have differing social class experiences, they also encountered differing racialized and gendered experiences as black men in the neighborhoods in which they lived. This difference was evident in how they described their experiences in and out of school, their opportunities to succeed, and the barriers they saw in their way. Rashaud did not see any barriers to achieving his goals, whereas Dwayne did. Further, they each were exposed differently to hegemonic and subordinated images of masculinities. And, different images of masculinities were sanctioned through their interactions with others. Dwayne encountered the comradeship and the activities of his peer group in Detroit, which surely influenced his version of success and masculinity. These activities and connections based on particular ways of being and acting were far removed from Rashaud's connections with his friends. His daily activities included going to movies or doing homework, and he spent little of his time hanging around with peer groups in his neighborhood. Hegemonic images of subordinate masculinities were not part of his daily encounters in the same way as they were for Dwayne. In addition, their differing access to resources was a significant factor in how they saw themselves. This difference in their ideas and images of others, and their differential access to resources, in part influenced how they viewed the high school diploma in their lives and how they thought its meaning served as an indicator to others about who they were.

Delving into this variation further, we learned that Rashaud believed that if he could be successful, then others could be too. Rashaud saw himself in the process of becoming successful. At the same time, Dwayne talked about success, but the limits of success to him seemed narrower than in Rashaud's version. Dwayne wanted success sooner than Rashaud. Rashaud was prepared to wait longer until he received a college degree. Dwayne talked about the negative impact of the daily experiences of living in inner-city Detroit on the hope and expectations of inner-city youth. Dwayne saw the high school diploma as a chance to become successful. The difference between these two young men is that Rashaud *believed* he was on the path to success, whereas Dwayne *hoped* to enter the path of being successful. Dwayne was perhaps the most deeply affected by the institutional racism and classism that pervaded his life in Detroit. And he was aware of this. He did not unwittingly blame himself for the decisions or choices he made. Rather, he focused on explaining the impact of the environment on his choices in Detroit.

Notwithstanding the variation among these young men, the high school diploma also was unanimously perceived as a symbol of potential mobility and potential economic success. On a general level, there is a pattern across these six young men involving the connection between the high school diploma and the world of work. The connection between the high school diploma and the job-acquiring process has been noted by many writers (see, for example, Collins, 1979; Labaree, 1988). Not only was the high school diploma viewed as a ticket to employment, it also was viewed as a symbol of economic security and success. Rashaud, middle class and attending school in a white, middle-class neighborhood, was perhaps the most convinced of this connection; it represented a "guaranteed future," he told me.

In essence, the high school diploma symbolized success. Although these young men had similar values and beliefs about the high school diploma, they differed in the kinds of opportunities they received to acquire the high school diploma, and also in the form and content of the support they receive at home and in their community. Thus, their orientation toward the high school diploma is where the similarities across these young men ends.

Such a difference suggests that these young men's explanations of why they went to school, and the meaning of the high school diploma, were shaped by the institutional and cultural arrangements in society. Interaction of culture and structure in their lives contributed to how they saw themselves in the world and in relation to others, and to how they viewed their potential in relation to others. Their experiences differed as young African-American men in a social world where class location shapes and is shaped by access to rewards, privileges, and cultural and material resources. Their class location seemed inextricably and dynamically bound to their experiences of racism, and the images of what it meant to be successful men. These young men's day-to-day explanations of their experiences with others, however, suggest that the social construction of the meaning of the high school diploma was influenced by more than experiences and location within a social class hierarchy, as Bowles and Gintis (1976) suggest. Their experiences appeared to be shaped not only by their relative position in the social class hierarchy, but also through the interlocking connections between the race, gender, and class structures and practices of domination and oppression (Collins, 1990). This theme of examining the interplay of race, class, and gender structures and cultures of domination and oppression in the context of each of these young men's lives is discussed in Chapter 8.

Although much of this discussion has been about accepting the diploma as a vehicle to economic and social advancement, several questions arise that need further consideration. One important question concerns the relationship of meanings of the diploma to these young men's emerging social identities. Embedded in the question about who these men were in the process of becoming are also questions about the social cost of their commitments. What is it that these young men gained and gave up in order to acquire the diploma? To better understand some of these questions, the next chapter focuses on the process of schooling as a way to understand their experiences in classrooms. Subsequent chapters will further consider the process of identity formation.

5

Accommodation and Critique of Life in Classrooms

This chapter focuses on the six young men's experiences in school and the ways in which they simultaneously accommodated and critiqued the process of schooling. Most prominent in their talk about schooling and their experiences as young African-American men were issues about the relationships they encountered. Here, their encounters with teachers, peers, curriculum, and pedagogy in classrooms revealed that going to school was considerably complex as they went about acquiring the high school diploma. Through the schooling process, they also learned about what was valued by their teachers and peers in school, what was important to them, and their identities as young African-American men. For some of the young men, issues of conflict between themselves and their teachers was one of the strands that seeped into their conversations; issues of lack of engagement and connection to curriculum was another. In their quest to acquire the high school diploma, school was also a place where they experienced both knowledge and social relationships in complex and contradictory ways. These various experiences were all at play as they developed their social identities as African-American men. As Connell, Ashenden, Kessler, and Dowsett (1982) argued,

Schooling is a powerful institution through which people and their relationships are produced. That is not a matter of choice; schools *do* that, one way or another. The choices are about *how* they do it. Schools have the capacity to shape the way they do that work and determine which social interests will be advanced by their laborers. (p. 209)

Thus, examining the complexity of going to school begs an investigation of these young men's perceptions and experiences of schooling. While they went to school to acquire the high school diploma, this was only part of their story. Their relationship to schooling and the role of schooling in their identity formation process seem important as they developed meanings about the high school diploma and school. In the postfield analysis, I also learned that schools became places where they both challenged and confirmed the ongoing images they constructed of themselves and others as classed African-American men. These images in the making are important in understanding their perceptions of their experiences of school and the high school diploma.

As they shared their stories of their experiences in classroom and schools, it became clear that the task of acquiring the high school diploma was complex and neither straightforward nor smooth. They did not go to school in ways that consistently represented their needs, interests and aspirations. Schooling saw them pursuing their potentials[6] that were often constrained by barriers emerging from encounters and interactions in school. For example, at times they were confronted with individual and institutional racism, or seemingly denied opportunities to develop their voice through mainly authoritarian and traditional pedagogy. Their experiences in school and classroom contexts were ones of challenges, contradictions, and accommodations. They simultaneously accommodated and critiqued aspects of schooling. Such contradictory strands of their lives in school the focus of this chapter.

The notions of accommodation and critique are developed from critical education theory (see Anyon, 1983; Apple, 1982; Connell et al., 1982; Freire, 1974; Weiler, 1988). Here, I use *accommodation* to mean to tolerate, and/or consciously and sometimes unconsciously accept the dominant structure and culture of schooling. *Critique* I use to frame their talk as young African-American men about relationships, ideas, processes, and issues that challenged or called into question the multiple interests, purposes, and consequences of schooling.

In this chapter, I argue that the contradictory tension between their critique and accommodation of schooling manifested itself differently in the lives of these young men. This suggests that they not only experienced schooling in different ways, but that their participation in schooling had differing consequences.

This chapter focuses on those experiences and aspects of classroom life they talked about.[7] First, I provide a brief discussion about how they talked about classroom life, followed by an analysis of the aspects of school they critiqued. From there, I examine the complex ways in which they approached school, which reveal a tension between accommodation and critique.

TALK ABOUT CLASSROOM LIFE

Talk about school experiences involved two sets of relationships, one that centered on their encounters in the classroom, and the other that focused on their relationships with students outside the classroom—in the hallways, at lunch time, in between classes, and on the school bus. Thus, school represented, on the one hand, issues connected to their experiences of different aspects of classroom life and, on the other, issues connected to interaction with students. They talked about their relationships with the teachers and students they associated with, or students they rarely talked with, but talked about. Their relationships with other students at school will be discussed in Chapter 6.

In the main, their talk about classrooms, the homework and tests they were assigned, and their level of engagement or enthusiasm in classrooms seemed also to be about their perceptions of their relationships and encounters with their teachers. Such talk about teachers focused on teachers' personalities, attitudes, and the responsiveness of their pedagogy to students. They provided seemingly vague accounts of life in classrooms that revealed much about the aspects of school and classroom life that were important or unimportant to them or the aspects of school that stood at the forefront of their thinking. It seemed that going to school was less connected to their interest in various school subjects than to a desire to meet and socialize with friends and a long-term goal of high school graduation. Their accounts of classroom life also revealed their connection, disengagement, and the degree of alienation from certain processes within school that, in turn, provide us with glimpses of their social identities in the making.

Although conversations about classroom life seemed to vary among the young men according to the particular school and classes they attended, there were discussions that were common across the young men. For instance, talk about curriculum invariably was framed by a discussion of how the teachers taught a subject area; that is, the process, with little attention given to the substance—the topics, issues, or ideas they learned or were exposed to in classrooms. Farrell (1994) noted similar patterns of talk in his study of "successful" young men and women of color, attending schools in New York. He wrote: "Conspicuous by its relative absence in the dialogues between the students is mention of academic courses and course content. . . . When there is talk of subject matter, it was always in the context of the teachers who taught it" (p. 81). In my study, however, there was one exception: Most of them did talk about the history curriculum they encountered and the inattention of the history curriculum to the history and experiences of African-Americans in the United States.

In sum, there were similarities in the themes that dominated their discussions about classroom life. Notwithstanding, talk about relationships, curriculum, teachers, and pedagogy varied among the six young men through how much description they offered about their experiences in the classroom, the kind of critique they offered, and the aspects of classroom life they accommodated. Despite their critiques, they attended school daily and completed homework assignments and projects set by their teachers, and they strove to attain a passing grade for their tests and examinations. Grades were important to these young men, and completing the assigned work became a vehicle to the acquisition of a passing grade. Nevertheless, they did not just accommodate all their teachers' demands, nor did they encounter life in classrooms without passing criticism. I will discuss this uneasy tension between accommodating and critiquing their encounters in classrooms toward the end of the chapter. I now turn to the spheres of life in classrooms they critiqued.

CRITIQUE OF SCHOOL AND CLASSROOM LIFE

Being young African-American men and going to school was neither smooth nor uncomplicated for any of the young men. Complexities emerged that revealed their differences and similarities in their experiences in and out of school. One similarity is the racism encountered by all the young men. However, they viewed and talked about racism differently. Zakeev and Marcus seemed most insightful about the racism they encountered, while Rashaud and Shawn were critical, but less critical of how they viewed themselves in relation to their school. Their experiences in and out of school, on one level, seemed different from those of either Zakeev or Marcus, who passionately critiqued the racism they confronted at school. Rashaud and Shawn both argued that they would not attend another school because they believed the credential acquired from Cedarville High School had more value than the diploma from another school in the area. Not only was their critique of schooling different from that of Zakeev and Marcus, their school experiences as young African-American men did not enrage them in the same way as Marcus or Zakeev. During the postfield analysis, I began to learn that the critique of all six was as much influenced by their views of themselves as by their experiences, which in turn challenged or confirmed their images of themselves in relation to the institution of school. Notwithstanding, these six young African-American men had something in common: They managed not only to go to school but to stay in school. Further, they were committed to being successful as African-Americans and saw their potential success as a challenge to ideas and images about African-American youth. It is within this context of staying in school, their commitment to being successful, and their desire to challenge dominant images of African-American youth that I turn to a discussion of their critique of life in classrooms.

"Teaching Us to Kiss White Folks' Butt"

Of these six young men, Marcus was perhaps the most critical of schooling. In particular, he spoke disparagingly about the racist nature of the educational system in the United States. His perspective as a young African-American man reflected the racist nature and content of the education process he experienced in high school. It also reflected the complexity of being in school as a highly conscious young African-American man:

> To me how I feel about the education system, I mean they don't have the locks on our hands and feet no more, but they've got it on our brain. They've got the locks on our brains now. . . . They just try to clog our memory, you know trying to express how powerful white folk are.

Marcus here addressed the oppressive nature of the educational system for him and other African-Americans. His analysis suggests the constrained freedom wielded by African-Americans goes beyond physical control to consider ideological control—dominant or emphasized values, beliefs, ideas, and images. The educational system did not allow him the access to intellectual freedom he so urgently sought. Marcus often referred to school as a place of white domination and control, where the teachers are seen as instruments of such control. His criticism of the process of his schooling clearly attended to the racial nature of the culture and structure of schools.

> I don't really agree with the stuff they teach us all. I just do it to get my grade, because the stuff they're teaching us at school, they ain't teaching us, because basically what they are teaching us at school is what the white folks want us to know, basically. They are not teaching us what we need to know as black people. They're teaching us to kiss white folks' butt. That what it is. Kiss their butt.

Marcus had a particularly broad notion of what counted as education in school. He argued that the kind of knowledge to which he had access taught him to "kiss white folks' butt." Marcus's stance toward school revealed his abhorrence for the racism interwoven in the overt and covert curriculum where he learned about African-American subordination to whites. The knowledge he encountered at school represented "teaching you white is superior."

> Because basically to me, they ain't there to teach, they're just there to get their paycheck at the end of the week. They ain't teachin you nothin'. 'Cause if they was teaching' you somethin', they would be teaching you somethin' about your black African culture, instead of teaching you white is superior. Because that is all they are teaching you, white is so superior, they dominate everything.

Marcus readily identified himself as an African-American, and linked his experience and the experiences of other African-Americans at school to the broader oppression of African-Americans in U.S. society. Marcus criticized not only the culture of schools but also the very role of the institution itself. His critique suggests that power manifested and wielded through the institution of schooling is significant in the maintenance of the social location of African-Americans in a hierarchy of racialized social relations. Among the six young men in my study, he was the strongest critic of the racist nature of schooling, but certainly not the only one. The theme of racism in schools and society were, to some extent, addressed by all the young men. Their discussions about the history curriculum represented the most common strand of their experiences of racism in school that they talked about.

"Why Can't We Learn About Our History?"

The history curriculum these young men encountered in school was the most notable subject of critique of classroom life among them. In particular, they talked about the ways in which the school curriculum and their teachers gave little or no attention to African-American history. Jeff was the exception. He stood alone in his silence about his perceptions of the history curriculum at school.

Dwayne, Marcus, and Zakeev in separate conversations spoke about societal domination by white people and their relationship of control over the curriculum:

> *Marcus:* . . . that's all you hear is about in history, how white folks overpowered, where are the black folks in all this . . . this is something that I want to express I will, I don't really care if they get offended by it, really. Because if the truth hurts.
>
> *Dwayne:* It is basically about America, white people. I feel it is not right whatever, we built this country, we worked as slaves. . . .
>
> *Zakeev:* Because the white people, they don't want us to find out . . . they're hiding it, and it's white people wanting to hide that part. . . . It's important to me because first of all we were here without our will. Second of all, we are here now, we are part of history, we should have some part of say about something, and we got to learn something about what happened to us. If you say it the way the white man say it, if I'm the plantation owner, then of course I'm going to say they was happy. 'Cause I was happy. They say they was dancing and stuff. You've got to do the part about how you would feel if you was chained to a boat. Doing that stuff, carried to a foreign land without your will. . . . You're supposed to do this, and if you don't, you get beaten.

These three young men criticized the minimal way in which African-American history was conceived whereby the perspectives of the curriculum represented a white perspective of history and perpetuated white interests. Dwayne felt it was "not right" because African-Americans are as much part of this country as any other racialized group. Zakeev not only criticized the minimal attention given to

African-Americans in his history curriculum, he also criticized the perspectives that were offered about African-Americans.

Marcus passionately argued that the omission of African-Americans and the perspectives of the history curriculum reveal how white people wield control in the United States. Marcus elaborated on his point using an example from his history class about the study of Christopher Columbus:

> Like Christopher Columbus discovered America. Christopher Columbus didn't discover America. He didn't know in the world where he was going. How can they say that he discovered America? . . . Why do we want to hear about Christopher Columbus? What about our people, they act like we wasn't even there. . . . America was already discovered. He was lost, he didn't know in the world where he was at. That's all we hear about. Alexander the Great and all that. I don't want to hear about that man. I want to hear about my black people. How white folks doing everything, that's crazy. Like I said, they taking so much credit for what black folks did back in them days.

Marcus once again argued that the history curriculum offered him little as an African-American. Through linking his perceptions of the history curriculum to his critique of the racial nature of schooling, it becomes clear that such instances reinforced Marcus's belief that school and going to school meant learning about the dominance of white people in society.

These three young men were not the only ones who critiqued the history curriculum. Shawn, for example, examined his school's textbook to consider the extent to which African-American history was part of the curriculum:

> Me and a couple of my friends, we go through our history book, and see how many chapters they have on Marcus Garvey, and how many they have on Theodore Roosevelt. . . . [There was] One and half paragraphs on Marcus Garvey, and then a chapter and a half on Theodore Roosevelt. . . .

Marcus echoed Shawn's observations of the limited amount of curriculum material attending to African-Americans. "Oh, there's just one chapter about W. E. B. Du Bois," Marcus commented. The omission noted by Marcus and Shawn strikes at the heart of the maintenance of racism and the pervasiveness of racism in individual relationships and the institution of school itself. Despite Shawn's criticism of the textbook, however, he acknowledged that his teachers gave some attention to African-American history. Shawn, unlike Marcus, had a history teacher who provided material beyond the textbook. He distinguished between the content of the textbooks and the content of the lessons:

> But the books and the teachers are two different things. Now he [the teacher] does go into the detail about black history, black achievement. We do a lot of activities for Black History Month . . . a celebration of all the black achievements that they don't know about. Rather than things about where did folks go, family and so forth.

The teacher, while attending to African-American history, tended to confine such discussion of topics and issues connected to black history and achievement to Black History Month. But for Marcus, attention to African-American history during Black History Month seemed inadequate:

> . . . just like you've got Black History Month, every year. Black History Month should be every year, it should be all year round. It's not just a day, a week, a month. To me, that don't make no sense.

Despite Marcus's criticism of Black History Month and his history teacher's inattentiveness to African-American history, he did not ascribe such omissions to a conspiracy theory. Rather, he viewed the problem historically, and analyzed the cultural contexts that most of his teachers experienced. He said, ". . . that's how they been taught, so they teaching us to do the same thing, that's how I see it."

Zakeev did not accept the omission of African-American history from his curriculum. At the beginning of his semester at his new school, he challenged his history teacher about the omission of African-American history from the curriculum:

> I was like "why don't we study Africa?" And I asked him that, I was mad. . . . He told me, "it's just not in my curriculum." I was like, I was asking, I said "we're part of history, why can't we learn about our history?" . . . It was about the time he was telling us about the curriculum, it was the beginning of term. I was interested in what we was going to learn. I get interested in history now. . . . And they're saying something about Abraham Lincoln, saying he was a hero about slavery. He didn't really want to do that. Abraham Lincoln did not care about the slaves. . . .

Not only was Zakeev critical of the fact that the teachers focused on white history and history he deemed relevant to white people, but he also criticized the ways in which history was interpreted. So, the fact that Abraham Lincoln was discussed was one aspect of his criticism; the other aspect of his criticism was that the book's portrayal of Abraham Lincoln is but one perspective of his role in history. Zakeev's criticism brings to the fore an important aspect of the history curriculum that is often omitted in discussions about reform of curriculum. He demanded a more inclusive focus of topics relating to African-Americans and that multiple perspectives of topics be part of the curriculum. Zakeev's criticism did not just rest with comments to me during this study. He was adamant about his critical appraisal and said, "I'm going to write a letter to the Board [of Education] one time. I'm going to do that."

The inclusion of African-American history in the curriculum is one thing; another is how we teach, for example, slavery as a curriculum topic and issue. At one point, Shawn criticized the way in which slavery was taught in school and the ways in which white students reacted to him as an African-American in the classroom.

... Another thing that gets to me, is we're in history talking about slavery or whatever, and the other people are looking at you, or whatever, and then a white person
might talk about slavery and how hard it was, and black people might be offended.
What do you know about black history?

Shawn's concern was not just about what he was taught, but also about the opportunities for learning—it was about how the teacher conceptualized the relationship
between herself, learners, and knowledge. However, his critique was also about
how students can affect each others' learning. White students' reactions to the
content potentially offended African-American students in the classroom. Shawn
did not like his history classrooms; his grades certainly reflected his lack of connection to the content. He consistently received a grade of D for history. "Ever
since the seventh grade I've had trouble with history, out of all the classes. . . .
Maybe because a lot of it is boring," he noted.

Shawn's concern about his engagement in history, and how his teachers conceptualized the relationship between subject matter and the racial and ethnic experiences of students in the classroom, and how students interacted with one another
in such contexts, is a significant point that clearly needs further investigation. His
point, however, does not detract from the larger concern of all these young men
about their exclusion from their history curriculum. While attempts have been
made to address the inadequate attention to racial minority perspectives in curriculum, particularly the history curriculum dominant in their schools, invariably
such reforms emerge as an 'add-on' approach to reform of the history curriculum.
In many instances, providing and shaping curriculum that attends to the experiences of racial minority groups is not seen as a fundamental human right.

These young men in varying degrees desired a more inclusive curriculum, not
only of curriculum topics and issues but of perspectives of these topics and issues.
This exclusion of African-American topics, issues, and perspectives can be considered as a form of racism and the ways in which African-American history is
addressed reflect sets of values, beliefs, and ideas that may unintentionally reify
social relations of race (see Gillborn, 1990; Mac an Ghaill, 1988; Sarup, 1991;
Troyna & Hatcher, 1992). The omission clearly impacted the way they
approached history. But their critique, particularly Zakeev's challenge to his
teacher, suggests that these students did not accept such omissions with ease. The
acts of challenge and critique serve to remind us that they did not uncritically
accept or accommodate the dominant discourse and structures in school but
actively analyzed and challenged such structures and cultures. Such curricular
omissions and exclusionary perspectives suggest that the racism they encountered
was more than acts of individual racism, it represented acts of institutional racism
in that it was not individual teachers but a range of collective experiences across
the institution of schooling that were similar.

From their accounts, racism seemed the major challenge they faced in school.
The racism they experienced seemed more than acts of individual prejudice, but in

addition, institutional racism, which emerged from both the structure and culture of school. Their talk about the Eurocentric constructs embedded in the history curriculum reveal a pattern across the young men that suggests their experiences were not isolated incidents. The dominance of Eurocentric history curriculum across their schools points to how power and privilege is wielded and racialized privilege is sustained through schooling.

This discussion about the history curriculum provides a glimpse of the young men's experiences in classrooms. Significant to their conversations were the relationships they encountered not just in history classrooms but in other classrooms as well. To further consider their relationships with others in classrooms, I next discuss the pedagogy the young men encountered. The following discussion about pedagogy and relationships with teachers perhaps illuminates the understanding and respect afforded these young men by their teachers. More centrally, the discussion of the pedagogy these young men encountered at their different schools sheds light upon the *ways* in which they encountered and experienced knowledge in their classrooms, and provides further evidence for understanding race, gender, and social class in the lives of these young men.

Pedagogical Encounters in Classrooms

Teachers' pedagogy and interest in their subjects seemed influential in the formation of the young men's ideas and conceptions of the subject matter of the class and their attitudes and approaches toward a class. On the one hand, Rashaud, Shawn, and Jeff, who attended a middle-class, private parochial school, each talked about the interesting ways in which teachers taught their subjects and promoted student involvement. On the other hand, Dwayne, Marcus, and Zakeev each talked about the procedural ways in which they learned and participated in classrooms. Their contrasting accounts of their experiences seemed to mirror the discussions of Anyon (1981) and Oakes (1985), in which students from different social class locations experienced and encountered knowledge in different ways depending on their location in an academic or vocational track within a school, or the dominant social class interests of the school. The accounts also reflect the work of Kessler, Ashenden, Connell, and Dowsett (1985), who suggest that different forms of curricula and school organization separate out different forms of masculinity within the same school. Different kinds of experiences provided different kinds of opportunities in classrooms for masculinities to be enacted and negotiated. "Teaching inevitably involves emotional relationships. How these issues are handled thus depends on the construction of masculinity and femininity in the teachers' own lives" (Kessler et al., 1985, p. 43) and also how they are constructed in the lives of students. The different experiences of the young men in my study raises questions about the relationship between experiences of curriculum and pedagogy and their social identities, namely, their emerging race, class, and gender identities.

As I explore and contrast these young men's experiences of pedagogy and their teachers, I want to note that not one of the young men spoke about their relationships with students in their classrooms. When they spoke about relationships with others in the classroom, they talked only about their teachers and not about the other students.

Marcus criticized much of the pedagogy he encountered at school. For him, life in classrooms entailed completing and doing assignments. For example, his experience in algebra, described in the extract that follows, was mirrored in almost all of his classes throughout the year.

> *Marcus:*   Then after lunch I've got algebra . . . all they do is give us all the assignments, read all the directions, and that's it. That's basically how the class goes. We do that for the rest of the hour.
> *JP:*   So, do they explain anything?
> *Marcus:*   "Read directions."
> *JP:*   Really, in the book?
> *Marcus:*   Mmhumm.
> *JP:*   The teacher doesn't teach or what?
> *Marcus:*   Ugh, ugh. *(Laughs.)* Don't make me no do nothin'. I get an A off anywise.

Although Marcus claimed the teacher "don't make me do nothin'," the teacher did instruct Marcus to complete work sheets assigned in order to receive a grade. His algebra teacher seemed to lead a very teacher-centered class with few opportunities for engagement. Notwithstanding, Marcus suggested little effort was needed in algebra and he was able to achieve an A for the course. Thus, his grade became the main focus of the course and not what he learned. More significantly, Marcus's perspectives of his algebra class suggests a limited access and conception of mathematical domains of knowledge. It raises questions of not only how he came to know and understand mathematical concepts and ideas, but also what counted as mathematical knowledge to Marcus.

Algebra was not the only class where Marcus encountered apparent teacher-centered pedagogy. The description of the pedagogy in his biology classroom was similar.

> . . . biology. Which I can't stand that class. It's maybe 'cause of the lady. 'Cause I want to do some kinds of experiments or somethin' and she don't do none. She do like, she did one, that's it. 'Cause how she do, she gives so much paper, paperwork. 'Cause when we first got in the class, she gave us a thick packet. Thick 'ole packet, telling what we had to do by ourselves. I was like, come on. She talks like it don't look like a lot but you know, this, and this, and this. "You know, how to do it." Then we just had to go through it. Plus she gave us that, the next day she gave us some more assignments. 'Cause she just pile assignments on assignment on assignment. And we got to be giving in [assignments] all the time. I have more work from her class than I got from any other class.

It was not only Marcus's experiences in biology and in algebra that consisted of completing many work sheets and assignments. His American history class in the spring reflected similar experiences:

> *Marcus:*   . . . See to me he [American history teacher] don't teach nothin', he don't explain nothin' to me. Give you the packet, give you the worksheet, "go ahead it's in the book." The only thing he explains is the review for the test. He will go over it twice and still read it just as fast as he did the first time. Where somebody can't catch up.
>
> *JP:*   What are you learning about there?
>
> *Marcus:*   Nothin', we're learning all about white folk, and how they dominate everything. I think we've got off a chapter about when the Charleston dance came, when they were doing that. We just got off a chapter about that.

Marcus's encounters of mathematics, biology, and history suggest a pattern of little student engagement in these subject areas. Perhaps it is not surprising that Marcus talked little about what he learned in his classes and focused more on the work he was assigned, because being in these classes essentially entailed completing work sheets and taking tests.

Both Zakeev and Dwayne characterized the pedagogy of their classes at Central in ways similar to Marcus. But when Zakeev moved to Western, he noticed a difference in the teaching because it was "quicker." The pace at which teachers moved through material was faster than at Central. He ascribed the differences not to individual teachers, but to the predominance of white students attending the school. Hence, for Zakeev, the large proportion of white students at the school became a central factor in his assertion about the pace of the teaching.

> Western teaches you more. . . . The teachers, they go through things like that. I'm thinking, I see, soon as it's majority white, you start teaching people quicker and putting it in their minds, I should be able to keep up with something. In my history class, I'm doing a test almost every three days. Like at Central it would be every other week. It was weird to me. As soon as I got there, it was quick, and teachers were teaching like they were supposed to be teaching. They were teaching at a speed, you know we were supposed to be at. At Central, they were teaching at sixth grade level, not their teaching but their speed.

But when I asked Zakeev to talk about what the teachers did in his classroom, the pedagogy did not seem much different than the pedagogy he encountered at Central. For example in biology:

> *JP:*   You were talking about biology, what does the teacher do?
>
> *Zakeev:*   He loves to talk.
>
> *JP:*   So is there participation?

Zakeev: Yeah, no. Well, he gets into it sometimes: "Yeah, okay give me an answer."

There seemed little interaction between the teacher and students. Despite the difference in pace, student participation in his biology, history, and mathematics classes at Western echoed many of Zakeev's experiences at Central.

In contrast to Marcus and Zakeev, Shawn and Rashaud liked the teaching methods at their school, Cedarville, and also enjoyed the numerous discussions that predominated in classroom life. Both suggested they rarely used a textbook, and class discussions were very common and the norm in most of their classes. At one point Shawn said, "as matter of fact, except for courses like math and the career center, we rarely use textbooks. . . . I find it easier to grasp information easier like that . . . we have access to a lot more video equipment. We can always run down to the library."

Although Shawn preferred his learning experiences at Cedarville, he bemoaned the fact that there were not good relationships between teachers and students there. At his old school in the Detroit suburbs, the teachers "[tried] to get to know you," whereas at Cedarville he claimed that teachers and administrators "don't try to get to know you." Rashaud, however, differed with Shawn on this point and liked most of his teachers at Cedarville. He said that, "They like to teach. They like to be around kids . . . it's just their mindset." So while they both appreciated the pedagogy they encountered, they differed on how they saw relationships with teachers.

Jeff argued that the pedagogy he encountered at Allerton Christian School (ACS) was "better" than that at his previous school, Central. It was not really possible to tell what was better, nor whether he encountered knowledge differently than at his previous school. What did differ substantially at ACS was the predominance of white students in his classes and also his views of schooling, which changed as he went to ACS and emerged from his decision to work hard in school and acquire the high school diploma. Jeff's story is an interesting one, because he lived in the same neighborhood as Dwayne and Marcus, a predominantly working-class neighborhood, yet he attended a decidedly middle-class private school and developed a different approach and view of schooling.

From these various accounts it seems there was a difference in how these young men participated in the production of knowledge in classrooms, with Rashaud and Shawn, who attended a middle-class school, encountering more student-centered and engaging experiences in their classrooms as compared to the other young men. Dwayne, Marcus, and Zakeev suggested a pattern of participation in school similar on one level to the white, working-class males and females in Weis's (1990) study, where she argued the students were "involved in the *form* of schooling, but not its substance" (p. 30). Different for these three young men were their experiences of racism, woven through the fabric of their experiences of schooling.

While noting these six young men all encountered racism at school, their experiences of curriculum and pedagogy on a larger scale differed markedly. Social class appears to be a powerful explanation of the difference. The difference raises questions about what and how they learned, and how the knowledge they had access to influenced how they saw themselves in relation to others in the development of their identities as African-American young men. The difference also suggests that through the silencing and marginalization of some perspectives, and the privileging and centering of others, they learned through their experiences of knowledge about racial relations of power. Amid their learning about the privileging of Eurocentric perspectives of knowledge were differences in how they experienced knowledge, with the two middle-class young men arguing that discussion was integral to their learning.

For each of these young men, however, learning in classrooms was not only about *what* they learned, it was also about *how* the teachers related to them as students, as African-American students. Next I turn to an examination of the relationships some of these young men experienced with their teachers, as these the relationships seemed instrumental in how they viewed school, teachers, and learning in their classrooms.'

Relationships with Teachers

Amid the discussions about curriculum and pedagogy, these young men naturally talked about relationships with their teachers. Although relationships with their teachers were inextricably linked to the subject area and the pedagogy they encountered, for the purposes of the discussion, I separate this sphere of classroom life to better understand the kinds of relationships they encountered with their teachers and the kinds of relationships they sought from their teachers.

Dwayne, Zakeev, and Marcus offered similar responses when I asked them about good teachers they had encountered at school:

Dwayne:	Mr. Barrett, he taught me how to read good.
JP:	Was he a black or white person?
Dwayne:	Black person.
JP:	Was that like second grade or fourth grade?
Dwayne:	Fourth grade.
Zakeev:	My sixth grade teacher, Ms. Henley. She was the type who was strong, and told you why you missing something and get you along to do what you were supposed to do.
JP:	Tell me was she white or black?
Zakeev:	She was Black.
Marcus:	Err, I had one at Westview Middle School. Ms. Henley.
JP:	What was good about her?
Marcus:	She was black. And another one is 'cause you can really understand what she talks about 'cause she really broke it down.

Dwayne could not add any other teachers to his list. Marcus added his choir teacher from the fall semester, who was African-American: "She sees the shirt I had *Black Oath* . . . she really liked that." Zakeev also mentioned his band teacher, an African-American man. It is significant that the teachers they identified were teachers from their elementary or early middle school experiences and, after additional probes, that the teachers they identified were African-American. It is also significant that these young men found it difficult to come up with more than a couple of names. For these three young men, part of their frame of reference for what made a good teacher was influenced by their connections and relationships with teachers in classrooms. It seemed that the teachers they most connected to were African-Americans. The lack of connection they currently encountered in high school no doubt had a bearing on how they approached their classes. But what does it mean to be connected with a teacher?

I asked Marcus what the African-American teachers were like at school and he said, "I don't really know, because I've never had a black teacher. In the middle school I went to I had one, I liked the way she taught." For Marcus, the notion of a "good" teacher was not only about the racial identity of his teacher but also "how they treat you . . . how they accept you." His point is significant because he, together with Dwayne and Zakeev, did not seem connected to their teachers in high school. Zakeev elaborated on this point further by arguing that teachers' relationships with students also included providing opportunities for students to shape the curriculum and conversations in the classroom:

> The wrong people are going into the teaching profession and that is affecting our lives. . . . A good person would be a person that pushed someone to succeed . . . should say . . . what's boring for you in this class or something. They need to ask the people in the class what they like about the class, what's wrong, what's boring, or what's making you not interested?

Zakeev wanted to participate more in class. He wanted opportunities to provide feedback about his interest in the issues and ideas under discussion.

The relationships and connections with teachers of Dwayne, Marcus, and Zakeev markedly contrasted with those of Shawn, Jeff, and Rashaud. For Jeff, his best teachers were his current teachers at ACS, where he liked the teachers and the teaching. Although Shawn liked the teaching at Cedarville, he was not particularly enamored with the relationships he developed with the teachers there. "That's one thing I'm happy about here. I don't have the teachers that have me read the book, and answer the questions. I have a lot of enthusiastic teachers," he said. However, he preferred the teachers at his previous school, a predominantly African-American school where the teachers tried "to get to know you." So, while Shawn liked the teaching but was not connected to the teachers at Cedarville, Rashaud liked both his teachers and the teaching. He developed a list of numerous "good" teachers with ease, whose racial identity did not seem a consideration to him.

Compared to the other young men, Rashaud was not as critical of his teachers nor of his relationships with his teachers. When talking about their relationships with teachers, I asked the young men to talk about their perspectives of a "good" teacher. Rashaud's sense of a good teacher seemed to emerge from his experiences of teachers at the schools he had attended.

> A good teacher that I had at school, Mr. Whitiker and Ms. Jansen at elementary school, I had, let's see, Mr. Schinker, Ms. Hoffman, and Ms. Skula at middle school. In high school, Mr. Burris, a basketball coach, he was just a good figure, a role model, Mr. Turner, couldn't tell you that many 'cause I haven't finished [school].

I asked Rashaud what about these teachers was "good":

> A good teacher is somebody who lets you, who makes you learn, you don't have to fight all these people off and keep away from the bad stuff and spread through the bull, it's not like to have to sit there and you try to discover it for yourself . . . last year with Mr. Eisner's class, I think out of the whole year, no one skipped the class, no one did. And when they did miss something, they came back almost the next day, they wanted to come to this class. . . . It's not how they behave, it's just their mindset, they like to teach. They like to be around kids.

His response starkly contrasted with the responses of Marcus, Dwayne and Zakeev, who found it difficult to think about teachers who stood out to them, and struggled to disclose more than one name.

Thus, for Rashaud, a good teacher was someone who provided opportunities for students to be engaged in their learning, to not only participate in the classroom, but also feel as though they were somehow involved in their own learning. Interestingly, his focus seemed to be more on the process of what he was learning in the classroom than on the content, which both Zakeev and Marcus criticized. This is not to say that all relationships with teachers that Rashaud experienced were to his liking. Rashaud also had relationships with teachers he described as "bad." For example, he criticized his teacher at middle school, Mr. Rutherford, who provided few opportunities for students to develop their own personalities. "I think he wanted a bunch of Rutherford clones," Rashaud said. His point suggests an important thread that runs through all the views of these young men: Their views of teachers were connected to their notions of who they were as students.

The variation in experiences of pedagogy and relationships with teachers among the young men raises questions about how they came to see themselves as students and how they viewed knowledge and learning. It seems that issues of engagement and opportunities for connection, nurturance, and support from their teachers were significant to their emerging identities as young African-American men who continued to be shaped and reshaped as they interacted in classrooms. The form and content of what they learned was simultaneously influential in the shaping of their classed and raced identities. Such processes, however, were also about their gendered identities. The kinds of relationships they experienced with teachers and other students suggest the prevalence of certain forms of interactions over others that they preferred. Marcus's and Zakeev's desire for connected and nurturing relationships were at odds with the unconnected and alienated relationships they experienced with teachers and other students. At the same time, the opportunities for discussion in classrooms that Rashaud and Shawn encountered suggest that the potential for connected relationships was stronger in their cases than in those of the other young men. The kinds of relationships they all experienced would have bearing on the forms of masculinity they lived out in classrooms. The ways in which these young men accessed knowledge, the forms of communication, and the relationships with teachers and students each were at play in how the young men responded to schooling and the versions of masculinity they lived out in classrooms.

In order to consider further the connection between social identity, knowledge, and relationships with teachers, I will turn to Marcus's relationship with his history teacher, Mr. Hill. The story of his relationship with his history teacher illuminates how race representation in the classroom provides opportunities for the young men to both challenge and confirm their social identities as young African-American men. Furthermore, as the story unfolds, I argue that the interaction was not just about race but that, in fact, a subtext of gender was also embedded in the interaction.

"Makes the Black People in My Class Mad"

Marcus was not just critical about what teachers taught and how they taught, he also took issue with the ways in which teachers related to him as an African-American man. Marcus was much more vocal and emotional about his treatment as an African-American than any of the other young men. In one story, Marcus revealed his anger through telling me about the comments his history teacher, Mr. Hill, a white man, made about African-American men during a lesson. Marcus talked about the remarks during a lunchtime conversation with one of his friends, Tyrone McKay:

Tyrone:	He talks about how most black males die between the ages of 19 or 25 or something.
JP:	He talks about that?
Tyrone:	Yeah, he told us like, I'm not trying to be a racist. He says most Black males, most crimes and stuff. And I be ready to go off. I know he's trying to do that on purpose, makes me mad, makes the black people in my class mad.
Marcus:	. . . Oh yeah, he was trying to compare him to us, how he grew up and how we go on as black people. ...
Tyrone:	Welfare and all that other stuff, how he was on welfare, and how he thinks he grew up with blacks and stuff, and how blacks should have no right to

be the way they are and stuff. I was like right, he doesn't know what's going on with all the blacks around this world and stuff.

Marcus: OK, get this, he was talking about, okay, I never grew up with a silver spoon in my mouth. And I grew up poor and everything. And I say okay. If you grew up where I lived at, being black, growing' up in the neighborhood that I lived at. . . .

Tyrone: Wouldn't have made it.

Marcus: The kind of fact that he's white and he's got it easy anyway, 'cause he's going to get a job before the brother will, flat out, that's just how it is. It don't matter if he's poor. . . .

Tyrone: Or stupid. . . .

Marcus: He's goin' to get a job faster than the brother would, that's the comment that I had on it. And he's always tryin' to get on. He always says "us." He never say, he never includes us.

Tyrone: He says you guys, you blacks or whatever. . . .

Marcus: He never includes himself. . . .

From the preceding interaction, it is clear that Marcus and Tyrone were critical of the ways in which Mr. Hill portrayed African-Americans and also the ways in which he spoke to African-American students in the class. These two young men were incensed when they told me the story. This was not merely a polite discussion about their history teacher. Being in the class meant they not only had to endure topics they found uninteresting, but they also had to endure the explicit misrepresentations the teacher offered about African-American students. This story helps remind us of the power that a teacher wields over students, not just in the allocation of grades, but in the maintenance of racism in the United States through what and how they do and do not talk about students' lives and their collective histories.

But the story was not only about race and race representation, it was also about how the teacher defined a version of subordinated masculinity. Mr. Hill suggested that it was "black *males*" (emphasis added) who were involved in crime. Further, Marcus suggested of Hill that "he was trying to compare him to us." Through Hill's version of his own and African-American masculinities he set apart African-American masculinity from white masculinity. Marcus and Tyrone, however, seemed to respond more to the racialized aspect of the image that Hill painted rather then the gendered meanings and images embedded in the teacher's talk. Notwithstanding the racialized responses of Marcus and Tyrone, the teacher used and imposed his institutional authority to define a version of African-American masculinities.

As the two young men continued their account, they revealed their relationship was further antagonized by their teacher's continual criticism of their membership in an African-American youth organization, the Alphas.

[The teacher] don't teach nothing, he don't really, Tyrone has this class too. But [the teacher] gets real personal like, he gets in your personal life. That's why I'm in punishment now, 'cause he get in my business. . . . He'd told my Mom that the organization that I'm into, Alpha has some effect on my grade and all this and this and that . . . we don't do nothin' at school, all we go is have our gold sweats on. See he don't like that, he has a problem with us goin' around the hall all the time. Because one day he walks in the class, he says something to me. "Hey why do you wear that gold sweatshirt all the time?" This and this and that. I said "because I want to" . . . he don't know everything about it. All he think is, fraternity, that's what he thinking. It's not a fraternity, it's a brotherhood.

Marcus took the teacher's criticism of the Alphas as a criticism of his "personal life." For Marcus this organization had intense personal significance. As I discuss in a subsequent chapter, this was an organization that was important to Marcus because it allowed him a connection with other young African-American men. Whether the teacher's criticism was warranted was not of issue to Marcus; what was of significance was that the criticism drew a deeper wedge between Marcus and his teacher.

Marcus's story of his relationship with his history teacher provides a backdrop to his critique of the racism embedded in educational institutions. This story reveals how his relationships with teachers contributed or helped shape Marcus's connections with school and the interpretations and critiques he developed about schooling. Marcus's and Tyrone's responses also provide a window to the ways in which social processes in classrooms play out in the formation of their social identities. As young African-American men, they responded to the seemingly racist perspectives of their teacher, and their strong emotional response became the way they expressed themselves as African-American men. This form of expression could be seen as a strand of their version of their racialized masculinities.

Marcus not only criticized the kind of relationships he had with his teachers, he also criticized the decisions about who taught courses. For example, he criticized the fact that a white woman taught "an African-American class at school."

Like they have an African-American class at school and heard there's a white lady teaching the class too. I said how can a white lady tell us about our own culture. She don't know nothin' about us.

Marcus was angered by the appointment of a white teacher to teach the course, because it contributed toward his belief that schools do not serve the interests of their African-American students. This situation reinforced his belief that schooling was about "trying to express how powerful white folk are." In his mind, he saw the appointment of a white teacher as part of the overall oppressive nature of the educational system.

In summary, relationships with teachers were significant because they seemed to shape the young men's access to and experience of knowledge through what the teachers implicitly and explicitly included and excluded in their curriculum. Further, the nature of engagement in classrooms and representations in the curriculum were directly and indirectly interwoven into their lives and the meanings they made of schooling.

Their critique of their experiences in classrooms with teachers, particularly about the racist representation of knowledge, in some way contributed toward the ongoing formation of their identity as African-American men. To some degree, all the young men experienced implicit and explicit forms of racism in their daily live at school. They responded in different ways, however, given the contexts and their experiences in and out of school. For example, dominant ideas about the portrayal of African-Americans provoked them, but Marcus's and Zakeev's critiques addressed issues of power relations between whites and African-Americans, whereas this was not the case for either Rashaud or Shawn, the two middle-class young men. Marcus's and Zakeev's strong critique of the history curriculum confirmed their exclusion as African-Americans from aspects of school life and simultaneously provided them fuel to assert an identity in opposition to their white teachers and the Eurocentric curriculum. They seemed less resigned to the strands of racism in their lives than either Rashaud or Shawn. Social class differences in part may explain this contrast.

There seemed a strong link between their experiences and understandings of racism in schooling and their experiences of racism in the larger societal context. Notwithstanding patterns of racism in the lives of the young men, amid their complicated relationships in schools, they seized different opportunities to confirm and challenge images generally about young African-American men and set themselves apart from these dominant images. But how they critiqued school and what they critiqued was as much about their emerging social identities as about their experiences of schooling. The racism encountered by Dwayne, Jeff, Marcus, and Zakeev, in school and out of school, was much more overt and confrontational compared to the covert racism encountered by Rashaud and Shawn in and out of school.

The interplay of racialized, gendered, and classed experiences in and out of school in the lives of the young men seems to explain the different meanings developed by each of these young men. If we consider Rashaud's and Shawn's accounts of their lives at Cedarville and in their neighborhoods, there seemed a marked difference in what they talked about compared to the other young men. For instance, both Rashaud and Shawn provided cautious critiques of the history curriculum in classrooms yet declared they had not encountered racism in their school, nor in their immediate neighborhood. Dwayne, Jeff, Marcus, and Zakeev, however, spoke of their encounters of racism not only in school but out of school, at work, through the criminal justice system, and in general conflicts in their neighborhoods. Here, race and social class interconnected in the lives of these young men in such a way that their access to privilege varied according to their race–class location, which was shaped by strands of the culture and structure of race and class power and privilege.

Their race and social class experiences, however, were also interconnected with their versions of masculinities. They did not respond to schooling simply as African-Americans, but rather as African-American men. It is noteworthy that Marcus and Zakeev seemed much more confrontational than Rashaud and Zakeev. Zakeev challenged his history teacher, and Marcus responded with disdain when his history teacher attempted to define African-American masculinity. A comparison of the experiences of Marcus and Zakeev with those of Rashaud and Shawn suggests that processes within the classroom not only reflected their different classed experiences as African-Americans but simultaneously their different gendered experiences.

The intersection of race and social class, however, is more complex than meets the eye, as is evident in the stories related by Jeff. A working class young man, totally shaken by his experiences with the criminal justice system, Jeff moved from almost being pushed out of school to seemingly embracing both the form and content of schooling, yet provided little critique of schooling. It is Jeff's experiences that I will now turn to through raising questions about his engagement in classrooms and his connections to teachers. From his accounts, it seems that his approach toward school and work in classrooms changed as he began to experience connected and caring relationships with teachers. His stories, however, do not suggest different experiences in how or what he learned in classrooms.

FROM REJECTION TO ACCOMMODATION

Although many of these young men critiqued aspects of their experiences in classrooms, Jeff stood out as someone who moved from almost rejecting school to seemingly embracing every aspect of the experience. As noted in the previous chapter, an understanding of Jeff's current relationship with school needs to be contextualized within his encounters with the criminal justice system. Jeff did not suddenly and whimsically decide that going to school could reap rewards. He decided that going to school was better than the prospect of going to jail, a very real experience for him. His changed approach to school was also influenced by the fact that he attended a different school.

Jeff really liked his new school. In particular, he liked the pedagogy of the classes at ACS. Often, he contrasted the environment there with that of his previous school. He viewed ACS differently from Central on various dimensions of schooling:

> The teachers, the environment, your peers, the work, they expect a lot more out of you. The teachers are just with you a hundred percent. "Do you need this? Do you need that? Is everything OK?" . . . They encourage you to go by the Bible and everything. They are really nice.

Jeff embraced school more than any of the five other young men. He seemed to take delight in every aspect of school. In mathematics, for instance, he compared his experiences at the two schools:

> Well I didn't take algebra at Central, I took general math. 'Cause I was goofing around. But it's totally different 'cause there's a lot more kids, my teacher Mr. Murphy, he'd help me if you raise your hand, but usually he'd say "Well the assignment is on the board, go back and do something at his desk." So you're sitting there and writing and everything. So you get bored and stuff, so you start talking to your friends and stuff, or just daydream, or write a letter or something. But Algebra here [at ACS], if I don't understand it, I will ask, and he will say "Come here." And if it takes a whole hour, we'll work at it, you know. Sometimes I will do a little of it and everybody will start discussing stuff.

As Jeff described his experiences in math at ACS and Central, it became clear that he most appreciated the smaller classes and the contact with the teachers. His teachers were ready to assist students with their work.

What was not clear from his description, however, was whether he learned and encountered knowledge differently at ACS as compared to Central. This distinction between engaging differently in subject matter and interacting more with his teacher became more apparent in Jeff's comparison of his experiences in biology at the two schools.

> *JP:* If you have to think about the differences between Allerton Christian and Central. You said it's a better learning environment. What do you mean by that?
>
> *Jeff:* Better classes, they teach you more.
>
> *JP:* How would you describe the teaching at Central?
>
> *Jeff:* Biology, when I think of biology, biology is living. It means like the living life. At Central it's bookwork. You just read a book chapter, don't do no dissecting anything. At Allerton Christian, the only time he ever really sat at his desk is when he was doing slides. Wasn't really much, he was sitting at his desk, and we would say "Excuse me sir, where is such and such a slide?" And he would say "It's right here." "Thank you," and then you go back. . . . Biology at Central, you just had to do chapter such and such, or if you've got a project, "I want you to make an atom, that's your homework, bring it in Friday." . . . Now it's fun, we've got lab partners . . . the teacher he will come by the desk, watch, take time, watch a person for five to ten minutes and if he see you struggling to do something, he will say "Do you need help with such and such?" Or, he might even come on over, and say "Let me show you how to do this."

From Jeff's accounts of biology and mathematics, it was the connection and the rapport he developed with his teachers that were different. Although the environment was different to him, I became unsure about how different the pedagogy or the curriculum was from that of his previous school. For instance, in English he described his teacher, Ms. Schultz, as:

> ... wonderful. She's the type of teacher, she talks all hour, but you know you never get bored of her. You never like "Okay lady, shut up." When you're taking notes, she goes step by step with us.

Jeff never really talked about participating in classes at ACS in ways that were different from his experiences at Central. What was different was his interest and how teachers attended to him. Regardless of whether the pedagogy or curriculum was different, for Jeff the difference seemed vast, and maybe most significant was the difference in his relationships with teachers. These relationships were important to Jeff because he argued that such relationships were nonexistent with teachers at his previous school.

In addition, Jeff preferred the students at ACS. He did not encounter strong or good friendships with his peers at Central because "[a] lot of black people like to tease me though sometimes, 'cause they say, I talk funny, talk too proper." They called him a "sellout." For Jeff, talking "proper" meant talking like "white people." At ACS students did not tease him about the way he talked. His relationships with other students and particularly his identity in relation to other African-American and white students will be explored in the following chapter.

Jeff's apparent embrace of the very fabric of school also saw him turn to religion. After attending the school for almost a week, Jeff informed me that he had been "saved." Jeff said that his Bible teacher "encouraged me to get saved. And I'm kind of struggling to take away bad habits." Intrigued with his turn towards religion, I asked him if his family was religious. He laughed and said "no." As we talked more about his experiences at ACS, it became apparent that religion, and particularly Christianity, seeped into the lessons of his day. For example, in his Algebra class he told me,

> ... We usually read a verse in Algebra. 'Cause the teacher is like that, which. He's really, really religious. So, we read a verse or two, maybe a chapter. .... Then we discuss everything. .... "Would you like to pray for such and such. What is going on in your life? Do you want to talk about it and everything?" So it's kind of like a team discussion and everything, so you know and then. We pray for those that are sick at school and everything.

Although Jeff was afforded opportunities to share aspects of his life with the class, only one person at the school knew he had recently fathered a child. He deliberately chose not to share this part of his life with other students or teachers at the school:

> I'm the type of person, I don't want people to know my business. Just like at Allerton Christian, nobody knows that I have a daughter. I think there might be one per-

son that knows I have a daughter. And that's as far as it goes, nobody knows stuff about my life.

So, Jeff's involvement in the school created an uneasy tension in his life. He attended a new school which he claimed served him well. But he did not have many friends outside of this new school, nor did he retain any friends from his previous school. In fact, he argued that students from his old school distanced themselves from him. It seemed that Jeff accommodated almost every aspect of the new school, regardless of who he had to be in order to continue attending the school. For example, attending school meant Jeff chose not to share with other students that he was the father of a child, and he embraced religion in ways he had not. He wanted to reclaim his pride, he wanted the high school diploma, and attending ACS became a vehicle to accomplish such goals. This embrace of school, however, raises questions about the cost to Jeff, socially and culturally, as he embarked on the path of acquiring the high school diploma from ACS. Jeff's case reminds us that there were costs involved in the choices that all the young men made.

ACCOMMODATION AND CRITIQUE

Through their characterization of school these young men implicitly distinguished between going to school and accommodating the content and process of school. Going to school meant aspiring to acquire the high school diploma. That did not necessarily mean they embraced all they learned, or connected to the teachers they encountered in their learning. As noted in the previous chapter, going to school was essentially motivated by the promise of a high school credential. This goal was important for these young African-American men, determined to struggle against the odds, challenge stereotypes about African-American participation in school and society, and seek a dominant symbol of success and achievement. Going to school was influenced less by their interest in the subject areas taught than by the desire to meet and socialize with friends, and by the long-term goal of high school graduation. As already noted, Jeff was the exception here. Their accounts are in some way reminiscent of Weis's (1990) study, *Working Class Without Work*, about white working-class young men and women and their experiences of school. Here she argued that "the *school itself* encourages the emerging contradictory attitude towards school culture and knowledge that is evident among youth both by stressing the utility of schooling and by distributing a form of knowledge that maintains order" (p. 92).

Going to school became a contradictory experience in the lives of these young men. Although they varied in how they embraced school, and how they critiqued aspects of school, simultaneously embracing and critiquing schooling emerged as central to these young men's perspectives and encounters with school. For example, Marcus and Zakeev each criticized the racist nature of the curriculum, yet each was committed to taking tests, getting an acceptable grade, and acquiring the high school diploma. They valued the attainment of the high school diploma but resented aspects of the content and process of schooling in order to acquire the high school diploma. Dwayne talked about school in a very procedural way. He complained that he received little attention from his teachers, and that school "be boring," or "it's alright"; he commented with seemingly little enthusiasm, suggesting a level of resignation rather than acceptance or embracement of his experiences. Shawn hinted at a similar relationship with school and classroom life. Although he encountered different experiences than Dwayne, he was impatiently eager to graduate from school, and like Dwayne talked about his work almost as drudgery in a seemingly mechanical way. Jeff and Rashaud perhaps embraced school more than the other young men. Yet despite Rashaud's apparent engagement in school and pursuit of high grades, he criticized the learning process in school, arguing that "if school was about learning, you wouldn't need grades." Jeff was the lone person to embrace school uncritically. He remained uncritical of his experiences at ACS, and reveled in every aspect of his experiences in classrooms and school.

Perhaps most revealing about their views of school were their accounts of their experiences in classrooms. Many criticized the instruction they encountered. Some shared their struggles in their relationships with their teachers. A common thread among the young men was that the content of their classes at school seemed meaningless to them. Even though this may not have been as much the case for Jeff, I am convinced that attending school presented some currents of contradictions in his life. I will now turn to some significant stories that focus on the different ways in which these young men appeared to simultaneously accommodate and critique school.

"'How Can I Be Racist and My Daughter Went to See Michael Jackson?'"

Although Marcus learned little of value to him as an African-American at school, it was not only the curriculum or the pedagogy from which he was alienated. It was also the particular kinds of relationships he encountered with teachers at his school. Marcus provided few positive comments about any of his teachers at school, besides his social studies teacher. Much of his time with me was spent berating certain teachers, talking about how prejudiced they were, and how they spoke about and referred to African-American students.

Marcus's relationship with his biology teacher, Ms. Huffington, perhaps captures the extent to which he was not only disempowered as a learner, but reinforced in his belief that his teachers were "teaching white is superior, they dominate everything."

Marcus admitted that from the moment he entered the biology class at the beginning of the semester, he did not like the class. From the start this class meant completing individual assignments with no opportunity to engage in experiments.

> They ain't teaching us and giving us homework on top of homework. They don't explain, they just give it to you and expect you to do it. You don't know what the world you are doing. That's how I feel in this biology class, I don't know what the world I'm, well I know what I'm doin', but I don't know the world what I'm doing because she don't explain it. . . .

Marcus here provides a glimpse of his experiences in his biology class. It seemed that he understood what he had to do in this class in a technical and procedural sense, but did not really have the opportunity to grasp the substantive knowledge in his biology class. For Marcus, attending his biology class did not provide an opportunity to engage and learn about biology. It seemed Ms. Huffington provided few opportunities to understand concepts and ideas in biology, leaving him feeling very unsure of the subject matter.

He also suggested that the teacher did not like him: "She don't like me, she's being trying to flunk me ever since I got in that class." He described the problem he had over his grade for his first assignment in the class:

> . . . Like yesterday, she told me, 'cause like I asked her a question, I said "I wanna know how did you grade this?" Because we had so much out of a hundred, and I got 60. I said "How in the world could I get 60 and there was only a possible. . . ." I got A's on all my papers, I only missed two, so that was like ten points off. . . . Plus I turned it in late, so that's 30. I said, "30 from a 100 is not 60." I said "where's your mathematics?" And I was explaining this to her. It took about five minutes to talk to her, I'm like "Excuse me, can I talk to you?" And she was like, "Hang on," and kept going on talking to somebody. I just looked at her there, and finally she came over and said. She still didn't understand what I said, you know, she was thinking about someone else. I said yeah, yeah. She gave me the 70. . . . She went on and gave me the 70. She wasn't even listening to what I'm saying. That's how she is, she don't pay attention to you. She don't care what she doing, as long as she gets her work done. All she want is probably that paycheck at the end of the week.

The problem with the biology teacher continued through the semester. On another occasion, Marcus encountered difficulty with this teacher over a test grade. This time he failed to hand a test in on time because he was scheduled to speak with his new counselor and therefore was unavailable to take the particular biology test. He explained this encounter:

> . . . what happened, okay, I wasn't there for the test day, I had to take it the next day, so I was doing it, she gave it to me so I could do it during class, right. So I was doing it during class, and class was just about over, and she was passing out papers, and I accidentally mixed it up with my other papers, and stuck it in my folder and forgot I put it in there. And when she asked for it, and when I went to look for it, I told her I couldn't find it. So she told me, when I find it, turn it in. So, I took it upon myself, when I do find it, I turn it in. So, a week later when we was doin' that em, we had to clean out our folders and everything, and I was separating papers and stuff, and I

turned it in. And then she told me that she can't give me credit on it. And I said you told me that when I find it, turn it in.

Ms. Huffington did not give him credit for the test. At the end of the semester he was told that he would get an E for the course. "If I had have had this test in, credited on my test, I probably would have had a D or something like that," he told me.

Marcus was dissatisfied with his test grades for the semester, particularly the E he was awarded, which represented a failing grade. Consequently, during one class session, Marcus decided to speak with his school counselor about this failing grade, and left the classroom before the biology session had ended. This move of taking the matter to his counselor angered his teacher. Apparently, as Marcus left the classroom, she called him a "black fucking nigger."

> . . . she was mad at me because I told her I wanted to go and see my counselor. She didn't say it directly in my face. Some students in my class heard her say it, saying it towards me when I left the class. There was about two of them that heard because they were sitting right up on her.

Marcus was adamant he should not receive an E for the course, so he went to speak to his counselor about the problem of his grade. And in reliving the interaction with me it became evident that the problem of the failing grade was exacerbated by the teacher's apparent racist remarks about Marcus. Marcus later heard about the comments from his two friends in the class.

Marcus told me that he was unaware of the fact that he would receive an E for the term, and that if he was going to receive a failing grade, a procedure was in place for a letter to be sent home to parents informing them of such a possibility. Marcus explained his anger:

> . . . 'cause I don't think I was failing, because even if I is, they should have sent me a failure letter home. That's a requirement, you have to send a failure letter home. She sent everybody else who was a failing, a failure letter home. So that told me I wasn't failing, so I didn't think nothin' of it, 'cause I wasn't getting there. And then she comes off and gives me off an E.

Clearly, Marcus was unprepared to receive the E because he was not forewarned by a procedural letter. In response, Marcus went to speak with his counselor at school. Although he was appointed a new counselor at the beginning of the year, he decided to speak to his old counselor because he found him more trustworthy and reliable.

> I told my counselor that, and he said "I will go and talk to her," and he ain't did a thing. He say the same line just to get me out of his face. I don't want to go to my new counselor, 'cause she ain't gonna do no better, because she just all for him.

Marcus also spoke with his mother not only about the failing grade, but also about Ms. Huffington's alleged racist remark. His mother responded by going to the school, approaching Marcus's biology teacher and the school principal, Mr. Warton. "My Mom went to her, said my son said this and that, and she [Ms. Huffington] said 'No I did not.' My Mom knew she was goin' to deny it. And she [his Mom] went and to see Warton." The principal assured Marcus's mother that he would speak with the students who overheard the remark. "We had a lot of people on our side. They only talked to one person. They didn't talk to the people that I said heard it," Marcus argued.

The teacher changed Marcus's grade to "a D, nothing high. My Mom said she should have changed it to a C," Marcus argued. He then relayed to me how the teacher justified the change in the grade:

> This what she said. (Laughs.) "Well Marcus, an E looks kinda bad, I know you don't deserve no grade like that, you know you've been working so hard." It was so crazy, I was falling off laughing. She put a little line in here, she changed my grade. "I thought you didn't deserve no E, so I moved your grade up to a D." I was like, yeah right. It was so funny, and then she told me, "how can I be racist and my daughter went to see Michael Jackson?" I said "So." I'm just looking up in the air, because she's tryin' to prove to me that's she's not racist.

This last comment reveals an aspect of the tension between Marcus and his biology teacher that was one of a teacher and a student, and significantly, a relationship between a teacher who was a white woman and a student who was African-American man. It was an argument between a teacher who had the power to assign grades, and hence pass or fail, and a student who was to receive the grade. But in Marcus's eyes this incident was not just about teacher authority and control, it was also about racism. Ms. Huffington's reported comment of "How can I be racist and my daughter went to see Michael Jackson?" revealed her understanding of racism and, rather than pacifying Marcus, further agitated him.

This was a conflict over power—power to assign grades. As Marcus battled to get a passing grade, but also himself not only challenging the individual teacher he was simultaneously challenging a racist system, which she represented. The significance of racialized meanings in his relationship with the teacher is apparent when he talked about how white students portrayed the teacher's attitude toward African-American students in his class. He said "even the white folks say she's prejudice, I was like goodness, this woman must be."

This conflict over the way she used her power to assign grades had implications for Marcus because it had an impact on his goal of acquiring the high school diploma. Complicating the tension was his perception that the authority figure was racist. Whether the teacher was or was not racist, for Marcus the interaction confirmed his view that she was racist. Other teachers in the building also have told me that this teacher was known to be racist in the school; but she remained in the school.

This problem, however, is greater than Marcus's individual experience. My reading and experiences reveal that his encounters with his biology teacher are not uncommon. It raises larger questions not only about individual racism, but also about how Marcus saw school as a whole as being racist, and this teacher as part of that authority structure. This account also raises questions for me about connections between individual and institutional racism.

Despite his critical perspective of the racist nature of the institution of school, Marcus continued to attend school, even under difficult circumstances and hoped to graduate by 1995. Like other youngsters of his age, he had dreams of pursuing a career that would give him material rewards and success. He wanted a job, yet he readily admitted he "can't get a job."

Marcus occupied a contradictory position in relation to school. On the one hand, he openly challenged, dismissed, and devalued the content and focus of the classes and, on the other, he highly valued the potential to graduate and acquire the high school diploma. He did not value the content of the classes he took, but sought the extrinsic value of the diploma earned by attending such classes, and getting good grades.

Marcus strongly argued that significant learning opportunities would represent learning something about himself as an African-American, whereby teachers would be responsible for "teaching you somethin' about your black African culture." Such learned involved caring and connected relationships, where teachers understood him and his perspectives. For Marcus, the curriculum he encountered in school had little significance to him. Yet he admitted that he does the work required "to get [his] grade." So why did he continue to attend school? He said he attended school to acquire a diploma. With the diploma he intended to "get a job, but can't get a job." Marcus's quest to acquire a high school diploma reflects not only the complexity of what the diploma represented to him, but also a complexity of the process he needed to undertake in order to acquire the diploma.

Marcus did not totally disregard what he learned in school. Rather, he was selective:

> But they teach me stuff, some of it I will comprehend, some of it I will keep in my mind, and throw it out, and educate myself. Because as you know, I'm in that group UNITE, and I get taught besides what they are teaching me at school, my black way. How black people came up and did so much.

One class in which Marcus was fairly engaged, and which he enjoyed above all the other classes, was the social studies class he took in the Fall semester of 1992. It was a global studies course that spent some time focusing on Africa. Marcus told me that he liked the class because

> It's just an active class, 'cause the teacher gives us the work, we talk about. It's just fun, it's just hard to explain. I just love being in the class. I just love being there. ... I can just flat out work in there. I don't know why. It's just the nature of the room.

Marcus enjoyed this class and often spoke to me about the class's discussion topics and the support and encouragement of the teacher. One of the central topics for the semester was the study of Africa. Each student was required to choose a country and prepare a project about that country. Marcus was very excited. Although he initially chose South Africa, he ended up studying Ethiopia. Despite a study of Ethiopia not being his first choice, Marcus immersed himself in the project. On the day of his presentation, he cooked Ethiopian food for the class members. Social studies was a class where he revealed an eagerness to learn and engage when presented with opportunities to learn about subject matter that was relevant and connected to his interests and educational pursuits. From his accounts of the class, however, it is unclear whether he participated in knowledge construction differently than in other classrooms.

Zakeev, too, developed a contradictory and complex stance in relation to the process of acquiring a high school diploma. As noted in the previous chapter, Zakeev criticized the knowledge he encountered at school that "shows nothin' on" him. However, he generated a stance toward the knowledge he encountered in school wherein he argued it was better to know the "white knowledge" than "knowing no way at all." He argued that "if you don't know it that way, how can you change it?" Zakeev, while rejecting the knowledge he encountered in school because it shows nothin' on him," simultaneously developed a rationale for learning concepts and ideas in school subjects that reflect white power and privilege.

Thus, Marcus and Zakeev each developed critical stances in relation to school, teachers, and their relationships with teachers. In fact, they each challenged their relationships with teachers: Zakeev challenged his history teacher about the content of the curriculum, while Marcus challenged his biology teacher about the grade she assigned him. But they continued to go to school. This raises questions about the complexity of their accommodation of schooling in their lives. It seems more likely that they tolerated the institution not because they accepted ideas or the ways in which their schools functioned, but because of their overwhelming commitment to graduate from high school. Zakeev, like Marcus, was not just critical of the particular classes, he also noticed the structure of school and how it reflected white interests. In order to consider this point further, I will turn to Zakeev's observations about the distribution of students in mathematics classes.

Mathematics: "That's Where They, I Think They Discriminate"

On moving to his new school, Western, Zakeev requested to be placed in an algebra class but was placed in a general math class. Although he was unhappy about this, he was more unhappy about the way in which students were separated into two classes that seemed to be divided along racial lines. "They put all the white people in one class, and then they were going to say they were full, and pick all the black people out and put them at the end in the little classes," Zakeev said. Apparently there were too many students to be placed into one classroom, so the administration divided the students into two classes. Zakeev told me that these classes were the "middle classes."

JP:	What's the middle classes, I don't understand?
Zakeev:	Not the middle classes, the last resort. They kicked all the white people out.
JP:	You mean out of the enriched class.
Zakeev:	No, they have the regular math, and they got full. But I think they got full with white people and they kicked the white people out.
JP:	Where did the white people go?
Zakeev:	They got put in another classroom.
JP:	There's how many white people?
Zakeev:	There's three, and the rest are black. About fifteen people.
JP:	And that is strange, because the school is predominately white.
Zakeev:	Yeah.
JP:	They didn't say why?
Zakeev:	Yeah, they said the class is full.
JP:	And how many black people in the other class?
Zakeev:	Not many, two.

Zakeev constantly raised the issue of separation of African-American and white students, because he could not understand the coincidence of clusters of black people in one class, and clusters of white people in another. "That's where they, I think they discriminate," he told me.

This example reveals the subtle or, in Zakeev's eyes the not so subtle, ways in which racism operated within his school. The fact that a predominance of African-American students was found in Zakeev's general algebra class and a predominance of white students in another class, in a school with an African-American population of approximately 30 percent, and that this was not addressed as problematic or an issue of concern, points to the ways in which racism in the eyes of Zakeev emerged and was sustained. Whether the allocation of students to the two classes was racist or not, through Zakeev's eyes, the decision was racist. It is through this incident that Zakeev was not only able to think about the predominance of African-Americans in his mathematics class, but also was able to think about "discrimination" writ large. Such incidents may have filled Zakeev with despair, but ironically also may have helped him strengthen his identity as an African-American and the understandings he developed about race privilege and power. Notwithstanding, he tolerated such segregation, because of his commitment to disproving racist assumptions through graduating. Zakeev accepted the situation, but remained critical. His experiences of school reveal a tension between accommodation and critique, and contrasts with Dwayne's story and his relationship with school.

"Education Means Like Gettin' All You Can Get from School"

As noted in the previous chapter, Dwayne went to school so that he could "be someone successful." When he spoke about school, he focused on his experiences at recess and not the actual processes of getting the diploma, of getting good grades, or of learning the content of classes to get the grades. Possibly he chose not to further discuss his school experiences because he felt intimidated by me as a researcher and, knowing that I was a teacher, felt as though he was being evaluated. Yet there seemed little to entice him to stay in school. At one point Dwayne told me that "as far as that school, Central, I guess it's alright. I be looking at it, like it be boring 'cause there don't really be nothin' to do," he said. The highlights of school for Dwayne were the opportunities to play sports and to see his friends. "I like sport, seeing my friends or whatever," he told me. After he arrived at school in the morning, he said that he spent his time

> . . . basically, goin' around and say "Hi" to friends. . . . And then after the bell rings, I just go, I guess go to class, then have gym. I have gym then have lunch, get like an hour from there. Go out to eat from school, talk to your friends . . . talk to a lot of girls . . . Just go fourth hour, fifth hour, sixth hour.

On a number of occasions I asked him to talk about his day at school. He listed the classes he attended almost as items on an itinerary, rather than places of learning, engagement, or activity. He spoke very little about the content of classes, or about the students in the classes. In a few of the classes he mentioned the "work" he encountered in the class. For example, in English he learned words, in math he did "work and stuff," while in biology-science he did "experiments . . . work sheets, read, take tests and stuff." Gleaning from his accounts, much of Dwayne's work experience in school seemed to represent following teachers' directions and completing tasks. Although his accounts were not detailed, it is significant that the aspects of classroom life he chose to talk about centered on assignments or his regard for a teacher. As he did not describe the pedagogy or ideas he encountered in class, it is difficult to catch glimpses of what he was learning, or of the pedagogy he experienced in classrooms. Dwayne did not talk about what he learned in school, nor did he indicate whether he found the subject matter to be interesting or engaging. Notwithstanding, going to school was important to him. It was "makin' it" through school and struggling to stay in school that seemed to become his priority. Schools seemed to have offered very little to Dwayne in his quest to achieve the high school diploma and thereby "be no statistic."

I asked Dwayne about his learning experiences generally at school:

> JP: Tell me what you're learning in school or whether there are things that you'd like to be learning.
>
> Dwayne: What do you mean?

> JP: Okay, you're doing all these things at school, what would you like to be doing at school?
>
> Dwayne: Nothin' really, that's what school is for.
>
> JP: What's school for?
>
> Dwayne: To get an education.
>
> JP: So what do you think you are learning about at school?
>
> Dwayne: Huh?
>
> JP: Okay, you say you want to get an education, what's an education mean to you?
>
> Dwayne: Education means like gettin' all you can get from school.
>
> JP: Like what?
>
> Dwayne: You're learning everyday, you ain't gonna never stop learning.

Despite Dwayne claiming "you're learning everyday," he never articulated what he was learning nor did he elaborate about the meaning of education to him. In a sense, he provided certain responses that seemed to show what school and going to school represented to him as a symbol, but simultaneously revealed the content of schooling had little significance to him. He was physically in school but he talked little about actually accessing all he can "get from school." Dwayne seemed to believe in school as a symbol of achievement, but did not seem connected to the curriculum and pedagogy in classrooms that were vehicles to such achievement.

For Dwayne, school tended to represent a process to endure in order to acquire a symbol of potential achievement, the high school diploma. His approach to school raises questions about how he valued and perceived the process of schooling, how he participated in the process, and how he was afforded opportunities for engagement in school. His involvement with school begs the question, what did it mean for Dwayne to accommodate schooling? Did it mean to tolerate schooling with the hope of acquiring the high school diploma? Poignantly, the hope of acquiring the high school diploma was not enough to keep Dwayne in school given that he really was not very connected to his classes at school, nor to his teachers. As previously noted, Dwayne ran away from his foster home in February 1993 and did not return to Allerton. Ultimately, the question arises: Did Dwayne chose to leave school or was he pushed out of school, through both his disengaging and "boring" experiences at Central, as well as the pull of his friends in Detroit? School seemed to emerge as a place where Dwayne attempted to live out his goal of showing he was able to acquire the diploma, but it was also a difficult place for him to stay in.

It seemed that it was not only Central that was disengaging to Dwayne, he also mentioned that he found school "boring" when he attended school in Detroit. Thus, it is not surprising that when Dwayne talked about schooling he focused little on his experiences in classrooms and instead talked about his relationships. These relationships with other students may have been the sustaining factors that helped him continue to go to school. So, questions about whether Dwayne was connected to school, whether he was learning, or whether Dwayne had opportunities to learn need to be situated within a sea of his multiple encounters with school, the history of the schools he attended, and the particular contexts in which he lived. It is these cumulative experiences that perhaps represent Dwayne's relationship with school.

Going to school represented a symbolic act for Dwayne. He simultaneously seemed disengaged from the content of his classes, which he argued was "boring," yet acknowledged the fact that he needed to endure the classes to acquire the high school diploma. Whereas Marcus seemingly rejected most of the curriculum at school, yet continued to attend, Dwayne provided little criticism of his encounters in classrooms. At the same time he offered little praise. He seemed almost anesthetized by school. He neither strongly rejected nor criticized his encounters. Dwayne invested a lot in the act of attending school, but it is unclear what opportunities he was provided, or what learning opportunities he seized in the process of attending school.

"If School Was About Learning, You Wouldn't Need Grades"

The topic of learning was something that wove its way into all conversations with the young men. As in the case of Dwayne, most of these young men suggested they were not involved in the process of learning. The knowledge they experienced in classrooms did not seem connected to their thinking or the challenges they sought. The curriculum encountered by many of these young men echoes the work of McNeil (1986) and, in the main, reflected a view of knowledge distribution that is highly routinized with few opportunities for students to engage in ideas and issues. But, as previously noted, there were differences in both what and how they experienced curriculum. Not all the young men seemed as disconnected from school as Dwayne.

Dwayne's experience of school most starkly contrasts with that of Rashaud, who attended a predominantly white middle-class school. Not only was Rashaud in mostly advanced classes in his school, he was someone who achieved high grades in school. Despite his achievement in school, he hated the competition in school because it tended to detract from a purpose of school, "to learn."

> If school wasn't such a competition, there would be no need for grades. If school was about learning, you wouldn't need grades. You can see it's competition, why do you need grades to learn?

Rashaud's insight suggests that while he embraced school and the high school credential as a vehicle for success and potential social and economic mobility and security, he was also critical of aspects of the process of schooling, particularly of the relationship between learning and the evaluation of learning through grades. In the previous chapter, I noted Rashaud's commitment to achieving good grades and being successful. "Grades, that's what's on my mind, the biggest. I don't give a rip about anything else," he said. This stance was ironic given his critical view of learning. He portrayed himself as a role model of success in school, to his family, and to African-Americans in the larger community, and spoke about challenging white Americans about stereotypes of African-Americans in society.

Despite this apparent acceptance of a symbol of school, Rashaud developed a sophisticated critique of the process of schooling. He compared going to school and being in school to the production of movies:

> To me school is kinda like a movie, the scripts are memorized, you do the performance, it comes out, audience will give you a rating, and you go on to your next thing, you go on and do your next movie. And that's elementary school, middle school and high school.

Rashaud's view of learning in school reflected a critique that centers on the process of knowledge acquisition and the relationship between knowledge acquisition and assessment. Each level of school became a place to memorize "scripts" that are graded, and was followed by a move to the next level of schooling. This scathing critique of the learning process in school starkly contrasts with Rashaud's characterization of schooling in the previous chapter. Hence, Rashaud simultaneously embraced the process of schooling to get ahead, yet waged a mindful critique of the system that evolved.

Rashaud was not the only person for whom grades were problematic. Marcus also criticized school, while he too mentioned the centrality of getting "good grades." Despite the focus on grades, this did not mean that he thought what he learned in school was valuable, or that he learned anything of importance to him as an African-American. He claimed the teachers did not care about education, and that much of his encounters in schools were repetitious.

> Central, they don't really care about education to me, because of how they got the system there. They just want you to get grades, and get the hell out of their class. That's what it is. Because they just give you grades. I know because I haven't learned nothing from that, nothing that I ain't heard before, because I've been hearing the same stuff for years and years . . . all the teachers there is to get their paycheck at the end of the week and to be in class to give you that old stuff that you heard before, that's it. Give you a bunch of dittos and papers and all that stuff. They won't sit down and discuss stuff with you and everything.

For Marcus, learning was more than getting grades on a test, more than attending classes, it was being engaged. He wanted to be afforded the opportunity "to discuss stuff" that was important. The kind of education that he sought had to be acquired outside of the context of formal schooling.

> It's not a really major part of my day. Because I don't really acknowledge it really, it just something I have to do. . . . Just to survive, just have to do it, just to survive. Because basically what I feel is this. 'Cause what I've been learning now I'm understanding what they're doing, they're really taking us back. So basically I don't have a feel for school. I won't drop out.

Attending school then was part of Marcus's will to survive. His notion of "survival" links to issues raised in the previous chapter about his commitment to acquire the high school diploma. It also links to Dwayne's approach to school, wherein he seemed little engaged in the process, but went to school regardless. Marcus's statements about school provides a glimpse of the extent to which he and other young men in this study were alienated from the very process they needed to engage with in order to acquire the high school diploma.

Staying in school was part of Marcus's survival strategy. He was determined he "won't drop out" of school. Although Marcus felt as though he was not learning, staying in school and attending classes saw him develop an approach toward school in which he didn't "have a feel for school." Marcus not only critiqued the way in which he learned, he was also concerned about what he learned. Education, for Marcus, meant learning about himself, his culture, and the experiences of African-American in the United States. Marcus discussed learning at school:

> . . . Learn what? They ain't teaching us nothin'. The stuff I learned, I learned on my own. Basically that's why, I can't really say. . . .'Cause trying to get more people educated out of school, learn us what they teaching us, cause they aren't teaching us the right thing, learn on our own, try to educate yourself on your own. Get that knowledge for yourself, try to get tell other people. But that's basically what I want to do, we supposed to tell people about the thing, try and tell our brothers and sisters, explain things. We need to unite as one, you know.

Marcus was not only committed to engaging in education about African-Americans for his own ends, he was also committed to broadening the consciousness of the African-American community at large.

Marcus's stance toward schooling, as with the other young men, was complex and contradictory because he, like the others, critiqued schooling yet continued to attend school. In some ways they all accepted and accommodated some of their teachers' demands, and in other ways, it seemed they tolerated some aspects of schooling in order to gain passing grades as a vehicle to the acquisition of the high school diploma.

Merely because they tolerated aspects of schooling—teacher's assignments, the form of classroom work, topics, and ideas shaping the curriculum—did not automatically indicate their tacit approval. As Fuller (1980) argued, "It becomes only too easy to assume that academic striving and achieving are synonymous with subscribing (conforming) to these values, and to see school failure as necessarily indicative of rejection of those same values" (p. 63). Fuller raises an important point, as it became clear that these young men unevenly "subscribed" to academic striving, and they often did so in opposition to other beliefs and values they held. Their experiences in classrooms were contradictory and complex.

Weis (1990) elaborates on this point about the contradictory nature of lived experiences in schools. She argues that "poor black students tend *not* to reject totally school meanings and culture, and, at the same time, act as if they do" (p. 25). Ogbu (1988) argued a similar point in his study of African-American high school youth in Stockton:

> Black youths do not consciously reject school meanings and knowledge. In fact black youths say emphatically that schooling is important to them and they want to get an education to escape from poverty and other problems in their ghetto community. But although they verbalize a strong desire for education, they behave in ways that will not necessarily lead to school success. (p. 170)

Both Weis and Ogbu point to the contradictory and paradoxical nature of schooling for African-Americans. In my study, I argue that the stories these young men shared of their experiences in classrooms, and their views of classroom curriculum, pedagogy, and their relationships with teachers, were complex and contradictory. Amidst these contradictory and complex accounts of schooling, however, their participation in schooling had differing consequences for these young men. It is within this context that I turn to a discussion of their perspectives of their experiences in school and situate these stories within the context of their views of the high school diploma.

GRADUATION, ACCOMMODATION, AND CRITIQUE

In Chapter 4, I argued that these young men's views about why they stayed in school and the meanings they developed of the diploma were influenced by a range of events in their lives. Acquiring the high school diploma certainly was linked to their desire for economic or social rewards and, in some cases, mobility. This orientation, influenced by and influencing the various events and encounters in and out of school, was but one of the strands in their lives to which each gave greater or lesser significance. Staying in school and acquiring the high school diploma was not a single phenomenon that signified their embrace or acceptance of dominant ideologies about success, mobility, and advancement, or about the form and content of schooling. As Weis (1990) argues, "The diploma can be obtained whether one challenges and/or questions knowledge or not. In other words, one can be alienated and still obtain the short-term instrumental rewards of participating in high school" (p. 92). Notwithstanding, there is a distinction between obtaining the diploma, participating in the process to acquire the diploma, and the meanings associated with the diploma and schooling.

In the discussion thus far, I have argued that the meaning of the high school diploma is redefined through the process of acquiring the diploma, and the process itself is redefined as students experience other events and experiences inside and outside of school. The process of acquiring the high school diploma is complex. And the meanings these young men developed of the high school diploma were also complex. There was variation in how these young men experienced school, and there was variation in the meanings they developed about the high school diploma. The contradictory and complex interactions of critique and accommodation reflect not only their experiences of schooling, but also the meanings of schooling and the high school diploma in relation to their identities as young African-American men. In the context of their identities as young African-American men, I turn next to an exploration of the strands of the culture and structure of race and social class that intermingle in their lives.

Variations in Patterns

The forms of critique and accommodation emerging from the lives of these young men seem connected to their encounters in school and their experiences of race and social class as young African-American men. Despite the strong pattern of critique of the history curriculum and pedagogy across the young men, there was some variation in the nature of their critique and accommodation. Although they each developed critiques about their learning, they differed in how they approached school and responded to school, and in the kind of learning experiences they encountered. For example, Shawn and Rashaud attended the same middle-class school, but seemed to adopt different stances in relation to school and learning in school. In terms of engagement and connection in school, Shawn seemed similar to Dwayne, who also seemed anesthetized by school. Shawn seemed to go through the motions of going to school but exhibited little enthusiasm or fulfillment, a pattern similar to that of Dwayne and not Rashaud. Yet Shawn attended a very different school than Dwayne did and had very different experiences growing up. Both, however, both seemed to endure school in similar ways. But differences emerged in what they learned, how they learned, and what they could do with the high school diploma once they graduated from high school. Given Shawn's social class location, he seemed to have more possibilities on hand compared to Dwayne. Thus, they may have viewed school in similar ways, but the consequences of their involvement in school suggest a vast difference.

At the same time, it is significant that Rashaud waged the most sophisticated critique of knowledge acquisition in school, yet it was he who seemed most engaged in school and was most poised to acquire the high school diploma and enter college. Rashaud wanted to go to college and he went to school in ways that assured him of outstanding grades. His motivation for graduation and attending school was different from either Dwayne's or Jeff's motivations. They saw their success in school as confirmation that they were not representations of the dominant images of African-American men. Rashaud, however, wanted his success at school to signal him as a role model to his family and the larger African-American community. Rashaud's perspective speaks to the kind of educational experience he encountered, and the access to power and privilege he was afforded. Interestingly, he developed a critique that did not challenge the relationship between institutional power and privilege in broader society, but did challenge the hierarchical and meritocratic shape of schools from which he seemed, compared to the other young men, most suitably poised to benefit.

In contrasting the talk about schooling of Dwayne, Jeff, Marcus, and Rashaud, it seemed there were differences in how these young men intended to challenge dominant images of African-American men. Jeff and Dwayne believed that merely staying in school was a way to challenge such images. They wanted to challenge dominant images and messages about the overpopulation of jails by African-American men in order to prove they were not a "statistic" bound for jail. For Rashaud, academic success and not merely staying in school seemed most significant. He wanted to challenge emphasized images and ideas about African-American men and their role and participation in U.S. society and wanted to use his image as an academically successful student as a vehicle for such challenges. His stance was different than Marcus's. Marcus challenged the images and ideas about African-American men as he engaged in the process of schooling. Marcus's active critique was integral to his ongoing experiences of schooling and his version of challenging such images, whereas Rashaud saw his success as a symbol of the challenge.

On comparing Jeff to Marcus and Zakeev, who all lived in the same working-class neighborhood, questions emerge as to whether Jeff's diploma would afford him more or the same opportunities as Zakeev and Marcus, despite his attending a private school. Jeff seemed quite alone in his battle to acquire the high school diploma. He was alienated from his old friends from school, and developed few friendships at ACS. So, while it is unclear what rewards Jeff will reap through acquiring a diploma from ACS, on the immediate level the personal and social consequences are terribly depressing.

From the various accounts of life in classrooms, it becomes apparent that the ways in which these young men talked about and experienced school were not just influenced by the kind of instruction and pedagogy they encountered. Intead their perspectives and experiences were also shaped by myriad prior experiences inside and outside of school. These experiences also shaped the ways in which they viewed school and the kind of opportunities and ideas they constructed about the importance of school, getting good grades, and the acquisition of the high school diploma.

Exploring Intrasocial Class Differences

Maybe most surprising about these six young men are not the differences across social class groups, but the differences within social class groups. There seemed a difference between how Shawn and Rashaud talked about experiences in school and the consequences of their experiences. The same holds true for Jeff as compared with Marcus and Zakeev. This point is significant when one considers, for example, MacLeod's (1995) study, in which he noted congruency in aspirations, success, and mobility of a working-class African-American peer group attending the same school. Although my study is not about peer groups per se, there seemed little congruency among any groups of young men. The working-class young men, in my study did not seem to hold a view or hope that education would dramatically enable them to acquire economic success and mobility. MacLeod suggested that the "Brothers," an African-American working-class peer group, are "optimistic about their future employment" (p. 78). In my study, the working-class young men were very skeptical about their future on the labor market, where they believed African-Americans were at a disadvantage compared with white Americans. The middle-class young men, on the other hand, seemed fairly optimistic and talked little about any barriers that may impede their ambitions and goals.

These six young African-American men at once accommodated and criticized strands of the dominant norms, beliefs, and values about school. This is significant, because these young men contrast with the Brothers who "respect the standards, conventions, and judgments of the school" (p. 91). This cannot be said for all six of the young men in this study. They critiqued some of the standards, conventions, and judgments of school. For example, Marcus explained the function of the hidden curriculum in school and challenged a teacher about a grade, and Zakeev critiqued his history curriculum and questioned the predominance of African-Americans in his mathematics class. They certainly did not suggest a fully fledged respect for the standards, conventions, and judgments of their school. Thus, on considering the African-American participants of MacLeod's study and the views of the young men in this study, an apparent variation within social class groups seems to prevail. I am not arguing that there were not patterns of talk and beliefs across the young men. If any pattern emerged in common in the talk of these young men, it was a pattern of critique of racism.

Ogbu (1988) argued that racism cuts across class boundaries:

If, however, we take racial stratification seriously as a distinct type of stratification, we see that it generates its own oppositional process that cuts across class boundaries because it is tied to the minority-group members' sense of peoplehood or collective social identity. Thus the oppositional process may remain even after economic and other instrumental barriers have been removed. That is why some black students from middle- and upper-class backgrounds may still express their opposition to "acting white" in school just as black students from working-class, lower-class, and underclass backgrounds may do.

Although Ogbu raises a significant point about a pattern of "oppositional" responses to schooling by African Americans from varying social class locations, there seemed vast differences in how racism manifested in the lives of these six young men, and how they responded to racism in their lives. There seemed significant differences between Dwayne, of underclass background, and the other working-class and middle-class young men. There also seemed differences between the middle-class young men and the others in this study. Three of the young men— Dwayne, Marcus, and Zakeev—mentioned racism as a barrier to success. Racism was not as significant to Rashaud or Shawn.

The ways in which the young men responded to their teachers, participated in classrooms, or were passive or confrontational with teachers reveal aspects of their social identities in the making. Their experiences of racism may have been different, but the kind of racism they experienced saw them responding differently. These responses seem to suggest not only aspects of their classed identities, or their racialized identities, but also their gendered identities. For example, Marcus's response to the grade his biology teacher allocated him and his history teacher's attempt to define a version of African-American masculinity, saw him aggressively asserting himself. The ways in which he responded certainly suggest aspects of his version of masculinity in the making. Such responses were not evident in Shawn's or Rashaud's accounts of schooling. Instead, in the main, they seemed to passively accept or tolerate most of their experiences in classrooms. Likewise, their responses could be viewed as aspects of their racial-masculine identities in the making.

From the discussion, it becomes evident that these young men did interrupt and respond to options and privileges, barriers and constraints in different ways. In this way, the interplay among race, class, and gender in their lives and how this interplay manifested in their experiences on a day-to-day basis becomes significant in understanding how they produced their social identities. Thus, the social practice of these young men in a sense legitimated and also challenged social reproduction (relations of power and control). For example, Jeff's move to a private Christian school had the potential to provide him with access to knowledge and opportunities that may not have been accessible to him at Central. Jeff had virtually dropped out of school, and though it was unclear whether he would acquire the high school diploma from his new school, the knowledge and experience acquired through going to this new school had the potential to see him having different options than those acquired at his old school, Central. However, across the period of time that I knew Jeff, he did not seem to have any greater knowledge of life beyond high school graduation than Marcus or Zakeev. But for Jeff, the significance of going to the private school was seen by him as a move that would prevent him from becoming a high school dropout which in his eyes might lead him to further entanglement with the criminal justice system.

Connell and associates (1982) note that "under-privilege" is not always perpetuated—that is, it is not inevitable:

> . . . the interactions among kids, parents, and teacher are constantly being renegotiated and reconstructed, at times quite dramatically mutated in crises of the pupil's

school life . . . privilege is not always passed on and under-privilege is not always perpetuated. (p. 188)

Here, I am arguing that these young men's lived experiences in and out of school led them to accommodate and critique aspects of school in ways that reflect and are rooted in institutional differences and opportunities. At the same time, these young men may have transformed their experiences in ways that actually challenged the barriers and constraints that seemingly lay in their paths, as in the case of Jeff. Such a view of the meanings they made of the high school diploma, and their experiences in school, suggests that social actors make choices, albeit constrained choices, and may act in ways that redefine the constraints and potentials—just as the constraints are redefined by others inside and outside schools. Thus, constraints and potentials are defined and emerge dialectically. My intention is not to over-determine the views and choices of the young men. Rather, I would argue that these young men's perspectives in the making emerged both as an accommodating response to constraints, and also as an oppositional or transformational response. For example, Marcus's and Zakeev's challenge of teachers represent their developing stances about the value of the knowledge and experiences in school, yet at the same time they recognized that they needed this knowledge or grade to get ahead. This view of human agency acknowledges the interconnectedness of institutional and cultural practices, but challenges the degree of determinism or the level of predictability of experiences, consequences, and outcomes.

In making these claims about social class differences, I am arguing that there are constraints associated with the social class location and the culture of these young men's practice. As Connell and associates (1982) argue, the interaction is more complex than simple reproduction: "If 'reproduction' predominates in a given case, it is because that side of things has won out in a contest with other tendencies, not because it is guaranteed by some sociological law" (p. 190). As noted, not only were there differences across social class, there were also noteworthy differences within social class categories. Two of the working-class young men, namely Marcus and Zakeev, were the strongest critics of schooling. Yet Jeff, also of working-class background, not only accommodated school, but almost embraced school, providing little critique of his most recent experiences. At the same time, Jeff went to a private, middle-class school, yet seemingly encountered curriculum and pedagogy in ways similar to Marcus and Zakeev. However, the school Jeff attended may have provided greater access to knowledge and ideas about graduation and beyond that may not have been as readily accessible to Marcus and Zakeev.

The ways in which social class divisions are made in relation to schooling is a complex and dynamic process. Connell and associates (1982) argue that "to understand the relation between social class and schooling we have to understand the ways in which the education system shaped, and is shaped by, the processes of class construction and division" (p. 189). Such an approach is helpful for conceptualizing class construction and also in thinking about the interplay of race, gender, and class in relation to schooling and other social institutions. For Jeff and Dwayne, for example, construction of their activity in school was related to their encounters with the criminal justice system. Jeff and Dwayne each moved to a school they thought was going to keep them out of jail. Yet it was these two young men who provided the narrowest critique of schooling and who were also poised to reap the least from acquiring the diploma.

Rashaud, too, provided a minimal critique of the racial structure of school, and the barriers that lay before him and other African-Americans. In fact he did not see any barriers. Was this just because of the school he attended? Or, compared to Dwayne or Marcus, did he have different experiences out of school that would provide different signals about school and life beyond school? Analyzing the form and content of his critique suggests a complex and contradictory stance. Rashaud criticized the ways in which the school promoted competition, yet it was the competition and doing well at school that Rashaud thrived on. And he was most poised to acquire the diploma and enter a high status university.

In this discussion I have tried to show variation across social class categories and within social class categories. The ways in which these young men made sense of their world, through critique, accommodation, legitimation, and negotiation of their experiences is a complex and contradictory process that becomes difficult to unravel. My account of these young men's experiences with school, it is hoped, contributes to understandings about the dynamic and complex nature of the making of social identities in relation to schooling.

Schooling As a Gendering Process

Although I have attended to dimensions of these young men's versions of their masculinities as a subtext of some of the racialized interactions they encountered, clearly the different ways in which their social identities as men played out in their racialized and classed experiences requires further investigation. Mac an Ghaill (1994b) and Connell (1993a) write about the connections between stratification of knowledge in school, teachers' relationships with students, career ambitions and expectations, and the ways in which students experience their emerging masculinities. Connell has noted that within the schooling process, "some masculinities are formed by battering against the school's authority structure, others by smooth insertions into its academic pathways, others gain by a tortuous negotiation of possibilities" (p. 100). The examples of Rashaud and Shawn provide a hint of the complexity involved in exploring the masculinity formation process in relation to their experiences in classrooms. On the one hand, their masculinities seemed to represent a smooth insertion "into the academic pathways." At the same time, however, it seemed that such an insertion was also influenced by their own constructs of their masculinities as African-American men—successful, ambitious and remaining connected to the African-American community—and rejected dominant constructs of black masculinity.

In the case of Dwayne, Jeff, Marcus, and Zakeev, understanding their identities in the making in classrooms is equally complex. Some writers (for example, Mac an Ghaill, 1994b; Willis, 1977) have drawn a distinction between academic and vocational tracks in schools and make connections between forms of masculinity and knowledge experiences. In the cases of these young men, it was difficult to make such distinctions. Dwayne seemed involved in a vocational track at school, and the other young men were not in advanced placement classes. However, it was the glimpses of pedagogy, curriculum, and relationships with students and teachers that provide evidence for understanding masculinities in the making in classrooms.

The pedagogy and curriculum Rashaud and Shawn experienced were different than those experienced by the other young men—seemingly more discussion oriented and student centered. The other four seemed to experience knowledge and relationships in ways that seemed highly routinized with few opportunities to engage in ideas and issues. These different experiences would provide different opportunities to live out different kinds of masculinities. In the same way, their responses to the structure and processes could have also seen them participating in unintended ways. But these are only glimpses and do not allow an understanding of the actual processes they participated in and the forms of masculinity that were lived out in classrooms.

Marcus's and Zakeev's interactions with their teachers do provide us with a sense of how processes and content within classrooms influenced the ways in which these two young men interacted with their teachers. Their interactions with their teachers provide some hints of the ways in which masculinities were made through processes in classrooms. Marcus challenged the version of African-American masculinity his history teacher provided. His confrontational response seemed to be an integral part of the version of masculinity he lived out in this classroom. In the same way, Marcus's challenge of his biology teacher certainly reflected a version of his masculinity as he battled to change his grade. Likewise, Zakeev's confidence and will to challenge his history teacher (despite the fact that he was new to the school) about the lack of attention to African-American history in the curriculum bears testimony to the idea that classrooms became sites for the making of their masculine identities. Their stances in relation to pedagogy and curriculum raise questions about how interaction in classrooms influenced them live out particular kinds of masculinities through challenging the power of a teacher or the content of the curriculum. In some senses, their stances in classrooms could be seen as being oppositional to the power of the teachers and are examples of their gendered, and hence masculine, identities as men. It seems important that further attention be given to the ways in which young African-American men construct their racialized masculine identities in the context of knowledge production in classrooms.

In sum, staying in school and experiencing the process of schooling saw these young men develop similar and different meanings about schooling and the high school diploma. These meanings and experiences, shaped by their experiences in and out of school, were contradictory and complex. The young men both critiqued and accommodated aspects of life in classrooms and schools in ways that revealed patterns of experiences that were common to some young men and not others. However, amid the different meanings and experiences developed across social class lines, and within social class groups, the young men from working-class backgrounds experienced curriculum and pedagogy in ways vastly different to the middle-class young men. Despite these differences, they all experienced either covert or overt forms of racism in their lives at school. These experiences not only contributed toward their views of school, but also to how they viewed themselves in relation to others. Experienced of racism, for example, influenced how Marcus and Zakeev viewed themselves as African-Americans in relation to their mainly white teachers. Their responses to racism and schooling contrasted with those of Rashaud and Shawn. The process of racial identity formation, Omi and Winant (1986) argue, is shaped by "[t]he ways in which we understand ourselves and interact with others, the structuring of our practical activity—work and family, as citizens as thinkers . . . these are all shaped by racial meanings and racial aware- ness" (pp. 66-67). But the young men's experiences of racism were also about how they saw themselves as African-American men. While race may have been central to their response, the subtext of gender seemed intertwined with how they inhabited school as African-American men. Critiquing school, thus, was not just about their experiences, it also connected to a process of affirming who they were and wanted to be as young African-American men.

Although this discussion has primarily focused on the dimensions of race and social class, this does not mean that gendering processes were not significant in the young men's relationships in school. Rather, race was a central category as they talked about life in classrooms, and social class became significant in my dis- cussion because of their contrasting experiences. For example, two of the work- ing-class young men, and Dwayne, of the underclass, brought issues of power relations to the fore. The middle-class young men did not. Thus, while their accounts of schooling may help me learn more about their racialized and classed experiences, they also helped me understand the ways in which race and social class shape gender relations. The analyses here then, are only partial, in that a con- sideration of the dynamic interaction of race, class, and gender requires an inves- tigation of other dimensions of their gendered identities. The following two chapters develop more consistent, but still partial, analyses of race, class, and gen- der in their lives wherein I will further consider the process of identity formation. In particular, I will focus on their relationships in families and with peers.

6

Building Connections

The previous two chapters dealt with the meanings the six young men attributed to the high school diploma and their talk about encounters in the classroom. Being in school, however, involved much more than attending classes. It also involved connecting to people, particularly outside of classrooms. These relationships formed outside of the classroom, during lunch hour, on the school bus, and during the time before and after school seemed extremely important to the young men. But they were not the only relationships they experienced on a day-to-day basis. They also maintained relationships with family members and with other youngsters from various sports, religious, and recreational organizations and activities. These relationships with others included a range of family members and peers. The young men's relationships with the various people in their lives are the focus of this chapter.

Relationships they sought from their peers and the kinds of relationships they experienced became a significant theme in their conversations with me. There is no doubt that schooling played a significant role in the relationships these young men formed. By the same token, the relationships they formed outside of school, in their families, in their neighborhoods, and in various organizations and networks, were equally important to them and the meanings they constructed. There were two kinds of relationships that seemed central to their lives: relationships with family members and relationships with friends.

As I unraveled their stories about friendships and relationships with family members, I became aware of the various layers and levels of intensity that were interwoven through their relationships and connections with others. During the postfield analysis, my questions were no longer about who they were friendly with; they became questions about which kinds of relationships were important to them, and why. What were the patterns of similarity and difference across their relationships in and out of school? Which relationships counted as friendships, and which did not? What features of relationships did they value and seek? In considering responses to these questions in this chapter, I want to explain what these relationships tell us about these young men, and how they saw themselves. In essence, many of these questions have to do with the emerging identities of these young men, and are more than questions about *who* they connected to and why. They are also questions about *what* they talked about, what they valued, *how* they acted and interacted, and *why* they chose membership or connection with some people over others. In other words, they reflect decisions they made and experiences they had as they constructed their notions of who they were and wanted to be. Here, I use the notion of identity formation to refer to the ways in which these young African-American men, collectively and individually, came to see themselves in relation to others, and the meanings they made of themselves and others and events in their relationships. This framework of identity formation (Weis, 1990) is not only about their racial identities as African-Americans, it is also about the various masculinities and social class identities that were woven through the fabric of their lives.

Through talking with these young men, I came to think about the relationships they sought as *connections*. I use the notion as a frame to think about certain *kinds* of relationships they wanted and worked to build. A connected relationship was not just a relationship with anybody. First and foremost, a connected relationship for these young men was one with a person they could trust and share their thoughts and their feelings with—most significantly, a relationship with an African-American. Stern (1990) writes about the importance of connection in young adolescent girls' relationships. She argues that as girls develop their sense of femininity, their "relationships provide the support one needs to push one's own further development" (p. 85). There seem parallels between the need for connection in the lives of young girls (see Gilligan, Lyons, & Hanmer, 1990) and the desire for connection in these young African-American men's relationships. Connection seemed important to these young men's sense of masculinity. Ward (1990) argues that in the case of black adolescents, "Integration of the individual's personal identity with one's racial identity is a necessary and inevitable developmental task of growing up black in white America" (p. 218). For these six young African-American men, developing solid, trusting, caring, and understanding relationships with others, particularly other young African-American men, seemed not only paramount, but crucial in their lives. The kinds of relationships they sought and the kinds of relationships they experienced tell us a lot about these young men and their experiences as African-Americans.

It is within the context of understanding the kinds of connections, the nature of these connections they sought, and who the young men were becoming that I explore the relationships they built and maintained. I consider three arenas in which they developed connections: (1) family, (2) schools, and (3) networks outside of school and the family.

INTERACTIONS WITH FAMILY MEMBERS

"My Mom" was perhaps the most common response to my asking these young men to name the important people in their lives. This probably does not surprise many readers, as mothers are often significant forces in the lives of children, given that mothers are traditionally expected to assume the role of primary nurturers and care-providers of children. How and why mothers and families are significant in the lives of students such as these young men has been an area of great debate. Collins (1990) problematizes the image of the "superstrong Black mother" (Staples, 1973), whereby "glorifying the strong Black mother represented Black men's attempts to replace negative white male interpretations with positive Black male one's" (Collins, 1990, p. 117). Such glorification, amid the many "controlling images" about black motherhood, contributes to the contradictions and complexities in the lives of African-American mothers and their sons. In relation to schooling, few studies have explored identity formation within families and the embedded contradictions. Instead, much of the discussion within the education discourse community has focused on the relationships among families, schools, and students, and the values, beliefs, and ideas that social actors bring to and construct in the institutions of school and family.

Family and School

Connections between families and schools and the family's role in the success or failure of students attending school continue to be a significant issue. This debate has been significant in policies and practices that shape quests to provide educational opportunities and experiences that meet the needs and potentials of *all* Americans. Spearheading this debate was the Coleman Report (1966), which suggested family background was a determinant of school failure and success more than any other factor. However, Karabel and Halsey (1977) challenged Coleman's findings and suggested that "schools at least reinforce the inferior position of disadvantaged children with respect to educational opportunity" (p. 21). On the other hand, Jencks and associates (1972) suggested that schools are "marginal institutions" in their quest for a more egalitarian society and that the economy, not schools nor families, may be the most central sphere that needs consideration. And Clark (1983) challenged findings that suggested social status was the most important determinant of school achievement. In his study of African-American families, he argued that it was the "beliefs, values and cultural style" at home that was the significant difference in the lives of students and "not the family units' composition or social status" (p. 2). And so the debate continued.

Most studies, however, did not consider the dynamic institutional and cultural connections between schools and families, nor the multiple variations and historical situations of families through a frame of interlocking structures of race, class, and gender (see Collins, 1994; Stack & Burton, 1994). In other words, most studies did not explain how the institutions of school and family interacted and influenced each other, nor the connections and contrasting experiences of the day-to-day experiences of racial minority families with schooling. Moreover, there are few studies that actually consider the nature and form of the relationships between parents and students, and consider these relationships in the context of students' lives and emerging identities.

Connell, Ashenden, Kessler, and Dowsett (1982) provide an important contribution to our understanding of the relationship between school and family and how processes within school and the family interact with one another. In their study of the relationships between school, family, and social class in Australia, they provide insights about how social class and social division are "made." These authors challenge the functional explanations developed to explain the relationship of family background to school achievement. Through a lens of material and cultural experiences of teachers, students, and parents, they examine the relationship between school and the family and consider each of these groups' current and past relationships with schools. They argue that

> The family is what its members do, a constantly continuing and changing practice, and as children go to and through school, that practice is reorganized around schooling. For its part the organization of the school varies with the kind of families in its catchment and the nature of their collective practices (p. 78).

Connell and associates (1982) went "beyond the assumption" that family and school are independent spheres that contain separate processes. They argue that schools and families interact in ways that influence how each comes into being and continues to emerge, and that the social class experiences of parents and teachers play a significant role in how they view each other. Further, they argue that the issue is not solely one of how different parents viewed school, but how the parents came to view school in the ways they did, and how different actors within schools came to view different parents. More recently, Lareau (1989) has written a compelling study about the interconnection between social location, experience, and family–school relationships. She argues that working-class families felt separated from the experiences in schools, whereas middle-class parents not only saw themselves as tied to their children's schooling, but also had ideas about their role in schooling, and the kinds of interventions they should make in their children's schooling.

Connell and associates' (1982) and Lareau's (1990) explorations of the dynamic connection between school and family seem important in attempting to understand the school experiences of these six young African-American men. These writers moved beyond debates that "blamed" one institution or the other and instead tried to explain how the relationships between family and school come to be the way there are. Connell and associates and Lareau suggest that school experiences are influenced and constructed through orientations toward school produced by family members of the school's students. For example, the students', experiences in school are influential in the kinds of relationships they encounter in and out of school and the relationships they seek. By the same token, schooling becomes significant in the relationships and activities they encounter at home.

The various debates about how families interact with schools provide a context for my analysis of these young men's families. While I do not intend to explain the family's role in the achievement of these young men, I do want to provide a glimpse of what it is that their families "do" and how activities and relationships in families were influential in shaping the participants' meanings and social identities. My approach builds upon analyses that argue that families and school dynamically shape each other, and that each sphere is shaped by its own activities and interests. As much of this discussion thus far has focused on schooling, the following analysis primarily centers on the meanings the young men gave to "family."

Who Counts As Family?

There is no doubt that their families were important to these young men. However, it became clear that what counted as family was not the same, nor did the family unit signify all the people living in their household. While many readers may identify with their constructs, they may differ with the explanations for how and why their families come into being and function the way they do. Historically, families are often viewed through a narrow lens of Eurocentric constructs about responsibilities, role, and relationships in families (Collins, 1990). Many of these constructs have ignored the subjective conditions of families, particularly racial minority families in the U.S. context.

The terrain of the "American family" has been dramatically challenged in past years, as scholars, particularly feminist scholars, have questioned the myth of the American family, and have provided alternative viewpoints about the texture and structure of the family in relation to the social world. For example, there has been a dramatic rise in the number of one-parent households headed by women. Households headed by women are proportionally higher in the African-American community than in any other racial or ethnic community. Such changes in family structure can be seen as a consequence and interaction of structural and cultural forces in the social, political, and economic spheres of society, where, in the African-American community, "black female-headed households become the logical

TABLE 2. Household Members

Name	Household Members
Dwayne	Foster mother, foster father, two foster brothers
Jeff	Mother, stepfather, sister, brother
Marcus	Mother, stepfather, sister, brother
Rashaud	Mother
Shawn	Father, brother
Zakeev	Mother, brother

end product of a whole series of social, political and economic forces" (Brewer, 1993, p. 375). Thus, it is not unexpected that for these young African-American men there were differences in their family households and roles that different family members played in their lives, and their ideas about who counted as family members.

Most significant about the participants in this study is that they did not solely consider the people living in the same households as their family. Table 2 lists the people who shared the same household as they did at the time of the study.

For five of the young men, the household consisted of biological family members, and additionally, in the case of Marcus and Jeff, their stepfathers. Dwayne was the exception because he stayed with a foster family. On examining their conception of family, we see a conception that is much broader than the household members. Table 3 lists the people they considered as family members in addition to the household members listed in Table 2.

An investigation of the "families" of all the young men reveals that they included biological connections who did not live in the household unit as "family." In some cases, the young men also defined nonbiological connections as family. For example, Dwayne's family included his foster family in addition to his biological brothers and sisters, and his biological mother, father, and grandmother

TABLE 3. Family Members

Name	"Family" Members
Dwayne	Brothers, sisters, biological mother and father, maternal grandmother, friends
Jeff	Girlfriend, baby daughter
Marcus	Brother, cousin, biological father, maternal grandmother, maternal aunt
Rashaud	Maternal grandfather, maternal aunt
Shawn	Mother, brother, sister
Zakeev	Father, sister, aunt, uncle

in Detroit. He also considered his neighborhood male friends as family—they were his "brothers." Marcus, too, had a broad conception of family. It included his grandmother and biological father who lived in a neighboring town. He was very close to them and often spent time with them. He said he was also close to a maternal aunt who lived in the same town. They all, in particular ways, provided guidance about situations he encountered in his day-to-day living—for example, about the importance of not being involved in drugs, and the significance of going to school.

This brief examination of the nature and form of the participants' family units compared with their conceptions of family represents a significant point. These young men received support not only from the people who lived in their homes but also from other relatives and "family" members. The support was varied. It included support in the form of guidance about school and staying in school, and also included guidance on how to respond to drug problems and crime. These young men talked about the people whom they considered as family members with respect. The support they received from their "families" suggests that household structure alone is a narrow construct to use in examining students' support or to consider as a determinant of success or failure in school. Collins (1990) for example, suggests that black women play multiple roles in relation to children's lives in the African-American community. Children, then, experience relationships with "bloodmothers," "othermothers," and women-centered networks. Clearly, on looking at the lives of the six young men, a framework needs be developed that gives attention to the various support networks in the lives of the students. This is not to argue that the family household plays a less significant role. Rather, in order to understand the support and resources youngsters have access to, it is important to consider the various actors who contribute to the students' well-being. Exploring such networks seems worthy of further investigation.

Although these family networks were important to the young men across time, on a day-to-day level it was the members of their households with whom they had the most contact. Therefore, in the remainder of this section of the chapter, I consider the nature of the relationships these young men formed within households in order to understand some, but not all, of the forms of support and connection they developed with family members.

The landscape of the families of these young men certainly reflected a range of patterns and kinds of relationships. The relationships were significant in the meanings they developed of family and were also significant in the meanings they developed of schooling. The relationships with household members, however, not only revealed the kinds of connections they had with the family members they lived with, but also provided insight into the ways in which structural and cultural practices were interwoven through the relationships, responsibilities, and roles they assumed at home. These interactions were significant to the meanings and images they developed of themselves as African-American men.

As they talked about the family members they lived with, four of the young men cited their mothers as the most important person in their lives, one cited his father, and Jeff cited his girlfriend and baby. What was difficult to explore was the nature of the relationships they experienced with their mother or father, or their brothers and sisters. Four held back in talking about "personal" interactions at home, while Marcus and Jeff were extremely forthright. What they mostly talked about was what the household members "did," their roles and responsibilities, and the nature of these interactions. However, one significant pattern across the participants was the role of their parents in schooling.

School in Relationships with Family Households

As the young men talked about their family households, and how they both resisted and embraced their parents' ideals and commitments, I began to learn about how they were supported in their lives, particularly in relation to school. In part, these were young men growing up, trying to assert their independence, be it through how they spent their recreational time or what they did at school. At the same time, their parents exerted strong control over how they spent their recreational time. There was a pattern that stood out in relation to all of the young men: they *all* religiously spent a couple of hours every weekday afternoon doing homework. When school featured in these young men's relationships with their parents, in most cases it was their mothers who ensured that they maintained their homework responsibilities. This was different, however, for Shawn because he lived with his father, and thus it was his father with whom he spoke about his daily school homework.

Completing homework assignments was part of their routine at home, and their parents made sure it was routinized. The support they received from the parents was generally one of policing their homework and providing rewards or punishments for grades and performance in classes at school. Failing one test or not doing homework seemed to greatly influence the penalties and privileges these young men received at home: speaking with friends on the telephone, playing basketball at a local court, or going to social functions. On a day-to-day basis, it seemed that controlling homework was almost the only overt connection with school that their parents played in their lives. The content of what they learned did not seem to be part of the conversations or interactions between these parents and their sons. There was occasional talk about a teacher, or assignments, or conversations from a parent–teacher conference, but little beyond this. Schooling on one level shaped these young men's activities at home, and on another it influenced the patterns of interaction between mothers and their sons.

Notably, it was their mothers who mostly played a central role in the schooling. I am not implicitly arguing that they all did not have someone performing a "father" role in their lives. Most of them did. But it was their mothers who most frequently attended to their homework responsibilities, and with the exception of

Shawn, it was their mothers who *always* attended the parent–teacher conferences. Thus, despite the differences in their household units, and in the support they received various family members, it was their mothers who served as the major players in their commitment to do homework, reinforcing their quest to graduate from high school. As noted, Shawn was the exception because he lived with his father, and his father played such a role in his life.

The participants, then, appeared to have a stronger educational relationship with their mothers than with their fathers. In part, the form and substance of the relationships were dynamically shaped by the structure and culture of the family and the different roles that the mothers and fathers assumed. In part this was influenced by dominant ideas about the roles of mothers and fathers in family, but it was also influenced by other factors and forces in their lives. For instance, in the cases of Rashaud and Zakeev, both their fathers were absent from home and thus played a negligible role in influencing their sons' relationships with school. This suggests that an enormous responsibility was placed upon the shoulders of their mothers, who were at once the sole or co-breadwinners and also the nurturers and caretakers of their children. However, when a mother and father were present at home, as in the cases of Dwayne, Jeff, and Marcus, it was still their mothers who assumed responsibility for ensuring the completion of homework tasks and preparing for tests.

The interplay of school and work in the lives of these young men influenced the kinds of household responsibilities they assumed and the relationships they developed. For instance, Marcus and Jeff assumed major responsibilities in the care of their younger siblings and they did this because their parents worked and they arrived home earlier than their parents. I next turn to the relationships between these young men and their siblings as these provide further examples of the kinds of roles and relationships they experienced in their homes.

Relationships with Brothers and Sisters

These young men may have had uneven relationships with either or both of their parents; however, many of them seemed to develop relationships as "protector" and "provider" in relation to their brothers and sisters. From their various narratives, it appeared that Marcus, Jeff, and Zakeev did not seem to engage in traditional forms of masculinities that may be associated with the roles and relationships of brothers and sons. This is not to argue that they did not perform what some may call exaggerated forms of hegemonic masculinity. Rather, they tended to embrace a broader form of masculinity. It was clear that they established strong relationships with their younger brothers and sisters, and were "expected" to be responsible for their welfare in the afternoons after school. Through these relationships, they revealed the warmth and care they developed for their siblings. For example, Marcus had been very involved in the care of his four-year-old sister since she was a baby. He noted, "My Mom . . . taught me how to change the diapers, do [his sister's] hair. I know how to do her hair. Put clothes on her. I basically do that." His mother worked full-time and Marcus had to babysit most afternoons and on some evenings if his mother and stepfather went out. To the present day he often helped his sister get dressed and did her hair for her. He accepted this responsibility as one of his duties at home. Likewise, Zakeev was responsible for his younger brother. Zakeev's mother was the sole breadwinner, and her job often saw her working into the early evening. After school, Zakeev's brother had to accompany him wherever he went, be it to the basketball court or to the local library.

Jeff's mother worked an evening shift, but there was a period of about three hours—between the time his mother's job started and his father returned from work—when he was held responsible for his younger brother and sister. Even though he did not seem close to either his mother or father, he did seem to be close to his sister. When we talked about his sister, he tended to talk about her in a loving and caring way. He said that he felt as though he was responsible for his sister for much of the time because both his mother and father were working: "So, actually I kind of raised my sister on my own. 'Cause my Dad was gone [to work], then my mom would be leaving [for work]. It's just me and my sister staying at home by ourselves." He said he had cared for his sister in this way since he was eight years old, when he first moved to Allerton.

For these three young men, the demands of their parents' workplace significantly influenced the kinds of role they enacted in their families. Because their parents worked, they were required to assume a role that traditionally has been assumed by mothers. This is not to argue that their mothers did not continue to assume certain traditional roles and responsibilities in their families; rather, some of these responsibilities were shared by the older siblings.

And even though Dwayne was no longer living with his young brother or sisters, he still felt a sense of responsibility toward them. His conversations with me showed a connection and care for his family. At one time he said that he wanted to acquire the high school diploma for them. He would move back to Detroit, he told me, "So I can be close to my family. What if I make it? If I make it, my family going to make it. Going to look out for them."

Interestingly, the three working-class young men were expected to be not only protector, but also nurturer and caretaker. The roles of Jeff, Marcus, and Zakeev in their families seem to challenge the traditional roles of young men as signified in hegemonic conceptions of the family role they played: Jeff, Marcus, and Zakeev all were required to assume some dimensions of the parental role with their younger siblings. This was not a choice for them; they were expected to take on this responsibility because their mothers and fathers worked. The sharing of responsibilities in the home that the working-class young men talked about contrasted with the situations of the two middle-class young men. Neither Rashaud nor Shawn had to assume the same kind of responsibilities because they had no younger siblings at home. Shawn had younger brothers and sisters, but they stayed with his mother. Social class, then, was influential in the forms of masculinities they lived out.

In examining the various meanings of family, the role of schooling in relationships, and their relationships with their siblings, it is evident that structural and cultural practices dynamically interweave the activities and interests of their families in different ways. The activities also saw them "doing" masculinity in the home, where the activities, interests, and responsibilities in the family were as much shaped by interaction in the family as interests and activities in school or the workplace. Their lives were certainly shaped by the intermingling of cultural and structural forces. In order to consider further the nature of relationships within families, I turn next to an examination of the relationships Marcus and Jeff developed with their parents. The other participants in the study did not talk about the nature of their relationships with their parents with the same depth as these two young men. Thus, I focus particularly on the conflicts at home that Jeff and Marcus spoke about.

FAMILY CONFLICTS

Conflicts between Marcus and his parents and Jeff and his mother were discussed at length almost every time we met.[8] Jeff quite forthrightly said that "Me and my family aren't close." For Jeff, the disputes were about his responsibilities in the house, such as cleaning his room. Despite the arguments, his parents did exhibit a sense of commitment to what happened to him. They were very supportive when he was arrested and spent time in a juvenile detention center. Their response was to support his return to school and send him to a private school. They did care what happened to Jeff. Marcus, too, had problems with a parent, his stepfather. While Marcus's relationship with his mother remained strong, there were incredible tensions between Marcus and his stepfather.

Understanding these conflicts is important not only to unravel the relationships of Jeff and Marcus with family members, but also to better understand the complexity of family life in the context of these young men's experiences. Many theories of the family have argued that families are a unit shaped by affection and kinship. However, as Baca Zinn (1991) has argued, "Rather than viewing the family as a unit shaped only by affection or kinship, we now know that families are settings in which people with different activities and interests often come into conflict with each other" (p. 121). And in the cases of Marcus and Jeff, it was not only affection and kinship that dynamically shaped the family unit; conflict also significantly seemed an integral thread. These different activities and interests of their family members were dynamically shaped by the interaction of race, gender, and social class at the social and the structural levels (Dill, 1988; Glenn, 1987). Therefore, in order to better understand the conflict these young men talked about, we need to understand not only the nature of the conflict, but the ways in which family members went about their different roles not just within the family but in the workplace or school and in relation to other social institutions.

My analysis of Marcus's and Jeff's relationships with their parents is developed in part through an understanding that their interactions and experiences in families were dynamically shaped by their access to resources and experiences outside and inside the home. To acknowledge that there were conflicts in their households seems inadequate. Conflicts seem inevitable in human relationships. What is significant is the nature of the conflicts, and understanding the conflicts in the context of the situated experiences of family members.

Family As Site of Conflict and Attachment

The "family problem" Marcus most talked about was his relationship with his stepfather. He told me that he was angered by his stepfather's verbal and physical actions toward him, and he was resentful of his presence. But there were also disputes about how Marcus spent his recreation time outside of the house: "I was always in the house, I could never go out nowhere, I always had to stay home. I could never do all the stuff I wanted to do. That's why I used to get into trouble so much," he said. In fact, Marcus's relationship with his stepfather became so intolerable that he was forced to move out of the house in May 1992. For the next six months, he stayed with his cousin in an apartment in a nearby neighborhood. Eventually, he returned home to his mother and stepfather.

Marcus's mother had tried to persuade him to return on numerous occasions. In the following conversation, Marcus described his relationship with his stepfather and the conversations with his mother about him moving out.

Marcus:	...he [stepfather] never did like me from the getgo. Because he always thought I was like my father because I look so much like him. Everybody else look like my mother, plus I'm the middle one, they treat me totally different than they treat [his older brother]. He [stepfather] thought I was no good, I'm going to end up in jail.
JP:	Why did he say this?
Marcus:	We never did get along, we was always at each other. You know, he always wanted me to be fighting him. He always wanted me to do that. To this day, I still owe him, but I won't do that. I still call over there to talk to my mother and stuff.
JP:	What does she say about you moving out?
Marcus:	Oh, she was all for it, because I told her. Because the night that it happened when I left for good. She called me. Because it was not the first time that I got kicked out of the house. Because I got kicked out of the house about four times.
JP:	Oh really, by him?
Marcus:	And I told her, and she always used the crying routine to make me feel sorry and all this, you know, to sucker me back. And knowing that we

don't get along. So this time I wasn't going for it, for the fifth time. I told her, you know, "Mom you need to quit doing this. You know how you get to me. It ain't nothin' to do with you, it just him." I said, "I just want you to know that. I ain't got nothin' with you, I always loved you and everything Mom, you brought me up to be a real strong brother and everything. I ain't got nothin' against you and all this." You know, I explained to her and really broke it down that night, and she, after a while started calming down.

JP: He doesn't speak to you?

Marcus: He doesn't say nothin' to me. Not until I say somethin' to him. If I don't say somethin' to him, he ain't gonna say nothin' to me. Even if I do see him, and we by ourself, he ain't gonna say nothin' to me first, I have to say something to him.

Through the conversation Marcus revealed the strong bond between himself and his mother. "You know how you get to me," he said to his mother. His mother, too, seemed attached to Marcus. He commented that "she always used the crying routine to make me feel sorry and all this, you know, to sucker me back." But Marcus seemed prepared to sacrifice this bond in order to distance himself from his stepfather. On one level, the struggle seemed to be a struggle between Marcus and his stepfather. On another, the strife seemed a battle of competing masculinities in the context of his family.

It is clear that Marcus had a fragile relationship with his stepfather, and that the lines of communication and connection seemed extremely tenuous. Marcus resented the authority that his stepfather wielded as a parent in his family and resented the presence of his stepfather in his and his mother's life. Marcus at times was grounded and chastised by his stepfather for poor grades. At the same time, Marcus attempted to challenge the authority of his stepfather; his stepfather too was "doing" masculinity as he asserted authority and power over Marcus as the father in his life. Further, Marcus argued that the problem was further exacerbated because this "father" was not his biological father, whom he missed:

My own father, we get along real good. . . . 'Cause I basically like him though. He kind of babies me more than anybody. 'Cause we [brothers and sister] all got different fathers. My older brother and me, we got the same father. My little brother, he got a different father, my little sister, she got a different father.

It seemed that it was the affection that Marcus's biological father gave him that he valued most in this relationship. This relationship contrasted with his relationship with his stepfather which seemed distant.

Amid Marcus's relationships with his mother, his stepfather, and biological father, he was struggling to assert who he wanted to be. His stepfather, for example, disapproved of Marcus's connection with his cousin and the Afrocentric reading group to which he belonged. In fact, Marcus's stepfather barred him from attending any more group meetings because he disagreed with the substance of the conversations. Given that the reading group was a symbol of one of Marcus's passions, and the ideas and images he associated with the group strongly shaped his sense of his masculinity, the action exacerbated the tension between him and his stepfather and potentially heightened his commitment to Afrocentricism. Life was difficult for Marcus, because amid these relationships was a strained relationship with his brother. His brother was a high achiever, a first-year university student studying architecture. As noted, Marcus felt as though he was constantly being compared to and contrasted with his brother. Despite this comparison, the power wielded by his stepfather, and Marcus leaving home, he continued to go to school. Not only did he continue to go to school, he was successful in attaining passing grades in all his subjects. He used the apparent success at school to demonstrate to his parents that he could live away from home and be successful. Schooling became a mechanism to prove his success.

Schooling was not the only mechanism that he used to assert his ability to thrive in the newfound independence from his parents. He was also proud of the ways in which he could take care of himself. During a conversation about African-American women, he told me:

> Like you know how they say women supposed to do women's jobs, I say: "How can you say that? I do women's stuff. I sew, I iron." Ain't no one, frankly, I don't need no woman to take care of me, I can take care of myself. I can cook, sew, wash clothes, I can do all those things. I can do for myself.

Marcus reveals his sense of comfort with what he saw as appropriating "women's jobs" to assert his independence. However, despite his newfound independence through supporting himself and continuing to do well in school, Marcus did return to his family's home. He could no longer afford the expense of living away from home. Notwithstanding, he maintained his distant relationship with his stepfather and his connected relationship with his mother.

The conflicts at home reveal the struggles Marcus faced as he went to school and perhaps provide a glimpse of how the family can simultaneously be a site of conflict and attachment. He valued the connection and bond with his mother. In the preceding conversation he said to his mother, "You brought me up to be a real strong brother and everything." It was important to Marcus that he could prove to his mother that he could cope with the situation. This suggests the strength that the family provided, particularly his mother. His response to the conflicts was to "prove" himself to them, thereby proving his sense of manhood. But his response was shaped by interactions between him and his parents. Thus, the family becomes a site that dynamically shaped his identity. Such a process is complex and not as smooth or functional as portrayed by sex role theorists.[9] Here, Thorne (1993) argued that power is central to relationships among children, teachers, and parents, and that this by no means suggests that children or students are "passive or without agency" (p. 3). Marcus at once asserted a version of masculinity through asserting his independence, resisting the authority of his stepfather, and appropriating certain domestic responsibilities associated with "women's work." These relationships, therefore, and the form, content, and consequences of the relationships, were not just about power struggles between parents and their son, they were also about emerging social identities.

Distant but Supportive Relationship

Jeff, like Marcus, also experienced conflict with his parents. Jeff continually had ongoing squabbles with his mother. "Me and mom aren't close," he once told me. He claimed he "got kicked out of the house about four times" by his mother during 1992. Jeff did not call these problems conflicts, rather he called them "disagreements." He explained the conflict between he and his mother:

> She would go through my stuff, and she would go in my room and throw everything out, and throw it all on the floor and stuff. She told me to iron my clothes, and fold them up and put them in a drawer and hang them up. I did that, and occasionally she would come into my room and throw everything out of the drawer. I cannot stand that, I'm sorry . . . and I'm like come on, somebody's got to get out.

This conflict between Jeff and his mother had being going on for a few years. Jeff said that such conflict was "normal" for the black young men at his old school, Central.

> *Jeff:* Basically, the black community, as far as I know, being at Central and everything, they really don't have no family relationship. Unless it's a girl. Girls, white girls like to stay with their family. The guys they are like into gangs.
>
> *JP:* Why don't they have a family relationship?
>
> *Jeff:* Basically it has to do with the fathers. . . . They don't spend time with their sons and stuff, so the son tends to go out with his friends and stuff, and then his friends get to doin' this and such and such. Haven't been brought up, his Dad hasn't took the time to tell him, well such and such, and this is the rules of the house.
>
> *JP:* Your father hasn't done that really?
>
> *Jeff:* No, my dad is kinda low key.
>
> *JP:* Because he's away [working] so much in Hatfield [60 miles away].
>
> *Jeff:* Yeah, he doesn't know what goes on in the house, 'cause when he's at home asleep, I'm at school, and then when he leaves to go out to work, and then when I get out of school, he's at work, and when he's at home again, I'm in the bed.

Jeff suggested that one of the reasons why he felt disconnected from his home was because his father played a minimal role in the family. But his father worked in a factory almost 60 miles away from home, and thus left home early in the morning and returned well after 8 p.m. Jeff used the example of speeches given by African-American Emmy award winners to further argue his point:

> If you ever have to look at the Emmy Awards, you look at the black actors and stuff, they will say "I'd like to thank the people, I'd like to thank God most of all." And then they go into the producers and everything, and they also say "I'd like to thank my mother." You never hear them say "thank you, dad." The Dads aren't there.

As Jeff's father worked the day shift and his mother the evening shift at an automobile plant, the intermingling of employment opportunities afforded Jeff's parents and the need for both parents to work reduced the time they could spend at home with their children. At the same time, Jeff once attended a school from which he felt alienated. Thus, various influences seened to shape Jeff's life, through his own and his family's activities, roles, and relationships at home; through his relationship at school; and through his parents' work activities.

At first I thought the conflict might have been a consequence of Jeff fathering a child and his mother being a little disappointed in him. At one point, Jeff said his mother thought he and Sharon "were spending so much time together. My Mom thought I was possessed with Sharon." But Jeff claimed that his relationship with Sharon or his fathering a child was not the central reason for the conflict:

> JP: Was the conflict over the thing with Sharon?
> Jeff: No, once it was. Another time it was because of whoopings.
> JP: They were hitting you?
> Jeff: Yeah.
> JP: Mother and father?
> Jeff: No, just my mother.

So, the conflict was at one time because of Jeff's relationship with Sharon, and another time because of the "whoopings." Although Jeff provided these issues as points of conflict, and he also talked about how his mother responded, it was not really clear what the various "disagreements" were about.

He said, "From my behalf, when I was having confusion with my Mom and everything, getting thrown out of the house. I was like what was the point of going to school. You know you cannot wear the same clothes to school every day and stuff." Jeff talked about one occasion when he was "thrown out" of the house.

> JP: So, what's the longest you've been out?
> Jeff: About a month.
> JP: And where would you go?
> Jeff: Sometimes I would stay with Sharon.
> JP: And what would her mother say? Would she mind?

Jeff: Her mom kind of minds because of my mom, harassment. My mom was like [to Sharon's mom], "I want him out on the streets, you let him stay there. I'll prosecute you."

JP: Why did she want you out on the street?

Jeff: I don't know, I guess that's the type of person she is. She has a lot of her dad in her. I guess she meant it in a good way in her terms. But you're talking about wintertime. One time I got kicked out with no shoes and shirt and stuff.

JP: Where did you go?

Jeff: I went to a friend's house and he gave me a pair of his shoes and stuff. One time I stayed with friend, and I stayed with him for a while. Eventually, you've got to leave; you don't want to wear out your welcome.

JP: Your mother doesn't suddenly say "okay, Jeff is getting out today." Something happened, right?

Jeff: Yeah, basically, we have a dispute or something. Like today I was playing my radio, getting ready for school, she's yelling through the door, "turn that radio off!" And I thought, what's the big deal with having the radio on?

Another example involved Jeff cooking at home. He told me that he cooked a lot at home, but his mother said she preferred him not to do that. At one point he told me, "That's what my mom was saying don't go cooking your own food, eat what I cook, 'cause that just wastes food." Jeff said his mother was on a limited budget, especially since his parents were paying for him to attend a private school.

I wanted to hear more about these disputes and learn about them from the perspective of Jeff's mother. Although I spoke with Jeff's mother a couple of times on the phone, we did not have a prolonged conversation, nor would she grant me a formal interview. Notwithstanding, she was quite contented for Jeff to "tell his story." And Jeff's story was really one of seeming alienation from his mother and father and most of his friends. Jeff had few good relationships in his life, except for his relationship with Sharon.

Jeff's relationship with his father, while not as conflict-ridden as the relationship with his mother, seemed distant. As noted, Jeff said that he really did not have many interactions with his father because of the distance his father worked away from home. And then his mother worked the "second shift" at a local automobile plant:

She goes in at four, as soon as we get home from school, she's like running around the house and getting ready to go to work. So, actually I kind of raised my sister on my own. 'Cause my Dad was gone, then my Mom would be leaving. It's just me and my sister staying at home by ourselves. When I was about eight since we first moved up here. . . .

Jeff encountered much conflict at home with his parents; conflict that he said had been going on for the past four years. Despite this hostility, it is notable that

Jeff's parents were seemingly committed to Jeff completing high school and acquiring the high school diploma. Their commitment was most evident in their willingness to send Jeff to a fee-paying private Christian school which required some material sacrifice on their part to afford the tuition. And they made this commitment after years of conflict and battles between Jeff and his mother.

The relationship between Jeff and his mother and father was certainly complex. It seemed distant yet simultaneously supportive. Although Jeff seemed connected with his sister, the significant relationship in his life was the one with Sharon and their baby. This was relationship that he worked on, that he tried to build, and that he valued.

The comparison of the relationships between Jeff and Marcus and their parents perhaps reveals that their relationships with the adults in their homes were complex and not easy to unravel. Jeff's relationship with his parents seemed more distant and complex than Marcus's relationship with his parents. Although Jeff's relationship was marred by conflict, his parents continued to support him in his quest to attain the high school diploma. Marcus's relationship with his parents reflected ongoing conflict, yet the bond between him and his mother seemed to remain intact.

Jeff's case starkly contrasted with Marcus's case. While they each had squabbles with their parents, and each left home for a certain period of time, they responded to the conflict and breakdown of the relationship with their parents in different ways. Jeff attended school less frequently, then dropped out of school, at which time he intermittently left home. After Jeff's entanglement with the criminal justice system, he returned to school with support from his parents, and he did not leave home for periods of time.

In contrast, despite the conflict with his parents, Marcus continued to attend school, but left home and moved into an apartment which he shared with his cousin and attempted to pay for his share of the household expenses. He continued to perform well at school and pass all his tests and examinations. He too returned home, because of personal difficulties with his cousin and the financial burden of supporting himself, even though he was resentful of his stepfather. In each of their lives there seemed to be a marked difference in the reasons for returning home. Jeff experienced a key turning point, which had little to do with his parents, whereas Marcus had no single turning point but rather a series of crises that saw him returning to his parents' home.

Schooling intermingled their relationships with their parents in different ways. On the one hand, Jeff had two kinds of relationships with school in the context of his relationship with his parents. One kind of relationship, that of alienation and disconnection, emerged because as he became more and more disconnected from his parents he attended school less frequently.[10] Even though he felt distanced from his parents, "dropping out" of school became his response to the disconnection. The other kind of relationship he established with school was to embrace attending school in order to gain respect from his parents after, and because of, his entanglement with the criminal justice system. But it was Jeff's parents who spearheaded his new relationship with school. On the other hand, Marcus continually used his performance in school to assert his independence from his parents—whether he lived at home or not. However, proving his "success" at school became even more significant when he began living away from his parents. He used his success in school as a tool to regain the respect of his parents, and to prove that he could succeed even though he lived away from home, because he knew that his parents valued and rewarded success in school. Going to school was part of Marcus's strategy to define himself to his parents, whereas it was Jeff's parents who made school a new possibility in Jeff's life.

These two young men's relationships with their parents reveal that despite the apparent strains, they remained connected and supported by their parents. For Marcus and Jeff, building and maintaining connections with their parents was not easy. The other four young men, as noted earlier, also talked about the connection and support they received from their family members. Their stories provide glimpses of the ways in which relationships with family members are integral to the meanings they constructed about schooling. The stories also reveal how their African-American masculinities came into being in the context of their families. The peer group, too, was a significant site where relationships were influential in their emerging identities. I now turn to an examination of the peer group and its significance in their lives.

THE PEER GROUP EXPLORED

The "peer group" is perhaps the most common relationship represented in literature about young African-American men and is often cited as an extremely significant arena in the identity formation process of young African-American men. Oftentimes, such accounts are about young African-American men from the inner city. One image of masculinity is found in *Makes Me Wanna Holler*, in which McCall (1994) provides a powerful and insightful autobiographical account of his life growing up as an African-American man in the United States. He presents a compelling image of the strength and power of the peer group in his life:

> Through those guys, I discovered the strength and solace in camaraderie. It was a confidence booster, a steady support for my fragile self-esteem. Alone, I was afraid of the world and insecure. But I felt cockier and surer of myself when hanging with my boys. I think we all felt more courageous when we hung together. We did things in groups that we'd never try alone. The group also gave me a sense of belonging that I'd never known before. With those guys, I could hide in the crowd and feel like the accepted norm. There was no fear of standing out, feeling vulnerable, exiled, and exposed. There was a comfort even my family couldn't provide. (p. 33).

Majors and Billson (1992) have further examined this image painted by McCall in which the ways of being and acting that McCall describes are seen as "cool pose." They argue that "Cool pose gives the black male his greatest sense of pride and masculinity" (p. 34). They use Oliver's (1988) notion of "compulsive masculine behavior," and further maintain that compulsive masculinity emerges as an alternative to "traditional definitions of manhood, compensating for feelings of shame, powerlessness, and frustration. Being a man becomes redefined in terms that lead to destruction of self and others. Staying cool ensures that destruction remains palatable" (Majors & Billson, 1992, pp. 34–35). Majors and Billson suggest that many young African-American men may reject those "brothers" who reject the standards of being "cool." Therefore, going to the theater, a concert, or camping may be seen as "uncool," and African-Americans who engage in such actions are seen as "uncool."

The "cool pose" described by Majors and Billson (1992) seems to reflect Dwayne's ways of being in his Detroit neighborhood. The peer group seems important to many young African-American men living in inner cities. McCall (1994) certainly articulated this point: "The group gave me a sense of belonging that I'd never known before" (p. 33). Taylor (1991) considered the significance of the peer group and noted that,

> For boys, the peer group is the all-important tribunal, in which identity is shaped and validated by the "brothers" on the streets. Boys are expected to be "cool" in the face of all kinds of adversity, and learn to behave accordingly. The ability to stay cool under adverse conditions is not merely a matter of style. . . . In short, "being cool" involves emotional toughness, even callousness and indifference towards many of the problems and people the adolescent encounters. (p. 151)

Here, Taylor presents a form of peer group relations that would be familiar to Dwayne, and other inner-city youngsters. For instance, Dwayne described the display of such emotional toughness as part of the building of his "self-esteem." I became curious about his notion of development of self-esteem and pursued this further with him:

JP:	So, how do you get self-esteem?
Dwayne:	Like for me, fit in, smoking bud, drink brew. Rush people.
JP:	What does rush mean?
Dwayne:	Like a couple of guys on one guy or somethin'.
JP:	If you beat someone, who would you beat? Would it be a rival gang, or what could be the reason?
Dwayne:	It don't really matter. It may, sometimes we used to do it, just to be doin' somethin' on the streets. Just to do it.
JP:	So you can be hard and respected?
Dwayne:	Yeah it made it feel as hard and as one.

Just as it was important for Dwayne to "feel hard," it was also important to feel a sense of connection, unity, and "as one." As noted in a previous chapter, Dwayne talked about his friends as his "boys, they be like my brothers, NFL, Niggers For Life. When we do this and that, we go down together." At the same time, as the unity was engendered through feeling "hard and respected," Dwayne's "brothers" also "gave" him "love." There seemed tremendous comfort in the group of friends that he connected with when he lived in Detroit. This support and deep sense of loyalty may be built through "acting cool"; it was also peppered with "love" and "care" from the peers he called his "brothers." Acting in certain ways potentially ensured continued membership in a peer group. But his relationships with others were not only about "acting cool," they were also about bonding, connecting with others, and providing emotional support. The ways he and his friends acted in these groups reflected their identities in the making; identities that not only reflected a response to racism, and economic or racial oppression, but also a response to masculinities they associated with white and black middle-class men. These identities had them identifying with exaggerated forms of masculinity that emphasize toughness. In this way, the peer group may also be seen as a refuge from the world.

These young men's versions of masculinities may reflect their sense of powerlessness in larger society and create a sense of power through the connections and patterns of behavior that the peer group sanctioned. However, Dwayne's connection with his friends appeared to be more than the "being cool" that Taylor (1991) characterizes. His peer relationships led to my asking questions about the kind of relationships the other young men encountered. Were the caring and connected relationships that Dwayne experienced similar to those of the other five young men in this study? Was there variation across social class groups in the kinds of relationships they encountered?

These questions are considered by Franklin (1992), who examines the form of relationships among African-American men from different social class positions. He argues that many working-class men engage in close, caring relationships much more frequently than middle-class men do. He further argues that:

> When black men accept and begin to display societal definitions of masculinity, many of the traits thought to be essential for the development of close friendships are lost. Basically, what happens is that expectation for these males begins to change. Empathy, compassion, trust, cooperation, and other such traits are eschewed in favor of ones such as aggression, competitiveness, stoicism, rational thinking, and independence. (pp. 209–210)

Franklin (1992) suggests that embrace of hegemonic masculinity sees some African-American men, particularly "upwardly mobile" black men, suppressing other forms of masculinity. His proposition is interesting because it hints at different forms of masculinity emerging among African-American men where social class is influential.

The images that McCall (1994) and Majors and Billson (1992) present certainly represent an interpretation of a strand of masculinity considered dominant among inner-city African-American youths. But surely there are other forms of masculinities among African-American men in the inner cities and other locations in the United States? The stories of the young men in this study suggest the peer group did not play the same kind of role in their lives as is often cited about inner-city youth. I raise these questions as a way both to probe the significance of all relationships in their lives and, more significantly, to understand better the form and content of the relationships these young men encountered with their peers. The image of the young black man in the inner city is an image that commonly seeps into the headlines of the commercial media: the tough, resilient, and violent African-American man. For instance, a feature story in the Sunday *New York Times* (December 4, 1994) was headlined "The Black Man Is in Terrible Trouble. Whose Problem Is That?" Images of the "troubled" African-American man generally present one version of young African-American men coming into being, and often represent only one potential aspect of their identities. But there are others. This is demonstrated through the stories of all six of the young African-American men in this study.

"They Will Stand by Me"

Nurturance and care, at some level, seem to be woven through the culture of Dwayne's peer group. These dimensions also seemed to be part of Marcus's connections with his friends. For example, Marcus described his connections with his friends:

> Basically they grew up with me; they know me real good. They will stand by me. If I ever got into any trouble where I was going to get to beat up by a whole group of people, they would help me. Because that's how we are, that's how me and my best friends are. If somethin' happened to them, I would happen to stick up for them, I will stick up for them and stand by them, if somethin' happened to them. And they're goin' to stand by me. It's not like we are a big ole gang.

There is no doubt that these friends were important to Marcus, and despite his conflicts with his parents, it was his friends to whom he turned for support and connection. The group was maintained through "sticking up" for each other, "standing by" each other. His description of his connections with male peers reflected a version of masculinity that involved physical control and solidarity. Marcus, like Dwayne, developed a version of masculinity that reflected collective strategies and survival.

> *Marcus:*   I hang around Tyrone a lot. He likes me. He make time to see me. Anyway. 'Cause that's how close we is.
>
> *JP:*   How long have you known him?

Marcus:	Ever since middle school. I've got about five best friends that I can deeply talk to.
JP:	What kind of things do you talk about?
Marcus:	Like, you know, my parents and everything. 'Cause them was the only people that was there for me when I had problems with my parents. They know more about that than my relatives do. They are the only person I can talk to. I can't go nowhere. He the only one I could talk to.

The significance of the support of friends in Marcus's life as he went about interacting with his family, going to school, or going to work, cannot be overstated. Their solace and comfort helped him sustain himself in the face of the challenges he encountered as a young black man. Through his particular experiences in family, school, or work, he developed a close emotional bond with his five friends that reflected a strand of his version of masculinity that he lived out. Intermingled with Marcus's sense of a strong network of friends was also a wide network of friends.

Marcus:	I've got lots of friends. I'm very well known. I try to make myself have no enemies. Don't want none. 'Cause I ain't that type that goes around. . . . I have a lot of friends but I have five best friends, that I basically grew up with ever since I came up to Allerton. Well, we sort of spilt up after middle school. But we still keep in touch. I have all their numbers. Just this weekend we was all together. Down at the riverfront, walking around. I have three that go to Central. Two that go to Western. . . .
JP:	Who do you hang around with most then?
Marcus:	Well, I don't hang around the same people all the time. I have my best friends, but I don't hang around them constantly.

Apart from Marcus and Dwayne, the other young men did not seem to have such a strong peer group. Not only does this reflect their differing experiences and possibilities, it also reflects their different opportunities. The fact that the other young men did not have such a support group is significant, and particularly important in relation to arguments about the centrality of the peer group in the lives of young African-Americans, as articulated by writers such as Taylor (1991) and Mincy (1994).

As I explored the extent to which the peer group became a source of affiliation for these young men, I asked them to talk about the important people in their lives. While they most frequently identified with either a parent or friends, it was significant that most did not name a woman as a friend, with the exception of Jeff, or a teacher or an adult connected to their school. In fact, as the conversations developed, it appeared that their friends seemed to play an extremely significant role in their lives, but it was only their male friends that they talked about most. Although they all seemed to suggest that they wanted "good friends," they all did not seem to be able to negotiate relationships in the ways that Dwayne or Marcus did. In fact, many of the young men seemed to have very tenuous connections with other peers. This is not to say that they did not seek greater connections with their peers; rather they struggled to sustain deep, connected relationships with their peers, and particularly the male peers they wanted to be connected with. Although some researchers have argued the importance of the peer groups, how easy was it to sustain membership of the peer groups?

Interestingly, although the peer group was important to all of the young men, only four seemed connected to a peer group of some form. For example, Rashaud and Shawn had friends but not in ways represented by McCall (1994), Dwayne, or Marcus. Further, the friendships Marcus, Rashaud, and Shawn developed seemed to be formed and sustained within school or in an organization outside of school. In contrast, Dwayne's relationships were all formed in his neighborhood, "in the streets" in Detroit and, to a lesser degree, more recently in Allerton. Like Dwayne, the peer groups of Marcus, Shawn, and Rashaud were exclusively African-American. At the same time, Zakeev and Jeff, both working class, seemed to have few, if any, close friends. For Marcus, Shawn, and Rashaud, one of the most central criteria for belonging to their particular peer groups was not to "act white." Engaging in oppositional stances in relation to this image seemed significant in promoting peer cohesion.[11] In order to understand better their relationships with peers, I now turn to a discussion of trust in relationships.

"I Just Don't Trust Nobody"

Perhaps the most central topic of all the conversations with these young men was the topic of "trust" in friendships. This topic, together with how they had been "let down" by friends, came up time and time again over the months of our conversations. Although the theme is interesting, the vital significance of having strong and connected relationships with peers in their lives was the overarching issue that was part of many of their conversations with me.

That "trust" in friendship was a central topic of discussion is not surprising. Many teenagers talk about lack of trust and connection with others of their age. But these particular young men's concern about trust in their relationships also told me something about the kind of men they wanted to be. Talk about trust in friendships was not just about what they hoped for. It also emerged from what they had experienced with others as they were growing up. Most centrally, they all wanted connection, community, belonging, and sharing with others. Their discontent about the lack of trust in their friendships perhaps reveals the values they embraced and attempted to live out.

As they talked about their friends, they also talked about how over time there had been a shift in patterns of whom they related to and whom they trusted.

> JP: One thing I'm trying to find out are relationships that people have with each other. Do you have a lot of friends?

Dwayne:	Me?
JP:	Yeah.
Dwayne:	Yeah. I just don't trust nobody though.
JP:	Why's that?
Dwayne:	The things I've been through, and I've been let down.
JP:	Tell me how people have let you down.
Dwayne:	Like fightin' and everythin'. Let me down, hurt me, my fellas and things like that.
JP:	They did something bad to you, or they weren't there for you?
Dwayne:	They weren't there for me. I mean like the times I need them, or something like that.
JP:	What do you need friends for? For what kinds of things?
Dwayne:	I talk about family stuff to friends. You know, be there through thick and thin. . . . somebody to talk to, want the right angle so you won't do nothin' stupid.
JP:	Do you have good friends in Detroit?
Dwayne:	Most definitely.

Thus, although Dwayne had talked about being close to his friends, his relationships and friendships were not always smooth. He had been "let down" and "hurt," which made him feel wary about trusting people. This suggests that while Dwayne may have had a seemingly solid support group, relationships were not always smooth, and were continually changing in response to the members' individual and collective responses to their daily challenges.

Jeff also raised the topic of trust in friendships and argued that there were few people that he could depend on. In fact, Jeff didn't even use the word *friend* to describe the people he connected to. He called them *associates*.

Jeff:	Well you get people talking about you, you know.
JP:	What do they say?
Jeff:	Basically like "Jeff want to be white. He don't have so many friends." So that's why I don't say I have friends. I have *associates*. You might catch me once in a while saying friend, but don't take it to mind. I have *associates*.

Jeff distanced himself from other people through using a different term to label the people he connected with. In our conversation he also raised the issue of what and how other people perceived him to be. He argued that many people claimed he "acted white" and that he had few friends. Jeff agreed with this point and provided more evidence as to why he thought he did not have many friends.

'Cause to me a friend is somebody that is always there for you. No matter what you do to them. No matter what happened between you and him. Like you argue in a fight. If he see me out with my car broken down, he's gonna pull over and say "do you need some help?" Even though me and him have been in a big fight. . . . I think there's a few people who I can depend on maybe, but not really. Well, there is one person who I know is behind me one hundred percent, Sharon. I'm crazy about her. . . .

Jeff's image of a friend seemed to reflect the kind of connections that Dwayne and Marcus talked about, but he did not seem to be able to develop such friendships. As we talked more about his friends, it became clear that Sharon was perhaps one of the few people that he connected to daily and actually trusted.

> JP: Is it hard having a good friend?
> Jeff: No, it's just the way people are. Okay, I will say, like when my car is broken down on the street, the guys I associate with, they will help me. But what I'm saying somebody you've argued with, still they will go the extra mile with you to help you out, that's what I'm saying. Like a good, good friend. Somebody you can tell anything, so basically I wouldn't want many good friends. Another thing is I tend not to trust too many people anymore, because those that I did trust, turned on me. 'Cause some friends of mine, ever since I've moved up here [to Allerton], they've been my friends. They recently turned on me, basically 'cause of Sharon, spending too much time with Sharon. Me being out of the house and everything.
> JP: So they didn't support you at all?
> Jeff: No, not at all.

Intermingled with Jeff's conception of a good friendship—going "the extra mile," "trust," "somebody you can tell anything" to—are certain codes of conduct. I also discovered from Latasha (Sharon's best friend) that some of Jeff's friends were not happy with Jeff, not because he was dating Sharon, or because he made her pregnant, but because he had liaisons with other young women while he was dating Sharon, and he did this without Sharon's knowledge. But more significantly, I learned from Jeff that as he began to act more and more "white," his childhood circle of friends slowly disintegrated. Jeff seemed to develop ways of being that were in part in conflict with those sanctioned by his group of friends. Part of this conflict seemed to be centered on his embrace of "acting white." Significant in the changed relationship with his boyhood friends was that the friendships themselves became part of a process of racial identity construction.

Over time I began to realize that Rashaud, too, had few friends. He seemed very outgoing, sociable, and easy to talk with. But as the months progressed, it seemed that the only person he really connected to daily was a school friend, Siko. This was a friendship he had only developed over the course of the past year. "I don't have a lot of different peope. My true friend, that I can honestly believe in no matter what, Siko, he's from Ghana. That's my boy," Rashaud shared with me. They spent a lot of time together after school. For example, on one occasion Rashaud told me, "Me and my friend last night, talking about going skydiving sometime next year. And I was going to go to Costa Rica, and go out to California, I just like to go to have the experience and then talk about it."

Rashaud did have other friends, at school and out of school, but these other friendships were not marked with constant interaction. In fact, when I asked Rashaud what he liked to do for fun he said, "Homework, hang out with friends. Basically it's cold now, so I like to try and do well in the winter." Here, Rashaud placed his homework at the center of his out-of-school activity. The only youths Rashaud regularly hung around with were Siko and the people he saw at the Jack and Jill club, although he did not regularly interact with these peers outside the confines of the club meetings and activities. Thus, the friendship with Siko suggests there were few others that he felt he could connect with at school. It could also reflect his not wanting to connect to a particular subgroup of friends. But this seems a choice possibly constrained by the social separation of racial groups at his school. This separation is explored in the following chapter. Significant in understanding Rashaud's relationship with others is what he talked about with his friend. For example, he discussed going on vacation to California or Costa Rica, which reflects middle-class possibilities that I doubt would be imagined as a possibility by Dwayne or Marcus. Through this relationship we are provided a glimpse of his version of masculinity that seemed to reflect his loneliness, his emphasis on academic individualism, and his personal career ambitions.

Marcus talked about the different kinds of conversations he had with different friends and acquaintances. For example, with the friends that he played basketball with in the early evening, he rarely talked about his home problems. In fact, I learned later that although he had five "best friends," he was still cautious about what he talked about with them. He was frightened of being "hurt" by revealing personal thoughts and feelings.

> *Marcus:* I can't talk in the same way I talk to my best friends.
> *JP:* How come?
> *Marcus:* Because they wouldn't be able to understand what I be talking about. A lot of them know about what I'm into.
> *JP:* But about your family problems, you wouldn't speak about it to those guys?
> *Marcus:* No. 'Cause myself, I don't trust nobody.
> *JP:* You don't trust me yet, right?
> *Marcus:* Not to the certain point where I will just tell you everything about me.
> *JP:* You're holding back?
> *Marcus:* I'll tell you basically the stuff that you want to know.
> *JP:* Like which stuff wouldn't you want to share with me?
> *Marcus:* My real background of my family. . . . I would never discuss that to nobody, 'cause that's me. I just holding myself up. I can to a point, I can, like I don't like people to know too much about me. I always been like that. To me they can hurt me in the long run.
> *JP:* Because they will make fun of you or what?
> *Marcus:* No, just they can hurt me in the long run.

> *JP:*   And your friends, what kinds of things do they talk about themselves to
> you?
> *Marcus:*   Their family and things. We always talk the same things. Basically talk
> about problems we have.

Thus, although Marcus may have had opportunities to share some of his problems with other friends, a possibility that did not seem available to Rashaud, he was selective in what he talked about with them. Once again this speaks to the tenuous nature of the friendships, and it also reveals how he did not want to make himself vulnerable. Through his selectively sharing aspects of his emotional and personal self, we are able to learn about the significance of maintaining an image of emotional control in the eyes of others. This can be seen as reflective of his masculine identity in the making, in that emotional control, while seen as a way of protecting himself against hurt, also suggests a barrier or the limit of the way he interacted with other men. Their talk about trust in friendships tells us a lot about the kinds of relationships they sought. It also informs us about the kinds of identities that they made in the context of their different experiences of the structures and social practices of race, gender, and social class.

Nevertheless, what they talked about, and with whom, and the ongoing relationship among their friends seemed primarily shaped by a quest to connect through a bond of loyalty, which seemed paramount to these young men. All the young men saw loyalty as one of the most fundamental features of their friendships with other men. But for Marcus, Jeff, and Dwayne, their sense of loyalty seemed to be contradictory, in that they wanted their friends to support them, "go that extra mile," but they were still reluctant to fully trust their friends with inner thoughts or feelings for the hurt that may follow. These young men's accounts of untrustworthiness in friendships perhaps reflected the intense nature of their relationships where solid support was expected. The bond that connected and disconnected them with their friends was around issues of consistency and supporting each other in personal daily struggles.

Franklin (1992) writes about a similar pattern in his study of friendships between African-American men. He argues that much violence that African-American men are involved with "is certainly associated with accelerated use and selling drugs. However, a relatively large proportion of black male same-sex violence ... may be related to *violations of friendship expectations*" (emphasis added, p. 208). Friendship expectations seemed high for these young men. Therefore, because they highly valued their friendships, they were careful not to jeopardize these connections. This meant that there were certain strands of their personal self that they did not share. For instance, Marcus shared with me instances of his personal life that he had not shared with his friends.

Although many of the young men may have sought the intense peer group that McCall (1994) and Taylor (1991) describe, it was only Marcus and Dwayne out of the six young men who had such a support group. Shawn and Rashaud had one or two male friends who supported them; however, Zakeev did not seem to have any close friends in the ways the other young men experienced friendships. Jeff, on the other hand, had a close friend, Sharon, who was a young white woman. The different levels of intensity of friendships across the young men suggest the complexity of the role of friendships in the identity formation process. The variation can be explained through taking into account why and how they formed certain relationships in and out of school; the meanings they gave to their own and others' identities through social interactions; and the racialized meaning they and others gave to schooling that caused them to be alienated from or connected to many of their peers and teachers. It was through the different individuals and groups they connected with and separated themselves from that they were able to display and live out versions of their racialized masculine identities. Although many of these relationships may have provided the potential for them to feel connected to people they could trust, ironically they were also sites that saw them developing stances where they did not "trust nobody." In order to consider their relationships further, I examine next the particular relationships they experienced. I explore these relationships in two contexts: (1) friends at school, and (2) friends outside of school.

CONNECTIONS WITH FRIENDS FROM SCHOOL

One of the most interesting aspects of the talk of these six young men was their desire to be among their friends at school. This is not surprising. Friendships are important in the lives of all adolescents. What did these young men mean when they talked about their "friends"? Who were they friends with? What did it mean to be a friend? What kinds of things did they like to do and talk about with their friends? Did they only connect with peers from their own school, or did their network reach others who attended other schools, or who dropped out of school? These are just some of the questions I explore as I consider their relationships with their friends.

Except for Jeff and Zakeev, all the young men had an African-American peer group with whom they met daily. This seemed the case for Marcus and Dwayne at Central, and for Shawn and Rashaud at Cedarville. They also hung around with these friends after school in their neighborhoods and in various recreational activities. As the semester progressed, Zakeev did develop a closer relationship wtih two African-American members of the school band. Jeff really did not have any friends besides Sharon, who is white.

As the months progressed, I began to realize that few of these young men had really close friends, as they defined friends, in their lives. Further, as I began to explore their friends and the institutional connection of their friends, it became apparent that in their personal lives outside the classroom, they did not have strong connected relationships with people outside of their homes. This is interesting, and potentially explains the emphasis they placed on their desire for more connected relationships with teachers.

Schooling and Close Friends

Five of the six participants identified with African-American peers as friends, and most of these peers were male; no one except Jeff identified a white person as a friend. Yet, they all attended multiracial schools. And, in the case of two of the young men, they were very much in the minority at school as African-Americans. These young men distinguished between close friends and peers called acquaintances or friends, but not "close friends." Table 4 suggests that few of these young men had peers in their lives that they called close friends; the extent to which both school and nonschool affiliations became important in their patterns of friendship were also significant.

Two participants who had close personal friends at their current schools were Rashaud and Marcus. Both these young men were the only ones still residing in the same house they had lived in while they attended middle school. The other young men had moved, attending different schools in their ninth- or tenth-grade years. This mobility surely must have influenced their opportunities to connect with others in school. The mobility was brought about as a consequence of family circumstances, activities, and interests. It perhaps reveals how decisions emanating from the family unit may influence relationships developed in school. The move from school to school saw some of these young men leaving friends from old schools and trying to develop new friendships in their new schools.

It became apparent just how precarious it was to build friendships at school and to make connections with their peers. In the previous chapter, I noted that the young men loved to spend time with their friends at break time or lunchtime. In fact, apart from wanting to acquire the high school diploma, meeting friends was one of the other most consistent reasons they offered for attending school. Yet, when we began to talk further about their friends and their peers, it became clear that they had few friends. For example, at one point Shawn said:

TABLE 4.   Primary and Secondary Levels of Friendship

Name	Primary Affiliations—Close Friends	Secondary Affiliations—Other Friends and Acquaintances
Dwayne	Neighborhood male friends from Detroit	Friends from current school
Jeff	Girlfriend	Friends from middle school
Marcus	Male friends from middle/high school	Fraternity, reading group, basketball
Rashaud	Male friend from school	Friends from Jack and Jill club
Shawn	None	Fraternity, members of school wrestling team, church
Zakeev	None	Male friends from current school, church

Shawn:	I don't have any close friends. I've had in [my old neighborhood].
JP:	Part of that is that because you have moved to the area? Are there any other reasons; is it partly because of you?
Shawn:	A lot of my friends, I don't really tell them personal stuff, I don't really try to get too close.
JP:	Is there a reason for that?
Shawn:	I had a lot experience of people who says they are your friend, and behind your back they will do something.

This becomes a troubling picture for the young men in thinking about the extent to which they were alienated from the content and pedagogy in their classrooms. I am not arguing that they did not have friends, nor am I critiquing the nature of their friendships; I am merely stating that they really did not have many friends at the various schools they attended. They seemed fairly alienated. The image of the alienation they experienced at school is deepened when one considers their apparent alienation from the content of schooling. The need for friendships is heightened in thinking about the larger picture of their experiences at school.

Maintaining Connections

Rashaud and Shawn each met their peer group daily at a certain area in the school. Rashaud had always hung around with this group. Shawn, who entered the school in grade 10, initially associated with white students in a particular area of the school where the majority of white students congregated, then was beckoned by an African-American student to join other African-American students during the break time. Both these young men said that they were friendly with white male and female students, and claimed that race was not a significant factor in their choice of friends or girlfriends. However, when I asked them to name their friends from school, they only named students who were African-American. And when I asked Shawn to describe his relationships with white students, he said they were "superficial."

Marcus and Dwayne each met friends during the recesses of the school day. They each spent a lot of time with their friends. There was a particular area in their school that they hung out in, where mostly African-American students hung out, but they did not confine themselves solely to this area when they met with their various friends. They also hung out in other places on the school grounds. This was markedly different from Shawn and Rashaud who had only one designated area that they hung out in.

School for these four young men was remarkably similar and also remarkably different. There were differences between the Cedarville students and the Allerton student in relation to their experiences in classrooms, and students' culture outside of classrooms appeared somewhat different. But what was similar was the fact that they preferred and consciously worked at identifying with a group of African-American students at break time and in an area that was "theirs." What was different was that the places that Marcus and Dwayne traversed were much larger and more varied than those of Shawn and Rashaud at Cedarville High School. Possibly this may have been influenced by the proportion of African-American and white students attending Central as compared with Cedarville.

Zakeev and Jeff did not seem to have a peer network at school. Jeff seemed to suggest that Sharon was the only person he associated with at Central. And then when he moved to Allerton Christian School, he said he had no school friends. Zakeev had a few students he talked with at Western. However, he did not have any peers at school whom he called friends and would hang around with after school. Zakeev's story of his attempts to make friends at school provides a glimpse of the difficulties that face youngsters at school as they try to develop connections with others.

"What Am I Doing Wrong?"

Zakeev missed his friends from his old high school, Central. Unlike the other young men, Zakeev did not congregate with a group of friends at the beginning of the day. "I get off the bus and go to my locker . . . then I go downstairs, my class is in the basement. I go down there and I just wait for my class," he said. Zakeev did not find it easy to be accepted at school by African-American or white students. At one point, he said that at his previous school, "Central, they accept people no matter what. They accept people better. I'm not saying all people do, but most people accept people for who they are." At Western, it was difficult for him to make friendships, but this was something that he tried to work on daily at school. "I really keep to myself now. . . . I talk to some people, I try, I always congregate with people, black or white, I'm a nice person, and I talk to people. And that's what I'm saying, the acceptance. . . ." He believed that essential to being accepted and connected with other students was being "popular" regardless of racial identity:

> Zakeev: It's to me, it's not really black or white [racial identity] at Western. It's really a popularity thing. It's like popular people, no matter if you are black or white.
> JP: How do you become popular?
> Zakeev: I don't know exactly, that's what I'm trying to figure out. I've sat back and said how do you do this?

Zakeev talked about a number of different students he spent time with outside of class when he was at school. He spent time in the morning before classes talking to a white guy, Aiden, and sometimes an Asian guy, Vinh. During his lunch hour he spent time in the library where he spoke with a young black woman, Trisha. He did not speak with these particular students outside of school. And he also spent time with two African-American male friends who, like him, were members of the school band. In fact, although Zakeev said he tried to congregate with white, Asian, and African-American students, after about the first six months at the school, it was mostly African-American male students that he hung around with. He spent most of his time with two other young African-American men who were in his band class. As the year progressed, these were two students that he remained friendly with, but he did not consider them friends.

In the end, Zakeev claimed that the white students at his new school were very much the same as the white students at his previous school. In the main, he did not associate with white students, and it was the black students that he tried to be accepted by.

> I don't know why these people are acting like certain way . . . to me and to other people . . . and it goes back to the acceptance part. At Central, they accept people no matter what. They accept people better. I'm not saying all people do, but most people accept people for who they are. . . . And I'm trying to figure out, okay, what am I doing wrong? I'm trying to be nice, that's worked on some people. I'm not trying to say that I'm trying to use people to see if worked. I'm just saying that nice is the way I am. And the people, sometimes I say, "hi" to them, and they just turn their back on me, and say nothin' to me. And I really don't like that, but I just figure out that's the way they are.

Thus, it was difficult for Zakeev to connect with any student at school. He did not connect with white students; in fact, toward the end of the interviews, Zakeev started telling me how he had never interacted with white students until he went to Western. This is an interesting comment, because many of his classes at Central and Western were multiracial, yet, in his mind, he had not interacted or connected with white students. Despite Zakeev's openness and willingness to make connections with other students, he remained considerably alienated.

African-American Connections

For the participants, there seemed two distinct patterns of friendship at school: one in which a group met and congregated with a set of African-American peers daily, and another that consisted of a racially diverse group of individuals. The latter was the case for both Jeff and Zakeev, who at both their current and previous schools did not seem to have many friends that they connected with daily. Dwayne, Marcus, Rashaud, and Shawn, in contrast, each met with a particular group of students every day. They spoke with the same students every day and usually met the students in a particular place in the school. This is interesting because they attended very different schools, with very different student compositions. Cedarville had a majority middle-class white student population, with no more than 10 percent African-American students, whereas Central was multiclassed and almost 50 percent African-American. Yet in each of their schools, they sought and preferred to hang out with African-American students. In the cases of Marcus and Dwayne, the net was cast more broadly than for either Rashaud or Shawn in that they connected with a number of subgroups. Thus, despite these four young men encountering different kinds of pedagogy and curriculum, and despite the differing student compositions, they all formed groups with African-American students during recess and lunch-time. In fact, on asking them to talk about school, it was the interactions with other African-American students, who were male and to a lesser degree female, that they spoke about. The identity of these students they interacted with was important and foremost in their accounts of the students they were connected to.

The relationships they formed in school seemed significant to their sense of their emerging identities. The students they associatd with were students with whom they shaped or developed common values and interests, and who were thereby able to sustain them in school. Because they felt alienated from relation-ships in classrooms, the relationships with peers took on a greater significance. Spending time with school friends became an important activity in their experi-ence of schooling. The peer relationships became significant to their identities as African-American because they served as a context in which to define them-selves—their racial masculine identities—in relation to the meanings of the insid-ers and outsiders of their peer groups. The significance of racial identities in the connections they formed is discussed in the following chapter. Of most signifi-cance here is that they encountered different kinds of peer relationships, while they had at most a small handful of friends whom they relied upon. The images portrayed by writers such as McCall (1994) and Taylor (1991) about African-American peer relationships perhaps do not capture the complexity of peer rela-tionshps in these young men's lives. Many of their relationships seemed plagued with uncertainty and lack of trust, yet four of the young men did have at least one person they relied upon. Their relationships were uneven and complex. Peer groups at once seemed to be both sources of connection and sources of alienation.

In addition to the friendship patterns that seemed to emanate from school, some of the young men also developed friendships outside the context of school. These friendships were important to them. Although they did not list the friendships with the people they connected with in these outside organizations as significant in their lives, they still mentioned the opportunities to meet and socialize with other peers at significant recreational opportunities that they enjoyed. All the organiza-tions they belonged to were African-American. It seemed that formal networks and organizations outside of school played a significant role in the lives and the identities of these young African-American men. It is to these various forms of networks, however formal or informal, that I now turn.

NETWORKS AND ORGANIZATIONS

Although they all appeared to have friends from school, it was only Marcus who had a consistent and sustaining circle of friends at school who showed connection and care that most of them sought. While I note that most did not find such friend-ships in school, a larger question looms, and that is: Why should they be able to develop friends at school? Their schools did not seem organized to promote caring and connected relationships among students over time; they were rarely in classes with their friends; and they suggested that in the classes they did take there was very little interaction among students in classrooms. What they yearned for at school was to spend time with their peers—not just to talk about school, but also to talk about girls, sports, television, and the like. Many of them turned to organi-zations that were not connected to school as an avenue to develop friendships and connected relationships.

Although each of these participants was involved in organizations outside the school, they varied as to the kinds of organizations they belonged to. These orga-nizations ranged from church and youth organizations to informal basketball games in their neighborhood and friends they hung around with in the streets. The membership of these organizations in the main was largely African-American. It seemed that the young men gravitated toward organizations with predominantly African-American membership. But this is a generalized picture of their associa-tion with organizations outside of school. For Jeff and Zakeev, their association with organizations was minimal, and Dwayne was not connected to a formal orga-nization but rather to an informal network of friends.

"Black Brothers Getting Together Being Just Boys"

The relationships they sought outside of school need to be seen in connection with both their experiences in school and their experiences in family. Four of the young men were involved in a range of organizations. Table 5 provides a sense of the range of organizations they participated in.

Marcus was involved in a "brotherhood," an organization closely connected to a college-based fraternity. He attended weekly meetings with other young men, who were all African-American, of varying social class backgrounds, and they talked about issues and ideas affecting African-Americans. They also planned social get-togethers. In addition, Marcus was involved in a college-based group that met to discuss ideas around Afrocentricism and attempted both to understand the plight of African-Americans in the United States and to develop strategies to build and strengthen the solidarity of the African-American community. Many of the members of the groups he belonged to lived in working-class and middle-class neighborhoods, which suggests that racial identity was more significant than social class in memberships of these organizations.

Shawn was also involved in a "brotherhood"—although a different and rival organization from the one Marcus belonged to. He joined the organization so that he could meet people. He told me, "To me it is always having somebody you can depend on, the guys will be there for you. That's one of the reasons I joined, I didn't know too many people (at school)." All the people that he met and main-

TABLE 5.   **Peer Organizations and Networks**

Name	Peer Organizations and Networks
Dwayne	Neighborhood friends in Detroit and Allerton
Jeff	Church group
Marcus	Brotherhood organization, reading groups, basketball
Rashaud	Mother-sibling organization
Shawn	Church, school wrestling team, brotherhood organization
Zakeev	Church group

tained contact with were African-American and lived in the greater Allerton area. "They talk a lot, they are going to do this or that, but they don't do too much. Kind of like hang out with a lot of the guys." The other members of the group did not attend Cedarville, and many were working class as well as middle class. He needed this group of peers so that he had others he could "depend on."

In addition, Shawn still maintained contact with his mother's church in Detroit, attending the church when he visited her. Even though it was almost four years since he had lived in Detroit, he still maintained the contact. During the summer of 1992, he participated, as part of a group of young African-American men and women, in a church-sponsored tour of African-American colleges around the United States. Tuskegee and Fisk were among the colleges he visited.

Rashaud, who attended the same school as Shawn but at a different grade level, was also involved in a community-based organization. The organization was established by single African-American mothers as a way for them and their children to get together. Most of the women, although not all, lived in the middle-class neighborhoods of Allerton and Cedarville. The Jack and Jill organization met most Sundays, and Rashaud looked forward to connection with other male and female peers. Like Shawn, membership of this organization saw Rashaud developing friendships that cut across social class lines.

Zakeev really did not have many friends in or out of school. In fact, he spent most of his outside of school time watching TV or practicing the saxophone. Occasionally he would go to the library or watch a movie with his younger brother. On a Sunday, he would go to church with his brother and mother. Sometimes he attended church events.

Dwayne, since moving to Allerton at the beginning of his tenth grade year, was not involved in community-based organizations. In Detroit, however, he belonged to a subset of young African-American men with whom he hung around in his neighborhood. This group of young men served an important role in his life. As noted in a previous chapter, the friendships he formed in his neighborhoods were his solace: "My boys, they be like my brothers, NFL, Niggers For Life. When we do this and that, we go down together. . . . They gave me love, they were there for me." In a way, it served as a place to go, to feel connected and respected:

JP:	Were you a member of a gang? You don't have to tell me if you don't want to.
Dwayne:	I mean it was somethin' like that.
JP:	Why was that important to you?
Dwayne:	(pause)
JP:	I'm trying to understand it, not in a negative kind of way.
Dwayne:	The reason it was important to me was because, the time I had problems, I ain't able to see no way out, you know I had problerms, had a lot of pressure, easy influenced and all that. And just hangin' with friends and when we do all that stuff, it just make me feel good, fighting, drinking, smokin' bud, and all that, made me feel like I was hard and all.
JP:	Was that important to feel hard, why was that important?
Dwayne:	Yeah. Like you can't touch me, nobody can mess with you. Or if you step against me, then this is goin' to happen, no such thing.
JP:	Why is no one going to touch you?
Dwayne:	'Cause you're hard, you know. Like you beat on people, you get into a, and you win. You got to hate, making money and all that. You've got a lot of boys together.
JP:	So alone, if you are hard, it's no good. You need to have your friemds with you?
Dwayne:	Not all the time, you might be you and someone else.
JP:	If someone sees you as soft, what does that mean?
Dwayne:	It's just like weak. It's like an image you're trying to portray, trying to hold up, like an image, in the streets. People in the streets, you know for the girls, you want people to know flat out you ain't fine, this is how you cut it, I'm going down like this flat out. It's like when you're raised up in the slums, it made black people down, that's what they're doing out there, is holding us down.
JP:	Why's it keeping you down? Explain to me.
Dwayne:	My opinion, kind of raised in a big city, a lot of crime, people poor with no jobs and all that, that's what going to go on, your family doing this and doing that, you crime, people sexually abusing their kids and all that, doing this to their kids, smoking drugs. That kid has so much hurt in him, he don't know who to talk to, don't know who to trust, don't know who to go to, you know, we getting little guys on the street, start getting into the road. Try to build ourselves up, so he have some self-esteem about him, try to get into the crowd.

The network that Dwayne connected with was significant to him in that it arose out of the conditions and experiences of his peers' encounters in the inner city. In a way the network, or "gang," represented the ingenuity of his peers to connect and form relationships around particular values and norms that helped them sustain their relationships. It became a context for them to develop meaning and a sense of themselves. Ironically, while the "gang" was important to his survival on one level, on another, its activities also saw his demise. He became involved in drugs—taking drugs himself and selling drugs—and was eventually arrested and sentenced.

But for Dwayne, while he did not belong to an apparent institution, there is no doubt that his neighborhood and hanging out with his "fellas" represented a significant institutional affiliation for him. Connell (1987) writes about the significance of "street life" as an institution in the identity formation process. For Dwayne, it was clear that his friends from his neighborhood in Detroit were the most significant people in his life. His connections with his friends were also opportunities to talk about personal problems. These connections were not just about trying to be "cool." However, Dwayne was no longer living in Detroit, and while he had a few friends from school and played basketball after school, he no longer remained constantly connected with his friends in Detroit. But he always hung out with his peer group from Detroit whenever he returned home for a visit. He still considered these peers as friends and valued his connections with them.

In sum, four of these young men found some level of connection with other young African-American men in organizations outside of school. Their stories suggest that the kind of organization they connected to varied according to their experiences outside the school, the kind of resources to which they and their parents had access, the situation at home, and the degree of control their parents wielded in their relationships with their sons. The fact that they belonged to organizations is not surprising. What is significant about the organizations is that they were organizations comprised almost exclusively of African-Americans. Of equal importance is that three of the four young men were connected to organizations with exclusive male membership while Rashaud belonged to a mixed gender organization. It is also significant that for the working-class and middle-class young men their institutional affiliations blurred class lines and highlighted race and gender, rather than class identity. Significantly, this was *not* the case for Dwayne, an underclass youth. These organizations seemed to provide them with an opportunity to affirm their sense of social identity as young African-American men.

Franklin (1992) has written about the nature of relationships African-American working-class men develop. He suggests that "because often young black males resist their mothers' primarily single socializing efforts, many of them develop their masculinities according to their own and their peer groups' inventiveness and ingenuity" (p. 212). It seemed that both the working-class and middle-class young men saw the peer groups as very significant in their lives. Their peer groups did not consist solely of youths from school; rather, they also consisted of other friends they met through organizations outside of school. Thus, the peer group formation became an institution that both shaped and was shaped by cultural and structural dimensions of the family and school.

RELATIONSHIPS AND CONNECTIONS

Thus far, the discussion has uncovered these young men's different relationships with families, peers in school, and networks outside of school. Yet these stories are also about their emerging identities. Important to note is the fact that the relationships in their lives were uneven, and that the relationships they sought in school were complemented with relationships they developed through organizations outside of school. In this concluding section, I focus on some of the themes that have dominated this chapter: friendships as sites of connection and alienation; trans-social class relationships; community and family connections; and the sense of fragility in the relationships they experienced.

Connection and Alienation

Most centrally, the young men's talk about their relationships raises some interesting questions about the dynamics and conflicts among friends within peer groups. Many writers characterize the peer group as an all-encompassing place of reference, and rarely articulate the multiple layers of conflict and connection that interweave peer relationships. This is particularly true for literature on young African-American men. For example Taylor (1991) argued that

> The peer group becomes the principal means through which they seek both a sense of belongingness and feelings of self-esteem. In fact, for males whose fathers are absent from the home, affiliation with street-based peer groups is a crucial step towards learning many of the socially defined and normative aspects of the male role in the black community and the larger society. (p. 150)

Taylor raises some important points about the significance of the peer group. In my study, the peer group was important for all the yong men, *including* the two who had fathers at home. They all sought peers in and out of school. Within the various contexts, the young men acted out their versions of masculinity. They were also places where they helped create it, through their talk about their lives and the lives of others, and through the beliefs and values emerging from and dominating the very group to which they belonged. But these peer groups not only became a place where they developed a sense of "belongingness," as Taylor argued, they were also places where they learned about conflict, hurt, and alienation. Thus, although the peer group could be an agent of affiliation, it could also be seen as an agent of alienation. Peer relationships were complex and while they might influence the young men's sense of self-esteem, they also sometimes inhibited some of the young men from sharing aspects about their personal lives.

Taylor (1991) also argues that many youth who are alienated from their homes because of "insufficient support, physical abuse, or family accords, and from

school because of repeated failure and humiliation often find street culture a welcome relief from the anxiety and stress associated with their other environments"
(p. 150). Taylor is convincing in his analysis about the need for the peer group,
particularly among African-American men, given their experiences in school,
with family, and beyond. Notwithstanding, many young African-American men
in this study had good connections with their parents, albeit occasionally plighted
with family conflict, and they still sought connections with a peer group, not just
any peer group, but an African-American peer group.

Noting the significance of a group identified as African-American is one issue;
another is the complexity of how group membership is sustained, or lost, as in the
case of Jeff. Perhaps amiss in many of the discussions of the African-American
peer group is the sense of conflict, frustration, affiliation, and alienation that were
also defining aspects of the groups these young men belonged to. Notwithstanding, these groups are multidimensional and conflict producing, and they often promote contradictions. Like Taylor, Mincy (1994) also tends to underplay these
dimensions of the peer groups. He writes:

> Adolescent black males have a propensity to exhibit real, honest, and authentic
> behavior in all interactions—that is, for "being for real" or "telling it like it is." They
> tend not to stifle their true thoughts, feelings, or behaviors in most social situations.
> While such authenticity may not always be appreciated or understood by others,
> black male youths tend to cut to the heart of a matter with their genuineness. (pp. 37–
> 38)

Mincy argues an important point about the authentic nature of interactions
among black men, but I wonder if he manages to capture the variation—in social
class, race, sexuality, masculinity, and geographical location—and the multiple
and complex ways in which African-American men interact with each other and
with others. I am not arguing authenticity might not be a part of peer relationships,
but rather, that the dynamic, contradictory, and contextual aspects of authenticity
in friendships may be underplayed through his characterization of authenticity in
friendships.

I have argued that peer group and friendships were complex and multilayered
as a context for the shaping of the young men's racial masculine identities. At
the same time, however, there were differences in their relationships and in the
forms of connections they developed that reflected individual choices they
made. These choices were not made arbitrarily; they were influenced by structures of power that were reflected in school curriculum, the different classes
these young men took, and the formation of racial peer groups in relation to
other groups in their particular schools. The emergence of their racial masculinities, as Connell (1993b) notes, "is a collective process, something that happens
at the level of the institution and the organization of peer group relationships"
(p. 96).

Transgression of Social Class Boundaries

For all the attention to peer group importance, there has been very little research about the friendship patterns of African-American males, and particularly African-American males of differing social class experiences. In a study about the perceptions of "impoverished and affluent" youth about social class, Brantlinger (1993) asserted there is a dearth of literature about social class influences on friendships, or about the differences in friendship patterns of different social classes. Based on her study, she argues that the "shared-taste aspect of friendships served to firmly establish class identity. Many of the commonalities in high-income adolescents friendships were simply inaccessible to low-income adolescents because of lack of funds" (p. 164). Her study is about the friendship patterns of youth, with a sample of about 85 percent white students and 15 percent African-American students. Nevertheless, she did not differentiate racial or ethnic accounts for the differences. Her study is interesting because she asserts that patterns of friendships rarely cut across social class lines, *except* in the case of working-class African-Americans. She noted that four of the six African-American participants in her study appeared to have close connections with middle-class peers. While Brantlinger pointed to the patterns among the African-American participants as an "exception" to her hypothesis that patterns of friendship rarely cross social class lines, she did not fully elaborate or explain her understanding of the exception. Her study clearly raises interesting questions for race/class/gender researchers to address as they try to explain the interconnection of race, class, and gender in the relationships of schoolgoing peers. In the end, while I understand that Brantlinger may not be trying to explain the differences between white and African-American relationships, I wonder whether her hypothesis is more about *white* working-class and *white* middle-class youth than about an all-inclusive working-class and middle-class youth. Brantlinger's exception, in fact, emerged as a dominant pattern among the participants of my study: friendship patterns did cross social class lines, and there also were trans-school relationships. But it was the middle-class youngsters who more commonly crossed social class lines rather than the working-class youngsters. However, most of the young men, with the exception of Dwayne, developed relationships across social class lines in some form or another as they maintained and constructed friendships with peers.

Community and Family Connections

Friendships were important to the young men. Along with family relationships, they were integral to the connections they formed with their community. Fine (1991) considers the connection of family and community in her study about dropout students. On contrasting community connections of dropout students with graduates she noted that the

Dropouts failed in traditional academic terms. But perhaps, ironically, they retained intact some connection, even if problematic and temporary, to community, kin, peers, and racial/ethnic identity . . . the dropouts appear more critical of social and economic circumstances and that graduates remain "optimistic" or "naive" about their social or economic circumstances . . . [and] pride themselves on sharing family, but the sharing ends at the boundaries of extended kin, not into the community. (p. 135)

Her argument suggests a definite contrast between graduates and dropouts. In contrast, among these six young men, all of whom were considered as potential high school graduates, a pattern of connection to both family and community appeared among four of the young men. Of the remaining two young men, Jeff and Zakeev, Zakeev certainly maintained connections with his family, while the connections that Jeff maintained with his family were tenuous, although in the last instance they seemed supportive.

It is through their family and the community connections that these young men were able to seize opportunities to connect with others and receive different kinds of support. Granted, their relationships with family members were complicated and often conflict ridden. However, although Marcus's and Jeff's relationships with their parents reflected conflict, they also reflected connection. Family households were also sites for these young men to develop caring and connected relationships with their brothers or sisters, or both. Their families were important and sustaining influences on their connections with school. The families were also sites where they made and lived out strands of their versions of their masculinities. In the same way, organizations in the community were extremely significant in their affirmation of their racialized and gendered identities. Significantly, for Dwayne, Jeff, and Marcus, the organizations they belonged to were comprised of African-American men. Thus, on one level we see the significance of race in the formation of groups; on another, these groups also became sites where they learned about each other as young men, where they developed their versions of masculinities.

At the same time, there is no doubt that schooling played a central role in these young men's friendship patterns. The fact remains, however, that few of them actually developed the kinds of relationships they fervently sought. Only two had friends that they said they could trust: Marcus and Rashaud. Examining relationships in school provides a picture of the complexity of relationships with peers in school. School became a place where five of the young men appeared to simultaneously strengthen their bonds with other African-Americans, and also a place where they felt alienated; they needed to seek bonds, but particular bonds, outside of school. Also, the out-of-school bonds could have lessened the need for in-school connections. It is through a combination of the various kinds of relationships across institutions that they were able to sustain themselves: through friendships in school, out of school, and with family members.

Tenuous Connections

The puzzle of the young men's relationships in school appears to be complex. Their various stories reveal that these six young African-American men did not have the same kinds of friendships. What they all had in common, however, was their desire for connected and trusting relationships. They all had acquaintances at school with whom they connected, but only Marcus and Rashaud were able to feel connected to some friends at school. The stories about their relationships with school suggest a somber and depressing picture of young men committed to acquiring the high school diploma, who tried to sustain themselves through school by having strong relationships, yet whose relationships in the end seemed tenuous.

Developing an understanding of the meanings of schooling that interwove their relationships in and out of school is the focus of Chapter 8. Before I turn to these analyses, I consider the various racialized and gendered images of themselves and others in and out of school that they talked about. These images provide us with glimpses of how they viewed themselves and reveal how meanings of their social identities were relationally constituted and negotiated.

7

Images of Self, Images of Others

In the previous chapter, I argued that for the six young African-American men in my study, *connection* was important in the relationships they developed. Such relationships involved respect, trust, and opportunities to share thoughts, feelings, and concerns with an African-American person. In the postfield analysis, I began to learn that although they viewed school as being about getting the high school diploma, it was also about negotiating the meaning of schooling, the diploma, relationships, and identities. There were aspects of schooling they used to shape their identity and there were also aspects of schooling that shaped their identities. For example, acquiring the diploma was integral to the people they wanted to be and how they wanted to be viewed by others. But the meaning of the high school diploma in their lives was not solely of their making. It was connected to larger institutional structures and practices inside and outside of school. These institutional structures and practices intermingled with their social practices as the young men gave meaning to the high school diploma and encountered relationships in school. As they continued to go to school, they continued to interact with teachers and peers, and continued to develop their social identities.

In this identity formation process, there were certain images that seemed to become central to them as they developed their sense of their social selves. Some of the most significant images they talked about were the racial images that students held of themselves and of each other. These images did not just have to do with the way individual people acted and talked. They were also about connections to students through peer groups that were formed on the basis of racial group membership. It was no accident that students separated themselves into racial peer groups. This mirrored divisions permeating the larger society in which schools become one of the sites where racial divisions may be made. Such racial divisions are formed through a process that Omi and Winant (1986) argued is a "racial formation process by which social, economic and political forces determine the content and importance of racial categories, and by which they are in turn shaped by racial meanings" (p. 61). Schools became a place where racial categories were made and given meaning, where these young men tried out their racial identities, and where they observed others trying out identities. Although many of the significant images they talked about were racial images, these images were simultaneously infused with social class and gender meanings. For example, they often accused other African-American students of "acting white," and in describing what this meant, it was clear that they were talking about their images of white middle-class, not working-class, students. Through these images, they were also implicitly defining "acting black." And when they suggested someone "acted white," they did not simultaneously suggest the person transgressed gendered boundaries.

The frame for this chapter is developed through considering the notion of *images* in their lives. This notion of images includes the ways in which they wanted me and others to see them, the ways they saw others, and the meanings and ideas they gave to these images. These images did not define their social identities; rather, they were a dimension of their social identities. Clearly, their identities did not emerge within a vacuum, but were relationally situated within a hierarchical social arrangement shaped by access to race, class and gender, power, and privilege. Here, their identities came into being and were giving meaning through their images of experiences with and about others. It seemed that their identities were comprised of many images developed in different contexts through different relationships over time. Through focusing on their images of themselves and of others in their lives, I also learned how these images were infused with values, beliefs, ideas, and behaviors.

Much of the chapter focuses on racial images because these were the images we spent the most time discussing and the images that seemed most significant to their emerging social identities. Toward the end of the chapter, I discuss Marcus's and Jeff's racialized gendered images of young women, and consider these images in the context of their own emerging masculine identities. I came to see how these various images seemed to intermingle their sense of who they were and who they wanted to be, and who they thought others were and wanted to be. This chapter focuses primarily on the schooling context as a site where they produced and discussed the images of others and themselves. Among the various images I discuss are those associated with "acting white." It is these images that I discuss first, followed by race–gender images.

"ACTING WHITE" AND IDENTITY FORMATION

As noted in the previous chapter, connections with people was a common theme across conversations with the young men. African-American people were important to these young men's sustenance, to their ongoing survival, and also to the building of their identity. Interwoven with these relationships were also the hegemonic and oppositional images, meanings, and symbols they believed African-American men should or should not embrace. Studies about the intermingling of aspects of hegemonic culture in the lives of racial minorities (Fine, 1991; Mac an Ghaill, 1988; MacLeod, 1995; Solomon, 1992; Weis, 1985), girls (Grant, 1992; McRobbie, 1991), and white, working-class students (Connell, Ashenden, Kessler, & Dowsett, 1982; Weis, 1990; Willis, 1977) all suggest simultaneous strains of resistance and accommodation as ways in which students respond to and make sense of their schooling experiences. Across the literature about racial and ethnic minorities' experiences, notions of resistance or accommodation, or both, have been addressed through exploring the racial images and identities embraced and rejected by African-American students.

In relation to African-American students, Fordham and Ogbu (1986) and Ogbu (1991, 1992) have addressed a theme of "acting white" as significant to understanding African-American students' experiences of schooling, particularly to understanding the relationships between their emerging social identities and academic achievement. They argued that the fear of being accused of "acting white" makes many African-American students avoid adopting certain attitudes and behaviors. For example, they avoid spending time on schoolwork because they and their peers consider such behaviors as "acting white." They further maintained that the problem of African-American students not performing at their potential in part is

> . . . because white Americans traditionally refused to acknowledge that black Americans are capable of intellectual achievement, and partly because black Americans subsequently began to doubt their own intellectual ability, began to define academic success as white people's prerogative, and began to discourage their peers, perhaps unconsciously, from emulating white people in academic striving. . . . Because of the ambivalence, affective dissonance, and social pressures, many black students who are academically able do not put forth the necessary effort and perseverance in their schoolwork, and, consequently do poorly in school. (Fordham & Ogbu, 1986, p. 177)

Fordham and Ogbu develop their frame through arguing that two factors are central to understanding the expressive dimension of minority–majority group

relations: oppositional social identity and an oppositional cultural frame of reference. "Acting white," according to the students in their study, included the following dimensions: speaking standard English, listening to white music on radio
stations, working hard to get good grades, getting good grades in school, listening
to classical music, and being on time. Those students who chose to pursue academic success were perceived by their peers as acting "white" and therefore not
truly black (Fordham & Ogbu, 1986; Weis, 1985). Ogbu (1991) has suggested that
a strategy of "cultural inversion" sees African-Americans regarding "certain
forms of behavior, events, symbols and meanings as not appropriate for them
because they are characteristics of white Americans; at the same time, however,
blacks claim other forms of behavior, events, symbols and meanings as appropriate from them because these are not part of white culture" (p. 441).

This work is further developed by Fordham (1996) as she captures the contradictions and dilemmas of "humanness" in her ethnographic study of the experiences of African-American high school students. In this portrait, she
problematizes notions of academic success for African-Americans in high school
and examines the relationship between students' academic motivation and the role
of schooling in the making of social inequality. Fordham posits two competing
versions of success: to play along and succeed without bringing into questions
dominate cultural practices or to disengage and resist being tainted by the cultural
of school success. Her work carefully unravels the life experiences of African-
American male and female students in school through two categories of student
responses to school: the "high achievers" and the "low achievers." Fordham
argues that high-achieving students resist "two competing yet similarly debilitat-
ing forces: the dominant society's minimal expectations for Black students and
their classmates' internal policing for group solidarity" (pp. 235–236).

The development of a framework for thinking about strategies such as "acting
white" that African-American students may use to cope in schools is helpful to my
study. Although I do not seek to explain the connection between coping strategies
and academic success of African-American students in schools, I do want to
examine and discuss the ways in which these six young African-American men
came to see themselves as African-American men and as students, and how
images of themselves and others were significant in that process. Various studies
about the coping strategies of African-American students provide a basis for
understanding the complex nature of schooling for African-Americans. These
works also suggests that it is not solely the institution of school that promotes success or failure. The ways in which students respond is also an important influence.

"Acting white" became a significant topic of conversation as I asked these
young men to talk about their time outside of classrooms. The topic was not one I
initially intended to explore. Rather, conversations about "acting white" emerged
spontaneously from all the participants of the study. For example, during a conversation about friends at school, Zakeev used the notion of "acting white" to talk
about an African-American, middle-class young woman who attended his school.

He said, "She tries to act white, but that's not how the white people act. She acts different, she stand out, and she's black. But she's farther than the white, she wants to be white, but she's farther than them. It's like she's more preppie than they are." Here, Zakeev argued that a young woman he knew embraced certain ways of being that were exaggerated behaviors and attitudes that he connected with white culture in the United States. As each of the young men raised the topic of "acting white," I began to explore their differences and similarities in the meanings they developed, and why this notion was important for them to talk about.

In talking about schooling, I asked them all to tell me who they hung out with, what they talked about, and where they hung out. As noted in the previous chapter, four of the six young men responded that they hung out with a group of African-American students. The two middle-class young men, Shawn and Rashaud, seemed to stress the fact that they hung out with African-American peers more so than the other young men. These two hung out only with African-American peers and congregated in a particular place in the school they called "the ghetto." Dwayne and Marcus, too, hung out with different but exclusively African-American peer groups that congregated in various places within their school. For Jeff and Zakeev, as discussed in the previous chapter, there did not seem a distinct pattern of meeting people in a particular place in school.

Hanging out with particular groups of students, mostly fellow African-American students, did not seem an accident. As Winant (1994) argued, "Race provides a key cultural marker, a central signifier, in the reproduction and expression of identity, collectivity, language, and agency itself. Race generates an "inside" and an "outside" of society, and mediates the unclear border between these zones" (p. 30). Race seemed such a cultural marker in the lives of these young men. In this chapter, I discuss how they used the groups and interactions and language within these groups to develop and validate the images of their social identities. The groups were also influential in the emerging behaviors and ideas that became significant to their identities as African-American young men. It is to the various groups they identified with that I now turn.

"Don't Hate me Because I Speak More Proper"

I begin by exploring some of the images of African-American and white identities that were part of Jeff's experiences at school. Racialized images and interpretations were significant to the formation of his emerging identity. I especially focus on Jeff because he was the only young man who acknowledged that other students accused him of "acting white." These students were the peers from his old school, Central. In the context of Jeff being accused of "acting white," he admitted that he would "change" his "culture" "to get ahead in life." However, he also suggested in spite of changing his "culture," "getting ahead" would not be easy because of structural barriers that lay in his path because he was an African-American.

"Acting white" to Jeff was seemingly part of his strategy to get ahead. He believed that he had to act and talk in certain ways in order to be successful. At one time he said to me:

> . . . if it takes me to change my culture, to change my speech, to get ahead in life, to get that big house with that white picket fence, I'm going to do it. As long as it ain't hurting nobody else. Don't hate me because I speak more proper, be happy for me, and in return, I'll be there for you. A lot of people don't want to see you achieve.

Jeff here presented an idealized symbol of success, a house with a "white picket fence." He believed a recipe for success included embracing talk and ways of being that he associated with white people. "Acting white" for Jeff was certainly about achievement. He saw himself as having to change his culture and be a different kind of person "to get ahead in life." At the same time, he recognized that his actions clearly evoked conflict. "Don't hate me," he said, as though he knew that his actions clearly represented a political act, one that may not be approved of by his peers.

But for Jeff, who spent 2 years as a sophomore and struggled to get good grades, "acting white" was not just about getting good grades. "Acting white" in itself was synonymous with being a "proper person." His commitment to believing in the importance of "acting white" in order to get ahead seemed to intensify after his entanglement with the criminal justice system and as he moved to the private school. But Jeff was not always like this. At one point he said that "I was brought up where I used to be around a whole lot of black people and stuff, but [now] I more relate . . . to more proper people. And at Central, you find people like with slang and stuff. I used to talk slang a lot."

Being "proper" was important to Jeff. This was not just about the way he talked or dressed. It was also his connectedness to symbols of "whiteness" such as school, or *being* with white people. Ironically, although Jeff may have attended a predominantly white elementary school, his friends were predominantly African-American, not white, throughout elementary and middle school. And it was during this time he acknowledged that he "used to talk slang a lot." He had a group of friends with whom he used to spend most of his recreational time.

> *Jeff:*   . . . we used to do everything together, they used to come over and spend the night. There wouldn't be a day that I wouldn't go over to their house, go to movies and stuff.
>
> *JP:*   Was it like a group of three or four people?
>
> *Jeff:*   Oh yeah, it was two brothers, and two others.
>
> *JP:*   About four people then.
>
> *Jeff:*   About four or five of us.
>
> *JP:*   And were they black or white?
>
> *Jeff:*   Black.

But Jeff no longer was connected to these friends. In fact, he had few friends. He said that he was not "hurting anybody" by talking "proper." But many of his peers were not enamored with Jeff's ways of being and talking. In fact, Jeff said that a lot of people at school said things such as "Jeff want to be white. He don't have so many friends." It seemed that Jeff's way of being had cost him his friendships with his African-American peers. I asked Jeff to elaborate on why some of his peers called him a "sellout."

JP: People say you're a sellout because of . . .?

Jeff: How I act, who I go with, who I associate with, how I talk. I like to talk with my hands.

JP: Is that a white thing to do?

Jeff: I don't know, but a lot of people are like "Why are you using your hands?" That's another reason why I like Allerton Christian, 'cause you get a lot of more proper kids there.

JP: Proper in what way?

Jeff: Like you know, they talk more proper, and you can kind of relate to them.

JP: You have to break it down for me now, what does it mean to talk proper?

Jeff: Basically, not to talk in slang. Like "hello" instead of "yo." I might joke around with my friends and stuff and say "watsup." (Inaudible.)

JP: What about dressing?

Jeff: You can say I dress kind of preppie.

JP: Is it a conscious effort for you, or does it seem natural?

Jeff: It seem natural, regardless. I used to say to a lot of black people too, "Oh you just want to be white," and all this other stuff.

JP: You used to say that?

Jeff: Well I used to think that. It's just a process, you know. . . . Another reason, 'cause I talk too properly, they say "Oh you just want to be a white person." . . . You might get a few of them, like "you act white" and stuff, they don't want to be involved with you.

It is interesting that Jeff's move to a predominantly, and almost exclusively, white private school saw him feeling more able to "relate" to his peers. Most significant is his account of the stance of "acting white" as "just a process." While he admitted that he used to say to some African-American peers, "Oh, you just wanna be white," he later began to live out the kind of identity he criticized.

The question becomes, how do we account for such a change? To argue that the change in schools or his entanglement with the criminal justice system were the influences upon Jeff's new ways of being, would be to discount his prior experiences in school and in the larger society where he had constantly learned about "proper" people. As he grew up, he learned about the value placed on symbols he associated with white people. His need and desire to appropriate the symbols has to be understood within a context of what Jeff thought he needed to do and be in relation to the dominant symbols and images of "whiteness." In the meantime, the friends he grew up with became disconnected from him, and it was students with whom he shared no personal history, but a common way of "acting," that he chose to associate with. Jeff suggested that the way he talked, acted, and dressed might have been the reason some African-American students disassociated themselves from him.

Although Jeff may have acted in ways that Ogbu (1991) may view as "choosing academic success" (p. 186), he was not a high-achieving student. In fact, academic achievement as such was not a crucial issue in his life. He was mostly in the low-track classes, and he did not achieve high grades at either school. And, until the time he moved to the private school, he was very disenchanted with school and disengaged from classroom work. In fact, while Jeff seemed to resist the pressures of his African-American peers to conform to certain behaviors and ways of talking that they sanctioned, he simultaneously was not an academically successful student. The cost for Jeff of "acting white" was the loss of his boyhood friends and connections.

Frankenberg's (1993) study of the social construction of "whiteness" among white women is helpful here as I unravel the complexity of Jeff's construction of his identity. She provides us with her conception of whiteness, where she argues that,

> First, whiteness is a location of structural advantage, or race privilege. Second, it is a "standpoint," a place from which white people look at ourselves and others, and at our society. Third, "whiteness" refers to a set of cultural practices that are usually unmarked and unnamed. (p. 1)

These three aspects of the social construction of whiteness are helpful to thinking about these young African-American men's constructions of "acting white." Most importantly, Jeff may have taken on certain cultural practices that are associated with white people, but his social location was not a position of structural advantage. Jeff may have been able to name and embrace certain cultural practices associated with "whiteness," but at the same time he was penalized through institutional and cultural practices because of the location of African-Americans in a race hierarchy in the United States.

For Jeff, much of his success was about how things *looked*. He wanted to dress certain ways, talk certain ways, and to go the "proper" school. For Jeff, acting these ways was important to him. To an observer this might not have seemed to add up to much. But for Jeff, his ways of being seemed important enough for him to continue to act, dress, and talk in ways considered as "acting white." Ironically, at one point he told me that "what white people do is they like to keep the white race, their brother man up there out of the level of poverty." Here, he seemed to suggest that it is white people who create the conditions to protect white people from falling into poverty, and the same privilege is not afforded African-American people. Thus, the fact that Jeff believed it was harder for an African-American person to get ahead than a white person and that he acknowledged being "proper" was related to "whiteness" suggests that he recognized some barriers ahead of him. Consequently, despite Jeff's "acting white," and resisting and rejecting connections with his friends and peers, his identity reflected a hegemonic culture and simultaneously acknowledged structural inequality.

Forging an identity, particularly within the context of schools that did not always represent their needs or interests as African-American students, undoubtedly heightened these young men's sense of their own racial identity and that of others. Being at Allerton Christian School (ACS), with an African-American population of 3 percent, must have further heightened Jeff's sense of his own racial identity, given the school had a almost exclusively white student body. I next turn to how the other five young men rejected symbols and images that were "white" and embraced those that they considered African-American as they shaped their sense of social identity.

"Just Trying to Be Someone You're Not"

Rashaud and Shawn, the two middle-class students, provided more detailed accounts about the racial identities and group formations at school than did the other young men in the study. They each told me that all students at Cedarville High hung out in a particular area of the school. They identified two main groups at school, namely the "preppies" and the African-American students. Rashaud said in one section, "the commons," there were "your little white kids and some of the wannabes." A "wannabe" was someone who "wanna be accepted by whites," he said. Some of these "wannabes" were African-American, while others were Asian or Latino. "I don't want to say sellout, oreo, Uncle Tom, it's not like that deep. You have your kids who don't want to hang out with us," he said. In his section, which he called "the ghetto," there were mostly African-American students, joined by a few Latino students. At the same time, he suggested that those students who did not hang out in the "ghetto" were not quite a "sellout." "It's not that deep," he said. Perhaps he was alluding to the fact that their actions do not represent an overt political act of rejecting African-American culture.

To Rashaud, "acting white" meant the way students "act, talk, dress." And while these ways of talking, acting, and dressing were about racial identities, they were also about their gendered identities in that the ways in which we dress, talk, and act reflect and make gender divisions. But the notion of "acting white," to Rashaud, overtly signified racial meanings. In addition to talking, acting, and dressing in particular ways, "acting white" to Rashaud also meant "acting fake....When I say someone's acting white, they are not in touch with being black." I asked Rashaud to elaborate on his idea that some African-American youth are not "in touch" with being black:

> Rashaud: They would rather disregard seeing, going to see *Malcolm X*, or learning about heritage, instead going to see *Home Alone* or something stupid like

that. Or to go, they would rather support something like, what's a good analogy or metaphor? They would rather support a country club which is predominantly white, which they couldn't possibly get into . . . instead of going to the Black Family and Child Institute in Allerton, and donating energy and effort.

JP: And getting good grades, is that anything to do with acting white?

Rashaud: No, that's acting smart.

Interestingly, Rashaud viewed getting good grades not as "acting white" but as "acting smart," whereas Jeff viewed getting ahead and "acting white" as being "proper." Jeff's conception of "acting white" was much broader than Rashaud's view. The fact that Rashaud attended a middle-class school and was a successful student with more options available to him than Jeff while Jeff, had not been an academically successful student, could in part explain their different perspectives. Further, Rashaud's view of students who "acted white" involved not only students who did not actively associate with black students at school. It also involved being connected with the larger black community through viewing certain movies about African-Americans, learning about African-American "heritage," and getting involved in community issues.

Maintaining a sense of *connection* was important to Rashaud, and his association with other African-Americans seemed to help him preserve and develop his sense of racial identity. This sense of connection was also important to Shawn, who attended the same school as Rashaud. About the African-American students who "acted white," Shawn said such ways of being "offend a lot of black people, you know, they [the students who "act white"] are ashamed to be black." He also hung around in the same area of the school as Rashaud, and admitted he "criticizes black students who hang around in the commons." He explained further, "It's not that I hate white people. It's just that I have more fun around black people." But Shawn had not always hung around the "ghetto" area. When he first arrived in the school in Grade 10 he used to frequent the "commons" area of the school.

I used to hang around there often, and one of the black friends said "Why are you hanging around here? Don't you know they're racists over here and everything?" And ever since that day, I've been hanging around [black students]. . . . But even in my sophomore year, I never really did associate with that many people. I was a new kid in my sophomore year. I was trying to find out where I fit in anyway.

Here, Shawn suggested he accepted his fellow student's remarks and recognized the need to distance himself from racism. He thus began to associate with students who hung around the "ghetto" area. It may be the need to distance himself from racism, rather than specifically wanting to connect with African-American students, that saw him frequenting the "ghetto" area of the school. Nevertheless, the fellow student's comments suggest that the African-American students at his school worked to maintain a culture of solidarity among themselves. This was in part accomplished by developing an oppositional stance in relation to the white students at the school.

Essentially to Shawn, "acting white" meant "just trying to be someone you're not." It also meant whom you associated with. "I mean if you are black, and always hanging around with white students, you never come over and hang around with the black students, don't speak to any of the black students"—such behavior was problematic to him. But division between black and white students was not only maintained through black students consistently being connected with each other through frequenting a particular part of the school building. It was also maintained through collective responses to white students. For example, Shawn told me that "the blacks in our area, they always tease the white people, and a white person walks past and they are scared. And they are not going to hurt them. One guy was leaving his school, and he saw us, and he started locking his car doors." Such collective actions by African-American students, combined with the responses by white students, served to reinforce the separation of African-American and white students and created tension between them. The actions also served to reinforce connection and to consolidate social group membership among the African-American students. It is perhaps the racial association aspect of their social group that was the most consistent aspect of "acting white" that runs through the conversations of Rashaud and Shawn.

Although Rashaud was extremely successful at school, he simultaneously seemed to reject aspects of "acting white." He was on the honor roll and in almost exclusively "advanced-track" courses, yet outside of class he hung around exclusively with African-American students and saw his connections with the group as important to his social identity. In Rashaud's eyes, academic achievement did not seem to be part of his sense of "acting white." In fact, the other young men in the study also did not see achieving good grades as part of "acting white." This was not surprising in relation to Rashaud or Shawn, as many students at their school were high achievers, with almost 90 percent of the students going on to college.

Interestingly, Rashaud criticized the students who "acted white," yet he also said he adopted a particular way of talking that consciously was not slang.

> I don't talk like, "yeah you," and all that. I try to use good English wherever I can. I don't smoke, I don't do drugs, I don't shoot dope, I'm not running in the streets all the time. And I . . . don't drink at parties and I don't boom music till all times of the night.

So, while Rashaud criticized others for "acting white," part of his own sense of his identity was to avoid involvement with drugs or alcohol, and not play "loud music till all times of the night." As noted earlier, Rashaud saw himself as a "role model," and how he acted as a teenager was important to that image. This image also included speaking "good English." In contrast, Zakeev and Marcus considered this kind of talk as "acting white." Their differing meanings of "acting white" could have been dynamically shaped however, by social class experiences.

In other regards, Marcus's and Zakeev's meanings of "acting white" did not differ dramatically from Shawn's or Rashaud's meanings. As noted earlier, Zakeev spoke of a young African-American woman who "acted white," and he suggested her affect was integral to her "acting white." "Acting white" to Marcus was "how you talk. It's just how white folks say stuff. It sounds crazy." Zakeev said that acting white to him meant, "The meaning is, what people say, white people are corny....They're like stuck up, like they are better than everybody else. . . . And there are some black people that way." Zakeev adamantly argued that despite the predominance of "white" ways of being at his school, he would not change the way he spoke.

> Zakeev: White people to me they talk . . . they try to keep proper English, proper that, proper this . . . everything's right, everything's perfect. They don't like to be wrong.
>
> JP: Do you have to change the way you speak when you speak to white people?
>
> Zakeev: I won't. I refuse.
>
> JP: Why's that?
>
> Zakeev: Because, I don't have to. I shouldn't have to, I'm American and that's the way I talk, you accept it or you don't.

Zakeev vehemently argued that he was not going to change his speech style. This conversation was not about African-American people who "acted white," it was a criticism of his sense of white people. Zakeev's criticism differed from Rashaud's, who did not criticize white people, but African-Americans who, in his mind, "acted white."

Marcus also said there were a number of students who "act white" at school. An example of the ways in which language use represented an embrace of racial identity became apparent in one of our conversations:

> JP: And the other thing I wanted to find out from you, being cool. Do you often say, "he's a cool dude."
>
> Marcus: Not cool. (Laughs.)
>
> JP: Is that a white word?
>
> Marcus: Yeah, that's what they say, "cool dude."
>
> JP: So what do you say?
>
> Marcus: Fresh, you don't put dude on it, that's the thing. (Laughs.) That's how you can distinguish a white person from a black person, because they always put their little words in there. Like dude, after a certain word. Like we say hard or something like that. Fresh. Can say something like "cool daddy," or something like that.
>
> JP: What's that mean?
>
> Marcus: It's just smooth.

> JP: What do you have to be to be smooth?
> Marcus: It's just a figure of speech, it's not really nothing, a lot of people try to be hard, 'cause wearing all their little stuff, pimpin' down the hallway.
> JP: What's pimpin'?
> Marcus: It's a walk, a certain walk.

This conversation reveals how use of language enabled Marcus to distinguish between "white" and "black" ways of being. He clearly suggested that the difference was not just a matter of how a person pronounced words. It was the very meanings associated with words that were significant. Like Shawn and Rashaud, "acting white" also involved "who you hang around with all the time." He suggested that his brother was someone who "flat out, he just act white. . . . You know, he'd do for his white friends all the time before he would do for his kinfolk." Marcus was very angry with the way his brother acted. Such a person to Marcus was a "sellout":

> To me it's people going against their own race. Like turning over their whole life to please the white man. Basically I have one at work. . . . When I started saying something black power stuff, and everybody hitting on it, Malcolm X stuff and all that. He don't want to hear about it. He blow me off.

This example of the African-American co-worker provided a glimpse of how work, besides school, became another context where Marcus learned about his relationship to white people and constructed his meanings of white culture. "Acting white" to Marcus was about relationships with white people. It was also about relationships with African-American people whom he suggested "acted white." So, his stance was constructed in relation to both white culture and the way it was manifested in the lives of white people and some black people. Marcus, like Rashaud, valued conversations about African-American culture and saw such conversations as significant in his relationships with other African-Americans.

Marcus said that the social context was influential in what people learned about culture, and in associated ways of being and talking. At one point he said that,

> Basically, I think it's because it's the environment that you grew up in too. Because if you going live in a white neighborhood, you're going to act that way just to please them. . . . To me it's people going against their own race. Like turning over their whole life to please the white man.

Here, he situated his notion of racialized ways of being through power relations between white and black people. He saw people who "acted white" as "going against their own race." It seemed that Marcus's conception of African-American ways of being was important to him because the ways of being in his mind stood *in opposition* to white ways of being. But the image is not a simple dichotomous one; it is relational. Marcus, like Rashaud, Shawn, and Zakeev, constructed the image of being African-American in relation to white people and in relation to African-American people whom in his mind "acted white."

In contrast to Marcus and the others I've discussed so far, conversations about the way people acted and the infusion of racial identity in talk and ways of dressing did not seem significant issues to Dwayne. In a sense, Dwayne's concern was less about trying to be "proper," "being someone you're not," or juggling tensions in order to get ahead. The issue for Dwayne, and his peers from Detroit, was "survival." Part of that survival, when he lived in Detroit, was living out social practices that his "brothers" collectively sanctioned. As he said at one point, "It takes street smartness, knowing the game, knowing how to survive." So, for Dwayne and his peers, issues of getting ahead were seen differently than they were for the other five young men. Dwayne said of his friends in Detroit:

> They feel there is no way out, all the odds is against them. That's what the world had gave them, you know there's nobody in the family, they look at the other people and they want to be like them . . . they want to make money, they want to be on top.

Dwayne talked at length about why and how people around him in inner-city Detroit got involved in crime as a vehicle to material wealth and status. For him, the battle to forge an image to his liking was not predominated by a tension between living out white or black culture, but by a tension between embracing street culture or not. Not to be involved with street culture meant not being involved in crime and staying out of jail. And while Dwayne lived in Allerton for a time, before running away from his foster home and returning to Detroit in February 1993, the issues relating to "acting white" did not seem of significance to him. Nonetheless, he told me that all his friends at Central were African-American, and he did not interact with white students at school.

Among the various interpretations of "acting white," it became clear that for the two middle-class young men the issue was about who they associated with, how people dressed and acted, and the beliefs and attitudes they held about the African-American community. For Marcus and Zakeev, the form of talk was significant too. Among these four young men, their critique of "acting white" was not just about a response to other African-Americans in school who "acted white." It was about how they wanted to represent themselves as African-Americans. "Acting white" also had to do with the images they themselves tried to live out as African-Americans. For Rashaud and Marcus it was also a criticism of white cultural practices.

These four young men—Marcus, Rashaud, Shawn, and Zakeev—tried to live out an image that was different from Jeff's or Dwayne's. All the while, the six were *all* committed to being successful in school. So what were the images that they embraced as African-Americans? While Jeff seemed to embrace a "white" image, did the other young men embrace a common image of being an African-American? Or, in the case of the four who opposed the "acting white" image, was it solely their opposition to "acting white" that they shared? Exploring such questions is helpful to understanding the images of African-Americans that these young men tried to build and negotiate for themselves as African-American men. Common among five of the young men, with the exception of Jeff, was their desire to challenge forms of racism or racist images through various forms of talk and actions. In order to consider the ways in which they came to see themselves as African-American men, I will now turn to the ideas they shared with me about their images of African-Americans.

IMAGES OF AFRICAN AMERICANS

Talk about images the young men embraced, or the images of "acting white" they rejected or opposed, was simultaneously talk about how they saw themselves as African-American men. As noted, four of the young men rejected certain ways of acting or talking, suggesting that particular "white" ways of being were inappropriate for African-American men. What was most important to four of the young men was being seen by others as associating with African-Americans. But this was not the only aspect of their image of themselves that they saw as significant. Marcus, Rashaud, and Dwayne saw challenging dominant images of African-Americans as important. Marcus believed that knowledge of African-American history and experiences was significant, and Rashaud believed that promoting himself as an "outstanding" student was significant, while Dwayne did not want to be classified as a "statistic." It is to these various images that I now turn.

Self As "Outstanding" African-American

Rashaud provided the most detailed account of various images of African-American people. He suggested a range of images of African-American identities. His various images included "militant," "mainstream," "outspoken but civil," "on-the-corner hanging-out type," and finally "the outstanding." He offered these categories in response to a question I posed to him:

> *JP:* People say the African-American community is diverse; how would you describe that diversity within the African-American community?
>
> *Rashaud:* You have strong militant, pro-black African-Americans, and then you have your mainstream African-Americans. You have your outspoken but still civil African Americans, you have your let's see, on-the-corner hanging-out type African Americans. Then you have the others—and others can classify as any type of person, anyone. . . .
>
> *JP:* Where would you put yourself in those groupings?
>
> *Rashaud:* I think there is other, then is outstanding. I probably would put myself with outstanding, just because, you don't try to be conservative, but you try to

be outspoken but you don't try to be militant, but you do try to put your
point across. But you don't try to be hanging out at the corner.

Rashaud's category of "outstanding" African-American represented an image
of someone who was *not* part of the other categories. It was someone who spoke
out but was not "militant." It was also someone who was not "hanging-out at the
corner." He elaborated on his position further by arguing that "I'm not very Afrocentric, but I do stand behind what my people say." Rashaud's images of African-Americans possibly captured both hegemonic images of African-Americans
and images shaped by responses from the African-American community as they
have challenged oppression and exploitation, and as some embraced white cultural practices. He seemed to weigh all these images in his mind and in relation to
these images, carve out an image for himself that drew from the array of images.
He described the image of himself as "outstanding." Through creating this image
he did not ignore his racial identity; he believed that the image of himself as an
"outstanding" student might challenge white conceptions about African-Americans and be a source of encouragement for African-Americans.

This complex image that he painted of himself perhaps reveals how identities
are situated and negotiated in context. In this case, the context included his family,
where the idea of "role models" was strong, and the predominantly white, middle-class school and neighborhood in which he was a racial minority. In Chapter
4, I noted that he wanted to be a "role model" to his family and peers to encourage
others to follow his successes. He was also committed to challenging hegemonic
images about African-American young men who drop out of school, who are
unemployed, or who are involved in the drug culture. Ironically, he used dominant
notions of school success to develop this image of "outstanding." His relationships with African-Americans and whites in his neighborhood and beyond influenced the ways in which he lived out his identity. Rashaud's sense of the image he
tried to live out as an African-American was different from Marcus's.

African-American Identity As Knowledge

Marcus, too, spoke about different ways of being among African-American students. Possibly, he could fall within Rashaud's category of "strong militant,
pro-black African-American." It seemed that for Marcus, being an African-American was not only about the way he talked, or acted, it was also "educating" himself about the history and experiences of African-Americans in the United States.
The image of the young African-American man he portrayed was not one shaped
solely by actions, behaviors, or way of talking. It was also shaped by displaying
knowledge about African-American experiences. *What* African-Americans talked
about was significant to him. For example, Marcus said that his commitment to
talking about the plight of African-Americans was well known among his peers at
school. At one point he told me that,

Everybody at school know I'm into that and they respect me for that. They always like to hear me talk about this stuff. I ain't got no problem talking about the stuff. That's what I'm trying to do, I'm trying to educate myself, so I can educate my other brothers and sisters.

Marcus was clear about how he wanted to be seen by others and how he earned their "respect."

If you can't accept me for who I am, I've got to dress up, look all pretty for you, you can forget it man. It ain't all about that, accept me for who I am. Not for who you want me to be.

Being an African-American also meant more than understanding the plight of African-Americans; it also meant educating each other. Just as Zakeev argued he was not going to change the way he talked, Marcus argued that he was going to dress and be who he wanted to be. But what was it that Marcus wanted to be accepted as? We are offered a glimpse of how he interacted with other students at school as he told me how he confronted students who wore Malcolm X T-shirts yet really did not understand what Malcolm X represents:

I say, "How can you wear something when you don't know what it stands for?" That's how I feel. I say, "How can you all wear that and go against what he says." One of the things he was saying was not to fight your other brothers. You know, you don't see him going around fighting his black brothers, he was going against the white man, he wasn't going against his own people. I say, "So how can you wear his shirt, and don't go by what he stands for?" That don't make no sense. I say to everybody, I say "Do you know what he stands for?" If they wear Martin Luther King [T-shirt] I say, "Do you know what he stands for?" 'Cause people don't really get down, they give you them little books and, um, church and all this stuff, but they don't really get deep down into the deep stuff about it. It just tells the basic stuff when he was on TV and all, it don't tell his life. Away from home, away from the media. People just read the basic, Malcolm X powerful, power to the people, just like you've got Black History month, every year.

The interaction Marcus described illuminates how he interacted with other African-Americans about his racial identity. For Marcus, it appears that wearing symbols of racial identity seemed inadequate. To him, it was important to understand the texture of Malcolm X's life, not just today's revisionist versions. He maintained that he was vocal with students about the importance of knowing African-American history, and he argued that efforts must be made to read and understand more than "the basics," such as "power to the people." He wanted his peers to understand how the ideas Malcolm X articulated are important in building the unity of African-American people. At the same time, it was only through the act of Marcus sharing his knowledge about African-Americans that he was able to validate his image among his African-American peers.

Challengers of Dominant Images of African-Americans

Understanding power relations between black and white people was certainly a strand of Marcus's sense of what it meant to be an African-American person. He asked the question, "How can a black person be racist? We don't have nothin' to be racist about. Basically, they [white people] got the power, we don't." His frustration was not just about power per se. It was also about how power was wielded. For example, at one point he talked about the images of African-Americans that dominate the media:

> Basically what I want white folks to know is don't treat me like . . . a person that just do their labor, that you can just boss around. We're people too, we're not just animals. And that's how they try to put black folks, like in the news, in the media. . . . You know how they say black folks are all bad. You know they always have something in the Detroit news . . . You don't see us going down and getting that stuff [drugs]. And if they really wanted it to stop coming into the United States, they can. Really, the government, has something to do with it. I think they are the one's that are doing the stuff. You *know* they doing the stuff.

Although Marcus challenged the images of African-Americans dominating the media, he also argued that relationships between black and white people are about the economic exploitation of African-Americans in the economy. Further, Marcus maintained that the current drug problem in the United States. is not solely the problem of the African-American community, and that white people were significantly involved in the drug industry, yet African-American people were portrayed as "bad." Dwayne argued a similar position in relation to the control of the drug industry by white people:

> My opinion, you know, I don't think it is right, because when you look down, you don't see no black man flying no plane over here, across the United States over to here. . . . I ain't got nothing against whites, ain't saying all whites is all wrong, you know, it themselves they're making it. They rich. Then it comes down to the little pushers on the streets, and they goin' to do what they got to do.

But these are the only two who developed economic analyses about white domination to the conversation. It was the images imbued with ideas about economic oppression that they wanted to challenge through the images they embraced and the identities they constructed.

In a previous chapter, I noted that Dwayne was trying to be a different kind of person than he was in Detroit. This was difficult for him. His experiences also influenced the images that he had of white people:

> I guess my experience, is like I say, kind of hard. Like we going in places like in the country when I went to placement, and things like that, mostly the majority of peo-

ple are white people around, I'm not prejudice at all, I don't know how they just treat people like that. We all can breathe or whatever, we got the same mouth . . . just a different color. . . .True, the United States of America was given to us, and they locked us up. As far as being, you know around white people, they plant stuff, doing those sneaky little thangs, and they just stood there laughin' in your face, to keep nigger boy down, or whatever.

Here, Dwayne is referring to his experiences in a juvenile home where many of those in authority were white people. These were the images that he carried of white people. Embedded in these images is the image of African-American people as oppressed.

Challenging racial dominance was also important to Zakeev. He noted that there was racial discrimination in the United States, and he wanted to do something about it. He said, ". . . there is a lot of black people standing up and saying discrimination is a problem. And I want to be one of those black people that stand up and says 'Hey there is a problem'." Zakeev's sense of racial identity and the importance of race in certain contexts varied and changed according to the situation. He told me that he really didn't always think about race. Yet when I began asking him about relationships between black and white students, particularly black men and white women, he said, "In a way I don't like it that way, deep down inside of me, like no, like ugh. I don't know . . . but after a while I try to accept it." Zakeev here revealed how he was resistant to the idea of interracial relationships but was trying to be more accepting of such relationships. Race was interwoven through the images and values and beliefs that Zakeev held. Sometimes he said that he didn't think about racial issues much, while other times he said that he wanted to fight against racial discrimination, such as the Eurocentric curriculum in his history classroom. In the final analysis, Zakeev, as an African-American, embraced certain values, ideas, and beliefs that he associated with the African-American community and his stance was not much different from that of either Marcus or Dwayne. "Knowing your roots" was important to Zakeev. At one point he said, "If you live by them [whites] a lot, you won't know your roots very much." His statement reveals his understanding of how he and others learn about culture through association and connection in context. Zakeev, Marcus, and Dwayne all spoke about and challenged issues connected to racial discrimination. In contrast, racialized power relations did not seem a significant concern to the two middle-class participants, Rashaud and Shawn, nor to Jeff.

"Hockey Is Just a White Sport!"

It was not just through people not being "fake" or being a "sellout" through how they acted, talked, or dressed, or what they talked about, that indicated these African-American students' commitment toward a collective identity. Symbols within school that were appropriated to affirm their racial identity were also significant.

Sport, for example, was a significant symbol to them. Just as involvement with sport is a major social context wherein masculine identities are developed (see Messner, 1992), so it is an institution where racial identities develop and change. For example, during a conversation, Rashaud told Latasha and me about an African-American student who had recently moved to Cedarville from Maryland, and who played hockey. Both Rashaud and Latasha, an African-American friend, considered hockey an inappropriate sport for African-Americans to play:

> *Rashaud:* Basically, Clyde came from Maryland . . . he was going to an all-black school where they had to bus in white kids. And he turned out, and he turned out white out of an all-black school. That's so uncommon. When . . . Clyde got here, and it was like a shock. It's like "what's up, what's goin' on?" And a couple of days later we see him walking around and we say "what are you doing?" . . . and my man had tried out for varsity hockey. Now this is like the only black kid on the varsity hockey team. Of all the hockey teams in the tricounty area. I swear Clyde is the only one [African-American]. And everybody is like "what?"
>
> *JP:* When you say everybody, you mean all the African-American kids?
>
> *Rashaud:* Yeah, and all the white kids were saying it.
>
> *JP:* Why is that? Are there certain sports that African-American kids play and white kids play?
>
> *Rashaud &*
> *Latasha:* *(In unison)* Hockey is just a white sport!

While some readers may argue that Clyde playing hockey actually challenged the attachment of race identities and meanings to certain sports, his actions also provide opportunities for students to further rally around a symbol they used to affirm their racial identity. They seemed to use their opposition to Clyde's practice as a way of reinforcing their own racial identities and symbols and meanings associated with their racial identities.

At the same time, five of the six young men saw basketball as a black sport. In the same way, this sport activity was seen as a symbol of their racial identity. By the same token, however, only three of the six young men played basketball almost every day. Dwayne, Marcus, and Zakeev all talked about playing basketball after school with friends. Most of the time, they played with other young African-Americans from their neighborhood. It is interesting that the two middle-class young men and Jeff, who was working class and had middle class aspirations, did not play much basketball but were spectators of the sport. Although sport activity, whether through being a player or observer, may be seen as a vehicle for expression of racial identity, it was simultaneously an activity that is deeply gendered. Messner (1992) argued that competitive sport for players and spectators alike becomes a vehicle for the construction of masculinities, where boys and men learn hegemonic ideas about what it means to be male. He further argued that "sport at once is a domain of contested national, class, and racial relations, at least symbolically, as a separate and superior group to women" (p. 19). Thus sport becomes an activity and a symbol not only of racial identity, but also gendered identity. Hence, their participation in sport—either as players or spectators—provided opportunities for the young men to live out their versions of their racialized masculinities.

The images presented here are only a few of the images of African-Americans they talked about with me, and only some of the images that shaped their racial sense of self and the racial sense of others. These young men were in the process of becoming, not just young men, but young African-American men. These identities seemed to be formed in relation to racialized divisions in sport that they reinforced, in opposition to their beliefs about white people's conceptions of African-Americans, and in the case of Marcus, in the tradition of historical figures who have powerfully shaped the struggle against racist oppression in the United States. As we discussed these various racialized images, for instance talk about "acting white," it became apparent that much of what they represented as African-American cultural practice was shaped in part by their opposition to conceptions of white cultural practices. This may not be surprising as they had had white cultural practices thrust upon them, with little or limited opportunity to learn and affirm their own histories and cultural practices that would strengthen their self image. Instead, they were struggling to define themselves in schooling contexts that were overwhelmingly shaped by institutional and social practices that seemed to perpetuate racial division through privileging some images, representations, and social practices, and subordinating others.

While most of these images have focused on the racial aspects of images they constructed, these images were simultaneously gendered. Of importance here is that these racial images were not dichotomous; rather they were relationally constituted. In order to understand better the interconnection between race and gender, I next turn to some ways in which race–gender images of others influenced them.

IMAGES AND RELATIONS OF GENDER AND RACE

Images of gender and race became prevalent as the young men actually talked about gendered images that were simultaneously racial images. However, few of the young men actually talked at length about their gendered images of women. Given that it was Marcus and Jeff who talked most about their images of women, this section focuses on their narratives about their images of women. These images are important in understanding their racialized masculine identities in the making. The images are also important in understanding how school contexts shape the versions of masculinities they enacted.

White Women, Black Masculinity, and Schooling

Jeff's relationships with others at Central and the friends he grew up with were not terminated solely because he transgressed an apparent racial boundary through the way he acted. The relationships also were tenuous because of his relationship with Sharon, who was white. Jeff said that a lot of his African-American peers did not associate with him because of the way he acted or talked. At the same time, because of the way he talked and acted, Jeff said, "It was just like a lot of more white girls was more attracted to me, dancing and start dating with them." In fact, Jeff began dating white girls more than he dated African-American girls. The picture of Jeff "acting white" seemed to be not only about getting ahead, it was also about him embracing images associated with dominant white culture. Jeff believed that his embrace of "acting white" was influential in him being able to date white girls. Further, "acting white" was enacted through dating white women.

But Jeff not only went out with white young women; he fathered a child with a white young woman. It was his relationship with Sharon that additionally provoked a tenuous relationship with his boyhood friends and many of his African-American peers at school, male and female. He said that,

> Yeah, a lot of people don't like me at Central also because of Sharon. They don't like to see somebody happy. You know you've got something good going on. [They say] "If I can't have nothing, you can't." You get rumors goin' around.

Probing Jeff further to uncover the nature of the rumors, he told me, "I think another thing is that Sharon used to be a virgin, a lot of guys get jealous, because 'how come I couldn't get it?' and all this other stuff." Thus, being "proper" was not just about talking and acting, it was also about his sexuality. As Lorber (1994) noted, "The social construction of sexuality is tied to the social construction of gender by marking off categories of who it is proper to mate and have children with" (p. 64).

The fact that Jeff mentioned Sharon losing her virginity, and that Jeff was her sexual partner, suggests ways in which sexual conquests are viewed as status symbols among *young men* and are integral to proving a certain kind of masculinity, a heterosexual masculinity. This talk about Sharon potentially confirmed not only Jeff's masculinity but also a kind of masculinity where his heterosexuality was part of the fabric of his masculine identity as an African-American. Another way in which he was able to live out his quest of "acting white" was not only to date a white girl but also to father her child. The image of Jeff becoming a father enthralled him: "I was happy, I was overjoyed," he told me. The relationship with Sharon may have contributed to the affirmation of the gendered identity he embraced. At the same time, his relationship with Sharon took on an important gendered significance in his relationships with other men, particularly African-American men. Notably, he did not share information about his fatherhood with the white male students at his new school. This suggests that gendered identities are not only formed in relation to women, but are also formed in particular contexts in relation to men through the various kinds of masculinities lived out by men.

Although the talk about Jeff and his relationship with Sharon may or may not have affected his relationships with others, what was significant was that this young African-American man, already aware of the damaging images of African-American men dominating society, aware of the hardships that face black young men, seemed to place emphasis on the need to assert his masculinity in the arena of school. It was through making public at Central his sexual relationship with Sharon that he was able to accomplish this. Through this relationship, "sex is prized not as a testament of love but as testimony to control of another human being" (Anderson, 1990, p. 114). The relationship became a vehicle to prove his self-esteem and pride and his heterosexual masculinity. As Massey (1991) argued, "Black boys engage in sexual activity earlier as a result of other blockages in the opportunity structure in our society" (p. 119). Sexual activity possibly becomes a way to exert his sense of masculinity, given a context imbued with distorted and hegemonic images of African-American men and his harrowing experiences with school and the criminal justice system. Although he fathered the child before his encounter with the criminal justice system, it was after the experience that he became almost entranced with the notion of fatherhood. It seemed as though the criminal justice system had stripped him of his sense of manhood and thus fatherhood became a mechanism whereby he was able to regain his sense of masculinity.

Interestingly, while Jeff made public his sexual relationship with Sharon at Central, he chose to be silent about his fatherhood at ACS. He decided that revealing such information to peers at ACS was inappropriate. His decision not to share these details of his life with white peers at ACS further revealed how Jeff used the social context of schooling to live out certain images of race and masculinity. At Central, it seemed important to his sense of masculinity to reveal aspects of his relationship, whereas at ACS he made a different decision. He seemed to use fatherhood to define his identity in relation to African-American men at his old school, but not in relation to the white men at his newer school, ACS. An interesting question that I did not explore with Jeff was whether he chose not to talk about his fatherhood because he thought sexual activity as a teenager would tarnish his image at ACS, or whether he chose not to talk about his fatherhood because he had a relationship with a white young woman.

Clearly, Jeff did not make these decisions arbitrarily. He seemed strongly influenced by the different institutional and cultural contexts of the two schools. These two different responses reveal how masculinities are actively and relationally made in context and the influence of the institutional and cultural forces in schools in the making of masculine identities.

Jeff's relationships with others in school, then, were not only about his racialized identity; they were also about his gendered identity. Although gender seemed to enter Jeff's conversations only in his talk about the sexual relationship between himself and Sharon, gender was present in *all* his conversations about his identity. When he "acted" in particular ways, he did not want to embrace femininity but masculinity. In this way, it seemed that his embrace of "acting white" was not only about his racialized identity, it was also about his gendered identity. When students accused him of "acting white," they meant that he "acted" as a white man as opposed to a white woman. There were implicit gendered meanings embedded and intertwined in his racialized ways of being and talking. This relationship with Sharon was important to his sense of racial identity, just as it was important to his sense of masculinity. It can be seen as giving him an avenue to assert his power and control as a black man.

Jeff and Marcus shared some similar experiences yet their social identities were somewhat different. They both lived with their biological mothers and stepfathers; they both had younger siblings in their homes; and they both had squabbled with their mothers to such an extent that they moved out. But that is where the similarities ended. What is interesting is the ways in which their identities as young African-American men in many ways were quite different. Yes, they were both working class, they were both young men of 17 years, and they were both African-American. They also shared commonality in the passing of their heterosexuality. But how they lived out their identities, how they went to school, and how they related to others in and out of school seemed different. What was strikingly different was the ways in which they talked about images and ideas of others, and used these images to develop a sense of who they were and wanted to be.

"What Do You Want with a White Girl?"

For Marcus, as with Jeff, gendered images intermingled in our conversations through talk about women and sexuality. For example, at one point, Marcus told me that he was "not really into relationship black and white thing. I hate to see my black sisters with white males. I think we need to stay with our own color." However, I suggested I occasionally saw black men with white women, but rarely, black women with white men. Curious about this, I asked Marcus if he agreed with my observations.

> *Marcus:*   Let me tell you about that. The reason is because, white girls are easier to get than black women. Black males don't want that challenge, black females will give you a challenge. They ain't gonna let you get them real easy. You have to prove yourself to them.
>
> *JP:*   Like what?
>
> *Marcus:*   The way you treat them. Basically you can get in their [white women's] pants easily. That's what it is. And I don't really like it, that's stupid. I don't really like it, I always say, "Come back to us."

Although Marcus related the issue of sexuality through his images of women, also intertwined with his ideas about women, sex, and men as "challengers" were ideas about race. His images were also imbued with the objectification of African-American and white women. He argued that having sex with African-American women was a "challenge" as opposed to the "easy" white women. He used the idea that black women are more difficult to "conquer" as a way to strengthen his image of black women, but this image of African-American woman was not only shaped by racial meanings, it was also shaped by his version of masculinity. Having a relationship with a black woman implicitly suggested Marcus's heterosexuality, and his sense of being a *black man*. Strands of sexuality, race, and gender identity came to the fore as he talked about women. Lorber (1994) correctly noted that sexuality is not just about behavior, it is also involves "desire and actual sexual attraction and fantasies" (p. 60).

Marcus, therefore, enhanced his version of masculinity as a black man through his commitment to, and the image he carried of, black women:

> Farrakhan says whites are an imitation woman. Anything black, you've got all the different shades of color in the black female, you've got big, you've got small, dark skinned, light-skinned. What do you want with a white girl? Hey, I'm not trying to cut. But ain't got no booty. And you know, black females, they've just got, everything is there, the perfect woman.

Marcus, like Jeff, used images and connections with women to develop his sense of self. However, it was a sexualized image that was interwoven through Marcus's talk about African-American women. In his mind, the black woman is "the perfect woman." He sexualized the body of African-American women and white women to argue his position about the beauty of black women. He denigrated white women, suggesting they are easy to "conquer." And conquest was part of the image of masculinity he constructed for himself. But his embrace of the beauty of black women was not arbitrary. It was connected to his sense of identity—his African American masculinity and heterosexuality.

Race–Gender Images of Women and Emerging Masculinities

These images of women and relationships with women and men were connected to the young men's construction of their sexualities. The identities were simultaneously gendered and racialized. Most important is that their talk about images of women was significant in their relationships with men. Talk about women with other men became a site for an affirmation of their version of masculinity, where men wielding power and control was a significant strand. For example, Jeff's relationship with Sharon saw him being rejected by his African-American peers but apparently the target of jealousy because he engaged in a sexual relationship with her. It seemed that Jeff's relationship with Sharon did not involve him having a relationship with a white woman, as a way to affirm his version of masculinity. He may be considered as "acting white" and rejecting other people's sense of his identity as an African-American, yet he asserted and affirmed his image as a man through the sexual relationship with Sharon and fathered a child. At the same time, his relationship with Sharon, a white young woman, could possibly be seen as a way of both challenging and trying to access white men's power (Collins, 1990). The relationship with Sharon, however, could also be seen as a story about competing masculinities among African-American and young white men at school: Jeff fathered a child with Sharon and thereby was able to prove his manhood to his peers, who seemed to place value on sexual conquests of women, yet the relationship could also challenge the power of young white men. This challenge is complex, however, because such challenging of power could have been an issue in relation to the young white men at his old school, Central, but at his new, mainly white, school, he chose to withhold the personal details.

Through exploring the ways in which these young men's sense of racial and masculine identities were constructed in relation to images, representations, and relations with others, we are able to catch a glimpse of the complexity in examining the ways in which race and gender interweave their lives. The discussion reveals that these two young men asserted their racialized masculine identities in different ways, but they both suggest images of men overpowering women through sexualized images and relationships as significant in their versions of masculinity.

RELATIONAL IMAGES, RELATIONAL IDENTITIES

A dominant theme that runs throughout this chapter is the *relational* nature of the images the young men constructed, which in turn speaks to the relational nature of their identities in the making. Through exploring the images they embraced, rejected, or criticized, we are able to capture glimpses of the different ways they came to see themselves and others.

The young men developed meanings and images of social identities in contexts that were historically shaped through relations of power and privilege. For example, their seemingly oppositional identities were constructed in relation to the hegemonic images of African-American masculinity—images of black men as violent, aggressive, and socially irresponsible. But they were also constructed in opposition to hegemonic versions of white masculinity. For instance, Marcus and Zakeev criticized white identities and tried to live out identities that were somewhat in *opposition* to the hegemonic images of black men; and at the same time, in *opposition* to images of white people.

Although I may have described some of the images being seen as in opposition to one another, this dichotomous representation of images does not fully capture the interplay of images in their lives. For example, the meanings given to "acting white" were formed not just in relation to white people, but also to African-American people who embraced aspects of white culture. Meanings were also shaped through their images about African-American people who embraced African-American culture. Further, these men were forming racial images even though they were not always interacting with white people. Such racial images were significant to their sense of self and identity.

Racial images and meanings, however, came into being not only through their individual practices. Collective actions, through their forming seemingly cohesive peer groups at school, also seemed to be a further force in their affirmation of identities. Many of these young men seemed to hang out with certain groups of students to validate their sense of their racial identity and concomitant behaviors and beliefs. Four of these men at once sought solidarity with other young African-American men and rejected aspects of white culture that they defined as not African-American culture. In their exclusively African-American peer groups at school, their talk and behaviors apparently were influential in their bonding. This sense of connection with other African-American students was important to them, not only because of how they came to see themselves in relation to teachers, pedagogy, and curriculum within school, but also because of the limited and negative images about African-American men that dominate society. Such a connection was not apparent for either Jeff or Zakeev who had few friends but still tried to embrace particular racialized images as they constructed their identities.

Their meanings emerged through social processes that were influenced by social practices and social institutions, which explains why the images they presented of themselves and others varied. Four of the six young men saw themselves acting in ways in opposition to "acting white," whereas Jeff embraced certain ways of being that he and others defined as "acting white." Dwayne did not consider issues of "acting white" to be as significant as the other five did. Rather, he was involved in a battle of embracing or rejecting African-American masculinist "street culture" in the shaping of his identity. Part of this street culture represented "hanging out with the fellas" and being involved in crime or drugs.

These images, while seemingly racialized, were also infused with gendered meanings. They defined their masculinities as African-American men in relation to versions of African-American and white femininities and masculinities. They tried to build an identity as men that represented distinctly African-American, not white, masculinities, and that did not reflect some of the dominant ideas, values, and beliefs about African-American men that permeate U.S. society. Such meanings about African-American men are given dominance in our society, despite these images representing only a few of the lived experiences of many African-American men. Many of these negative and limited images are constructed in ways that distort the reality of African-American men. As previously noted, the media and social science have largely contributed to this distortion. Constant stories on television and in our newspapers and magazines focus on the trials and tribulations of inner-city African-Americans. Shaping such stories are usually statistics about African-American men being a significant proportion of the prison population, or the number of African-American men who die before their 20th birthday. In social science there are many stories about the plight of inner city youth, their disenfranchisement, and their alienation from social institutions.

These hegemonic images and their own subordinated images played out in different ways in the young men's lives. They appropriated some images: some perhaps for their own use that may have served their own interests; others that seemingly served their own interests, but in fact may have acted to reinforce dominant social relations. And yet other images mitigated against their interests. For instance, the stance of rejecting "white" talk, ways of behaving, and dressing led Marcus, Shawn, Rashaud, and Zakeev to assert their membership, collectively and individually, as a distinct African-American group. While on the one hand this helped them forge a connectedness with other African-Americans, it also saw them consciously separating themselves from white cultural practices, yet unable to change the institutional and social practices that dominated the school so that their interests, concerns, and commitments were met. Through their practices, they seemed to reinforce their marginalization as a subordinate group and did not alter the relations of power in the school.

The images presented in this chapter have to do with the meanings given to social practices and the institutional structures that represent certain interests. Marcus and Zakeev not only challenged the racist practice of individuals, but also the power and privilege shaping the racial nature of institutions such as the media or the school. Many of the practices they opposed were deeply interwoven into the fabric of these institutions. Jeff's embrace of "acting white" as an African-American man seemed influenced by his disenchantment and alienation from school and his entanglement with the criminal justice system.

The interweaving of these various images in the lives of these young men suggests that the identity formation process is complex and linked to both institutional structures and social practices. The complexity of these images also suggests the complexities in explaining the interconnections of dimensions of race, class, and gender in their lives. In the final chapter, I investigate the complexity of the meanings they constructed of school in relation to the institutions they inhabited daily as young men. I also examine the challenges I faced as I tried to unravel the race, class, and gender dimensions of their day-to-day experiences.

8

Power, Privilege, and Inequality

In my discussion thus far, I have unraveled the meanings, images, and experiences that informed the narratives of the six young men and considered these meanings and experiences in the context of their interactions and encounters in school, family, and with peers. Each of the chapters provides a sketch and way of understanding how these meanings were interconnected with the making of their social identities. I have tried to show that their meanings and identities were not static, fixed in time, but were continually evolving. I have also shown that their meanings were not solely of their own making. These meanings were situated in contexts and relationships that are rooted in history with privileges, options, barriers, and opportunities that both constrained and supported their goals, ambitions, and desires. Through exploring these contexts and relationships, I have tried to show that the patterns of privilege and penalty they experienced were dynamically shaped through interlocking and interconnected systems of race, class, and gender.

Examining the various meanings, experiences, goals, and desires that the young men talked about, and simultaneously discussing the interconnection of race, class, and gender with the structures and cultures they inhabited is no easy task. There were multiple layers and interactions that were influential in making sense of their experiences. For instance, an understanding of their stories needed to be located within the context of the day-to-day experiences that were reflected in their individual biographies; within the context of their experiences as members of cultural groups that reflected their age, gender, race, and social class; and also within the context of the institutions they inhabited, such as schools and the family. These institutions in part reflected larger ideological and structural influences, which in turn had their own internal mechanisms reflecting some degree of autonomy, yet simultaneously mirrored relations of power in the larger society. To understand the complexity of the interaction of institutional and social practices in the lives of the young men, such explanations, on a conceptual level, need to be located at the level of concrete experiences. In this chapter then, I want to address three dominant themes: (1) the multiple strands to their meanings of schooling; (2) the interconnections of social institutions with the meanings they constructed; and (3) the interplay of race, class, and gender relations of power in these young men's experiences and meanings. Although I weave these three themes throughout the discussion in this chapter, I will examine elements of these themes by examining, first, the relationship between power and privilege and their differing meanings of schooling; second, the interconnections of experiences in institutions such as the family and with the criminal justice system in the making of meaning of school; and third, the complexity of the threads of race, class, and gender embedded within and interwoven through the meanings they gave to experiences, events, and symbols in their lives.

POWER RELATIONS AND THE MEANING OF SCHOOLING

One of the central institutions that I have discussed has been that of school. Throughout this work, I have learned how the meaning of school represented more than what the young men did in classrooms. Understanding their experiences in other spheres of school seems equally as important, for instance, in relation to their experiences with peers outside of classrooms. Their meanings of school were also constructed with their family members, and in relation to institutions such as the criminal justice system. For example, Dwayne's and Jeff's stances about going to school were constructed in opposition and in relation to their experiences with the criminal justice system. For most of the young men, going to school was integrally connected to their commitment to acquire a high school diploma.

In this section, I discuss the experiences in school that were influential in the meanings the young men gave to school and the diploma. I argue that although the meanings of school had to do with acquiring the high school diploma, it was also about their relationships with teachers and students, and their experiences of curriculum and pedagogy.

Schooling and the Diploma

For all the young men, school was about acquiring a high school diploma. But there were differences among the young men as to what the high school diploma and school meant to them. Understanding these differences can be explained by situating their meanings in their everyday culture and their experiences of different institutional contexts. Their meanings of the diploma were constructed through experiences such as their relationships with various actors inside and outside of school such as family members and friends, their access to knowledge and pedagogy, the courses taken, and the neighborhood in which their school was located. The structures of these institutions reflected complex political, cultural, and economic spheres of society that affected the kinds of meanings they carved out for themselves. Embedded in the culture and structure of these institutions were also dimensions of race, class, and gender power and privilege. These influences intermingled with their day-to-day experiences as they formed different meanings about the high school diploma. Through this complex process of making meanings of school and the diploma, they came to affirm and/or reject their own and others' conceptions of themselves and schooling. Invariably, the oppositional knowledge and stances they developed were unrewarded by the school, whereas engagement in the agendas of the school was rewarded.

An examination of the complexity of the making of meanings of school and the diploma, however, needs to consider the constraints that these young men encountered as African-American young men as they strived for goals beyond high school. Their opportunity to pursue their potential was often hampered by barriers emerging from encounters and interactions inside and outside of school. Within the context of school, the most significant institutional forces that shaped the barriers and penalties they encountered were primarily in the form of the disengaging and alienating pedagogy and curriculum they experienced, but there were others. They all had different grade point averages, they attended different schools, and experienced different kinds of support from teachers. They also had different access to knowledge of what to do with the diploma once they left the school, and their diplomas carried different social weight. These constraints were not of their making; they were various structural constraints produced in societal institutions. For example, Zakeev was not allowed to take an advanced mathematics class and was placed in a general mathematics class that was composed almost exclusively of African-Americans, whereas Marcus had to endure his history teacher's narrow conceptions of African-American experiences. These experiences of power relations that intermingled their social relationships influenced the making of their meanings of school and the diploma.

Pointing to the significance of institutional constraints and social practices in their lives further explains the differences in the meanings the young men constructed about schooling and success and how the diploma represented a *version* of success to all the young men. However, there were variations in the kind of success the diploma symbolized to them, just as there was unevenness in the kinds of resources they had access to and the penalties and barriers they encountered in school. There were also various strands to each of their notions of success, one of which suggested that the diploma could be acquired through hard work and that good grades could reap material rewards and social recognition. Meritocratic ideology, however, was only one strand of the meanings of success that the diploma embodied. The diploma, for some of the young men, was a stepping stone to college entrance, while for others, it was a form of achievement and an accomplishment in its own right.

For Dwayne and Jeff, for instance, the diploma may have represented an opportunity to go to college, but at the same time, more immediately it also represented a version of success. This version of success entailed not being entangled in the criminal justice system through staying in school. This version of the success they could reap from the high school diploma contrasted with Rashaud's version, which involved his hopes of going to a college, and Shawn's, which reflected his belief that the diploma was not worth much without a college degree. For Rashaud and Shawn, the diploma represented success in the future. They felt they could wait for the accrued benefits. On the other hand, for Dwayne and Jeff, and to a certain extent, for Marcus and Zakeev, doing well in school was intimately tied to seeking some form of immediate recognition—from their parents or other authority figures in their lives. These variations in the meanings of success that the diploma embodied were intrinsically connected to their access to resources and their concomitant location in a race, class, and gender order.

Variations in access to resources became most evident on comparing the two middle-class young men with two of the working-class young men. Zakeev and Marcus, both working class, and Shawn and Rashaud, both middle class, all had goals of going to college; but it was the two middle-class young men who not only knew which college they wanted to go to, they also knew and followed through with what they had to achieve in order to go a particular college. The two working-class young men did not possess knowledge about what they needed to do in order to gain college entrance, nor did they take courses that could enhance their quest to go to college. Further, the two middle-class young men gave less weight and social significance to the high school diploma than the two working-class young men did. Ironically, while Rashaud and Shawn gave less importance to the high school diploma, their diplomas carried more weight and social significance compared to Marcus's and Zakeev's diplomas, given the high school Rashaud and Shawn attended and the grade point average they accumulated. Through their experiences of the world, the middle-class young men came to see the high school diploma as being a vehicle to college. Though Marcus and Zakeev saw the diploma as a vehicle to college entrance, they were not as dismissive about the value of the diploma as a form of achievement in its own right. Their access to resources dynamically shaped their construction of the kind of success the diploma represented.

Amid these different experiences, social class seems to emerge as an explainer for their different experiences in and out of school, their differential access to resources and the different meanings they gave to school and the diploma. Dimensions of race and gender, however, seem integrally connected to the social class explanation for their different meanings. How they experienced social class as African-American young men, and how they experienced being African-American as young men seemed deeply intertwined with the meanings they developed and their relationships with other racialized and gendered class groups.

On the level of their individual biographies, their images of success, for instance, did not seem accessible for all the young men to live out. These images, although shaped by their access to opportunity, power, and privilege, were simultaneously rooted in the ways that race, class, and gender experiences shaped and were shaped by their definitions of manhood which seemed to be part of the different images of success they formed for themselves. For instance, Dwayne's access to opportunity—through the kind of school he attended and the classes he took—seemed more severely constrained than Rashaud's. In addition, these two young men seemed to experience race differently. The experiences of Dwayne in Detroit, and the kinds of relationships he developed with his "fellas" in the streets, his disconnection from school, and his entanglement with the criminal justice system were all at play in the making of not only his racial identity, but also his sense of manhood. Dwayne's experiences were in stark contrast with Rashaud's, whose experiences were not only far removed from those of Dwayne, but were also very different given where he lived and how he spent his time in and out of school. These differences suggest Rashaud had greater access to more privileges and options than Dwayne as part of his day-to-day experiences at home, in his school, and in his neighborhood. Clearly, their meanings were shaped by a *range* of cultural and structural influences in their lives and not just by economic interests. So, in thinking about the lives of these two young men, their goals were not solely tempered by class-based interests, but also were affected by their social class experiences, their racialized experience, and their experiences of gender.

Granted, the intersection of race *and* social class relations of power and privilege in part explains this unevenness among the young men, yet when I consider the various meanings the young men constructed of the high school diploma, the images of success they constructed seemed to be also intimately tied to their images of themselves as successful *men*. Images of success were simultaneously, and not in addition to, imbued with *gendered* meanings. Admittedly, all six of the young men did seem to hold an image of success whereby the diploma was a vehicle for a man to wield power in the labor market and to provide income to support his family. However, being a successful man meant different things to them. But what kind of successful men did they want to be? For Dwayne, being successful meant providing an income and not being characterized as a "statistic," whereas for Rashaud it meant pursuing a professional career, economic and social mobility, and a firm position in middle-class life.

Hence, the meanings they developed around the diploma reflected not only class-based but also racialized and gendered interests and experiences. Here, I am not arguing that social class dimensions of their lives were insignificant nor am I dismissing the ways in which gendered relations of power privilege the interests of men. Rather, I am arguing that a focus on the interconnection of race, social class, and gender helps me to better explain the different meanings of schooling and the diploma. For instance, in order to understand their location in a gender order, it is important to consider the kinds of resources they had access to as classed and racialized men. Also important to consider are the kinds of masculinities they lived out as African-American men in relation to other versions of masculinities and femininities—in relation to the gendered identities of their friends, peers, teachers, and family members, and in relation to dominant images of black and white women and men. Their location as men in a gendered order in itself narrows an explanation of their access to power and privilege. It is when I examine their social location in a gendered regime as interconnected with their racialized and classed experiences that I am able to better explain their different meanings of the diploma and schooling.

In sum, the different meanings, interests, and symbols associated with the high school diploma suggest that it is not solely social class location that influenced their meanings but the intermingling of social class, race, and gender in their lives. These versions of success and their views of the diploma were undoubtedly influenced by institutional and cultural practices. Such practices were in part the consequence of social class relations of power; however, their experiences were also enmeshed in racialized and gendered relations of power. The diploma became one of the central reasons for attending school, in part, because of and in spite of their disengaging experiences in classrooms. Though such disengagement may have been a common thread among the young men, there was some variation in what they experienced in classrooms, and the consequences of their involvement. Having noted that institutional interconnections, relations of power, and social practices were significant in the meanings of the high school diploma the young men constructed, I now turn to a more embedded examination of the meaning of schooling through exploring the complexity of their experiences in classrooms.

Missing Teachers, Missing Students

Through the young men's accounts of life in classrooms I learned about the nature of their relationships with teachers, their relationship with other students in and out of classrooms, and the form and content of the curriculum and pedagogy they experienced. I have noted that the pedagogy and curriculum they experienced did not reflect who they were as young African-American men nor did the experiences provide opportunities for them to develop understanding of their world and beyond. The relationships reflected relations of power between a student and a teacher where the curriculum and pedagogy, in the main, tended to marginalize and silence their perspectives and connections with subject matter. In many ways, the teachers were seen purely in functional terms: as curriculum giver, as allocators of grades, and as disciplinarians. This is not surprising, because it was the form of relation of power with teachers that they mostly experienced.

Although these six young men also sought respect from, care by, and connection with their teachers, not one of the young men talked about experiencing a form of connection with teachers. Thus, I have come to think of them not just as experiencing limited connection with their teachers; the teachers they are looking for were missing from their experiences at school. Many of their teachers were not African-American. They so needed teachers who understood them, who cared about their perspectives, who embraced their commitment to go to school, who provided opportunities for them to talk about their lives and their experiences, who would listen to them and nudge them as they learned about the world on their own terms.

Amid the experiences in classrooms and in school more generally, it is clear that these young men to varying degrees sought connections with others. Instead, it was only in the hallways, and in the spaces of the day when they were not in classrooms that they were able to maintain and sustain some level of interaction with others. Their experiences of curriculum and pedagogy in their classrooms seemed to hinder their ability to develop connected relationships with their peers. It is ironic, however, that they spent so much time with other students in classrooms yet classrooms did not seem to be fertile grounds for them to develop personal and intellectual connections with other students. Relationships with students in classrooms also seemed amiss. It is not surprising then, that the relationships with other students in their classes were not a central piece of the experiences that they cared about in school.

Despite these young men being unable to form connected relationships with other in classrooms, it was the middle-class young men, and in some instances, Jeff at his new private school, who *did* experience discussion and hence interaction around subject matter in some of their classrooms. Although I never learned about the *kind* of discussion they experienced, there seemed, from their accounts, to be *more* interaction among the middle-class students and their teachers than was the case for the other three young men. Their classroom experiences of Dwayne, Marcus, and Zakeev seemed to consist almost entirely of independently completing work sheets, answering textbook questions, and following teachers' directions. Consequently, even though the middle-class young men, Rashaud and Shawn, and Jeff, did not establish strong connections with others in their classrooms, there seemed the possibility that they could have experienced knowledge somewhat differently.

The eagerness of the six young to develop trusting, connected friendships, and the desire of some of them to learn about their own culture and history, beckons the imperative of crafting curriculum and pedagogy that would meet *their* needs and interests. Instead, these young men were alienated from their classrooms, from the teachers, from the content, and had little or no opportunities to develop relationships around the intellectual work of the classroom.

Although I have discussed the kinds of relationships these young men encountered in classrooms, relationships with teachers and students cannot be disentangled from the curriculum and pedagogy the young men experienced. These relationships they encountered emerged from the curriculum and pedagogy and, hence, the form and content they encountered. Significantly, these relationships and experiences of knowledge were intimately tied to the web of meanings they held about schooling and the diploma.

Curriculum, Pedagogy, and Power Relations

I have noted that these six young men had different experiences of curriculum and pedagogy in their different schools and that race and racism became a common thread in their experiences in classrooms. The classroom, then, became one of the sites where they learned about racial relations of power through the silencing and marginalization of some perspectives and the privileging and centering of others. For instance, in their history classrooms, they learned about race as a process and as a topic. Despite their critique about the lack of attention to the history and experiences of African-Americans in school subjects, race and racism remained at the heart of much of what many of them encountered through their time in classrooms and other arenas at school. Understanding the common thread of racism that they experienced can be explained by their location in a racialized order that privileges the interests and experiences of whites. But the form of racism they experienced was different, particularly when one compares the middle-class young men with the other four. Both Rashaud and Shawn suggested that there was some attention to African-American history. Moreover, these two young men were less critical of the lack of attention to African-Americans in school curriculum than Marcus and Zakeev, who were passionate about the exclusion of African-American history from their curriculum. Zakeev even challenged his history teacher about the omission, and his teacher said it was "Just not in [his] curriculum." Social class certainly may partially explain the differences in their experiences and their critique.

The variation in their experiences, however, needs to take into account the *interconnection* of race and social class. Previously, I have noted how the distribution of knowledge in their schools echoed the work of Anyon (1981) that caused students from different social class backgrounds to experience different kinds of authoritarianism in relation to their social class location. The middle-class young men seemed to have more opportunities to engage in curriculum and pedagogy that seemed to offer them a wider array of possibilities of coming to know and understand the world. They used fewer textbooks in their classrooms and engaged in more discussions that the other young men. Although they were provided different and less substantial opportunities, Dwayne, Marcus, and Zakeev were more critical of power relations than the two the middle-class young men. Perhaps it is not surprising that the high school diploma was the focus of their talk about schooling, given the oftentimes alienating content of school subjects they often experienced. The difference among the young men raises questions about what and how they learned, and how the knowledge they had access to influenced how they saw themselves in relation to others in the development of their identities as African-American young men. It is when I look at the race–class experiences as interconnected that explanations for their different experiences can be more thoroughly accounted for.

At the same time, while I note the interconnection of race and social class, and I previously have noted that they were silent about gender relations in the classroom, this does not mean that gender was not part of their discourse or the meanings and relationships they constructed. Gender appeared as important subtexts in their accounts of life in classrooms as I learned from the interaction between Marcus and his history teacher. Classrooms became sites were they lives out their versions of masculinity in relation to versions of masculinities and femininities. Marcus's interactions with his biology teacher about his grade also revealed the complex nature of the relations of the power between a teacher and a student. Race was clearly integral to the relationship because the teacher suggested to Marcus that she was not racist. "How can I be racist and my daughter went to see Michael Jackson?" she apparently said to Marcus. She gave racialized meanings to the interactions, as did Marcus. She articulated a view of race that trivialized racialized relations of power. Her understanding of race, rather than pacifying Marcus, reinforced his racialized images and his notion that she was racist, as were the institutions that he saw her representing. Although racialized meanings were interwoven through the interaction, gendered meanings also intermingled in the interaction. In this instance, the teacher was a white woman, and the student, an African-American man. This was not just an interaction between an African-American person and a white person; it was simultaneously an interaction between a white woman and an African-American young man. Marcus seemed to use his power as a man to challenge the women, and thereby to assert his gendered power, to challenge her power, not just as a women, but as a white woman. It would seem that race and gender, together, were at play in this interaction. Disentangling dimensions of gender and race would seem to loose the complexity of the social interaction. At the same time, Marcus's response to his teacher may also be seen as a working-class challenge to the authority and control that she wielded in a classroom that saw him learning in a procedural, technocratic way, offering him little opportunity to experience knowledge on his own terms. Such is an example of the interconnected ways in which race, class, and gender may interconnect through interactions that appeared to be centered on the dimension of race, but may also be imbued with subtexts of gender and social class.

The following questions emerge from my analysis: What kinds of gendered interactions did these young men participate in, observe, and create as they experienced pedagogy and curriculum in classrooms? Did they live out, experience and negotiate different forms of masculinities? What kinds of opportunities did they have to be the nurturing and connected young men they wanted to be? These questions are important to thinking about race, class, and gender interconnections and the versions of masculinities they lived out in classroom.

My analysis suggests that the variations in the young men's meaning of school and the diploma and the differential access to opportunity and resources can be explained through analyzing the ways in which race, class, and gender relations of power were interwoven through the lives of the young men. Ironically, while the young men shared a commitment to staying in school, and developed different kinds of critiques of schooling, they situated themselves in a process that did not always serve their interests, with the middle-class young men poised to benefit most from participation in school. The various meanings of schooling they developed, however, were not only formed through what they encountered in school. Equally significant were their experiences in other institutions as they went to school.

INSTITUTIONAL INTERCONNECTIONS

I have argued that it is difficult to understand the young men's commitment of going to school without understanding their prior and ongoing experiences outside of school and in the context of their differential access to power and privilege. Their meanings of school were not constructed solely in school. What went on in school for the young men was connected to dynamics in their lives outside of school, just as dynamics outside of school influenced how they went about going to school on a daily basis. This section explores the ways in which the young men's experiences with family and peers were each interconnected in the meaning they gave to school, and how schooling influenced the meanings they gave to relationships with peers and family. I also focus on the interconnection of the relationship between the criminal justice system and schooling. The different meanings they developed, however, emerged from the differential access to power and privilege that was created by and influenced their different experiences in institutions. In this way, family experiences were influential, but not determinant, of the meanings they gave to the high school diploma. This section is framed through considering the following twofold question: What were the relationships between family members, peers, and the young men, and what bearing did these relationships have on their emerging meanings of schooling?

Schooling and Relationships with Family Members and Peers

Family households were sites that reflected different kinds of relationships and competing interests among family members. Family household members for most of the young men, together with other family members, provide significant support for and advice about attending school. An examination of these six young men's relationships revealed that meanings of school were constructed through their involvement in the institution of school and through an array of other institutions.

Continuing to go to school became a way to seemingly strengthen the relationship between these young men and their family members, and in some cases, between mothers and their sons. For example, in the strained relationships between Jeff and Marcus and their parents, doing well in school was a way to strengthen their unstable relationships. By the same token, if Marcus did not do well in school, this affected his relationship with his parents. Sometimes it resulted in his being grounded at home. Another way in which the family and school interconnected in the making of meaning of schooling was through the monitoring of their homework by their parents. This action became a way for the mothers to follow through on their commitment for their sons to attend school. The interaction meant that homework tasks were central to their relationships in matters about schooling, and the subject matter content became marginal.

In the same way that staying in school and engaging in homework activities influenced their connections in relationships with family members, the demands of the parents' workplace influenced the kinds of activities these young men were expected to participate in at home. For instance, Marcus, Jeff, and Rashaud were the older siblings at home, and thus were expected to take care of their younger siblings while one or both of their parents worked. They had the opportunity to assume these responsibilities because they had the available time after school. The activities and responsibilities they undertook influenced the kinds of interests and ideas they embraced and rejected. Three of the young men took responsibility for the care of their younger siblings in the afternoon and developed caring relationships with their young brothers and sisters. Such experiences became part of their sense of membership in a family and also influenced the kind of young men they were becoming. In contrast with the three working-class young men, neither of the middle-class young men was expected to assume such responsibilities; instead, they spent their afternoons completing homework tasks and projects with little interruption.

The family, however, was also a context where different kinds of activities came into conflict with each other and was not just a place that was shaped by connection and affection. Following through with their parents' demands of taking care of younger siblings meant the young men were forced to place family responsibilities over other social commitments with friends they may have wanted to pursue. For example, because Marcus was expected to take care of his younger siblings, this often meant he could not spend time outside of the house with his friends as frequently as he preferred. The family responsibilities meant that he could not always play basketball when he wanted to, thereby strengthening the bonds with friends he considered important in his life: his boyhood friends, and the friendships he sought out during recess at school, friendships that he was not able to develop in classrooms. The friendships were important sustaining influences to him as he continued to go to school. On other occasions, when Marcus was not living at his parent's home, these friendships became central to his sustenance as he negotiated the fragile relationship with his parents.

School also played a significant role in the formation of the young men's friendships. Although some of the young men were able to develop friendships in school, the alienating relationships they encountered saw several of the young men look to African-American organizations outside of school to develop relationships with other young people. The young men seemed dissatisfied with the relationships they formed in school and thus sought avenues outside of school to develop connected relationships with youths of their own age. This was ironic: school seemed to become a place where they were able to strengthen their bonds with others, particularly African-American peers; but, schools were also a place where they felt alienated or unconnected with other students, particularly white students. Thus, it was through a combination of relationships in a range of institutions that they were able to sustain themselves. In this way, they were attracted to organizations in their communities with predominantly African-American membership. But they belonged to different kinds of organizations, and their parent's access to resources influenced the kinds of organizations they belonged to. Rashaud's membership of the *Jack and Jill* club was initiated by his mother. Whereas Jeff and Marcus belonged to brotherhood organizations, Shawn and Zakeev belonged to church organizations, and Dwayne did not belong to any formal organization. The kinds of organization they belonged to reflected the kinds of resources to which the parents and sons had access.

These young men's experiences in their various neighborhoods saw them interacting with different youths and adults. Most of the young men developed relationships with peers that cut across social class boundaries. However, the middle-class young men lived in environments that were somewhat removed from conditions of poverty and argued that they encountered few barriers in their quest for the high school diploma. In contrast, the other four young men were confronted daily with the conditions of poverty and hardship through their families, with neighbors, and with peers who were struggling to make ends meet or who were unemployed. These different experiences seem influential in the making of these four young men's views of the diploma as an achievement in its own right and the possibility of the job, and explains why the two middle-class young men seemed to be contented to wait for economic security through acquiring a college degree.

The Criminal Justice System and Schooling

A second example that once again illuminates the complexity of the institutional connections of race, class, gender privilege, and power in the making of meanings of schooling was Dwayne's and Jeff's relationship to the criminal justice system. Each was aware of the damaging images of African-American men that dominate our society. The ways in which they responded and became entangled with the criminal justice system seemed to be interconnected to their lived experiences. Where and how they lived was certainly about their racialized, gendered, and social class experiences. For example, Dwayne hung out in the streets with his "fellas," and developed ways of being with these young men, in an environment where he saw "no way out." At the same time, Jeff, who was disengaged from and had virtually dropped out of school, found himself being charged with armed robbery and the theft of a stolen vehicle. It was his social location in school and neighborhood together with his experiences with the criminal justice system that influenced his meanings of the high school diploma.

Neither of the two middle-class young men had lived in contexts where they were so vulnerable; rather, their lived in circumstances that saw them pursing different kinds of lives than either Dwayne or Jeff. Rashaud and Shawn were middle-class and had different options and privileges outside of school. Having a different relationship with school and different experiences outside of school meant that the choices they made, and the influences upon these choices, were different from those of Dwayne and Jeff, and hence had different implications. Not only did Rashaud and Shawn have a different experience at school, but involvement with the criminal justice system was far removed from their experiences. It was the interconnections of experiences of the criminal justice system and schooling that resulted in Dwayne and Jeff using schooling as a vehicle to regain and develop their sense of pride.

Institutional interconnections reflected an integral web in the making of the meanings of school. The various interconnected experiences in institutions suggest that there were a number of forces at play in the making of meaning of schooling. These young men's social location in school and in other institutions affected the very meanings they developed. It was not just the fact that their experiences of institutions were different, it was that these experiences intermingled with and reflected different kinds of access to power, privilege, and resources within the various institutions that explains the difference. I now turn to a discussion of the complexity of understanding race, class, and gender dynamics in explaining their meanings and experiences.

COMPLEXITIES OF RACE, CLASS, AND GENDER DYNAMICS

Throughout this work, I have argued that complex and contradictory processes were interwoven through the fabric of these young men's lives as I tried to unravel the ways in which they made their identities. A central strand of my argument has been that the interaction of experiences in school and with family and friends had different but sometimes similar consequences for these young men, even for those of similar social class backgrounds. Through examining both their differences and similarities in the meanings they developed of their experiences of schooling and beyond, I have tried to understand the ways in which relations of power were woven their experiences.

Explaining the interaction of race, class, and gender, however, has not been an easy task for me precisely because these dimensions are complex and contradictory. These are not only structural phenomena, they are also simultaneously cultural phenomena that are continually changing and evolving in different contexts over time. Throughout this work, I have also struggled with the complexity of trying to understand the meanings the six young men developed through a lens of the interconnection of race, class, and gender. This has involved trying to scrutinize each dimension in order to illuminate the complexity of individual circumstance in relation to social structure. For example, in some instances, I have tried to focus on the meanings of the schooling that reflected their experiences of race, and simultaneously brought into my analysis the subtexts of gender and social class, and considered the interactions of race, class, and gender in the meanings they gave to their experiences. I have also focused on the interconnected experiences at the level of personal biography, of a cultural group, and of social institutions. Through examining these various levels, at times, I focused on the way race and social class were woven through their meanings and the choices they made and the options that were available to them. More muted in my analysis was the strand of their gendered identities in understanding and explaining the meanings they developed.

Part of this unevenness in my analysis is a result of the difficulty I encountered in unraveling gendered dimension of their social lives. It was difficult to develop portraits of the gendered identities of the social actors they interacted with in and out of school. In noting this limitation, I am drawing from Connell's (1987) representation of a gender order that reflects three major structures: the division of labor, power relations between men and women, and sexuality. My conversations with these young men included occasional references to two of these structures, but sexuality was far less frequently raised, thus constraining my ability to evenly explore their gendered identities. Furthermore, the young men often did not differentiate the gendered identities of the students they interacted with in and out of classrooms. Notwithstanding, gender was a subtext of their experiences. These young men in differing contexts were in the process of becoming young African-American men who were formed not only in relation to women, but also in relation to men. Their masculinities were also formed and influenced by their ways of being and acting as young men in their groups, or with their friends; they were also influenced by the structure of relations in school. Such a structure involved the ways in which they experienced knowledge, the ways knowledge was organized in school through the various tracks within and across schools, and the forms of student–teacher relationships they encountered. Complicating the versions of masculinities coming into being were patterns that sometimes cut across the young men, for instance racism. This pattern, however, was manifest in different ways and had different consequences because of how the young men experienced and responded to racism and because of the resources that were at play in their experiences and responses.

The difficulty in understanding their meanings through a race, class, and gender lens is not only one of being able to examine the various dimensions; the larger difficulty is one of unraveling the complexity of the *interconnectedness* of race, class, and gender. For example, there were small incidents such as the interaction between Marcus and his biology teacher, Ms. Huffington, that were filled with intertwined race, class, and gender power relations. In the courses of Marcus's daily experiences of school, these "small" incidents accumulated and affected one another in ways that probably were not additive, which in turn further adds to the complexity.

In sum, their stories can *only* be understood if seen in the context of power, privilege, and inequality. This helps us understand how they experienced school, how the complex interplay of race, class, and gender affected them each differently, and how they shared both a commitment "against the odds" to go to school and a simultaneous critique of it.

Shawn Braxton, Jeff Davidson, Rashaud Dupont, Dwayne Reynolds, Zakeev Washington, and Marcus Williams provided rich accounts of the complexities of going to school as young African-American men in the 1990s. They all went to school with the hope of acquiring the high school diploma. Not everything in school, however, was meaningful to them; they invariably seemed alienated from others and encountered seemingly insurmountable challenges along the way. Notwithstanding, they did develop a consciousness, a critique of the world around them through their experiences with others in and out of the school.

A poignant quote form Marcus reveals the intensity of the critique: "To me how I feel about the education system, I mean they don't have the locks on our hands and feet no more, but they've got it on our brain. They've got the locks on our brains now." Marcus's voice of critique emerged from his experiences in the classroom, during basketball games, at work, and on the telephone with his friends. In the same way, Dwayne's voice of critique spoke to the harsh realities of his life as an African-American man:

> Like when you grow up in the ghetto, they are like slums, basically set up for to keep a black person down. And when you grow up in that, you see things like that, and you be around it, it's just like you're going to be into it. 'Cause the steps already stand up so high, that you know, you ain't gonna get no black male in inner city, crime city, like Detroit where I'm from, he's not going to make it. No. And that's how it is. You know you are going to start getting in trouble, hanging out with the fellas, smoking bud, 'cause it's set up to hold us black people down.

Such voices of critique suggest that human consciousness, and particularly critical thought, not only emerges through and in response to the actions and choices of teachers in schools, but is also very much organic to the students' day-to-day experiences both outside and within school. All of young men spoke about the problems that face young African-American men in the 1990s. Their voices of critique and discontent became a central strand of their identities in relation to their friends and families. This discontent with and critique of power relations and social position stand in the face of the idea that school passively socializes students into their roles. Rather, these six young men manipulated their situations, and given the constraints that shaped their lives, went to school to acquire a high school diploma. But ironically, while they critiqued school, their experiences of school could see them unable to pursue their goals and ambitions. They articulated the values and beliefs that the diploma signified and situated themselves in a process that did not always serve their interests. Yet against these odds, with incredible courage and remarkable strength, they continued to go to school.

Notes

1. For an excellent discussion about the complexities of the social distance between white researchers and participants of color in research studies, see Andersen (1993).

2. All ages provided are as of the beginning of the 1992–1993 academic year.

3. I often questioned how much his responses were a manifestation of me being a white male, and his sense of what he thought he was expected to say, given I was a white male. He told me that he liked talking with me because no one really paid any attention to what he had to say, and that he trusted me. But there is still no telling to what degree he spoke about the high school diploma in ways that seemed almost rehearsed.

4. Farrakhan also argues for the need for black business expansion. Farrakhan argues that such expansion is a vehicle for "black enhancement and black expansion" (West, 1993b, p. 214).

5. See Mickelson and Smith (1992), where they argue a persistence in educational inequality for members of subordinated groups. Also see Mickelson, Smith, and Oliver (1993) for an informative discussion about how African-American candidates are excluded from a pool of "qualified" candidates in the hiring of academic faculty through seemingly "neutral" criteria.

6. I use the notions of potentials and constraints from the work of Connell and associates (1982). The notions are helpful in attempting to capture the opportunities, barriers, and penalties embedded in the dynamic and complex daily interactions and relationships these young men encountered in school over time.

7. This talk was obviously influenced by the relationships I established with each of the young men. The fact that I am a foreign, white, middle-class man associated with a university, the nature of the questions I asked, and how they perceived me and interpreted my questions seemed influential here.

8. It was as though they wanted me not only to hear them but to respond to them. I felt a social responsibility to respond to their concerns in meaningful and helpful ways. This was at times difficult, because I did not know the relationships with their parents, nor did I have a full picture of their lives. Furthermore, I was only peripherally involved in their lives for a relatively short period. But where I could I tried to be supportive, to listen, to care

about how they were feeling, and help them think about different situations from various perspectives.

9. For an excellent critique of sex role socialization views ofgender identities see Connell (1987) and Thorne (1993).

10. This is the period prior to Jeff's entanglement with the criminal justice system. In noting the distance that developed between Jeff and his parents, I am not arguing that his experiences of school itself may have simultaneously caused him to become more disengaged from school.

11. This image of "acting white" is discussed at length in the following chapter.

References

Andersen, M. L. (1993). Studying across difference: Race, class, and gender in qualitative research. In J. Stanfield & D. Rutledge (Eds.), *Research in race and ethnic relations* (pp. 39–52). Newbury Park, CA: Sage.

Andersen, M. L., & Collins, P. H. (1992). *Race, class and gender—an anthology*. Belmont, CA: Wadsworth.

Anderson, E. (1990). *Streetwise: Race, class and change in an urban community*. Chicago: University of Chicago Press.

Anderson, G. L. (1989). Critical ethnography in education: Origins, current status, and new directions. *Review of Educational Research, 59,* 249–270.

Anthias, F., & Yuval-Davis, N. (1992). *Racialized boundaries: Race, nation, gender, colour and class and the anti-racist struggle*. New York: Routledge.

Anyon, J. (1981). Social class and school knowledge. *Curriculum Inquiry, 11,* 3–42.

Anyon, J. (1983). Intersections of gender and class: Accommodation and resistance by working-class and affluent females to contradictory sex role ideologies. *Journal of Education, 166,* 25–48.

Apple, M. W. (1982). *Education and power*. Boston: Ark.

Apple, M. W. (1994). *Official knowledge—democratic education in a conservative age*. New York: Routledge.

Baca Zinn, M. (1979). Field research in minority communities: Ethical, methodological and political observations by an outsider. *Social Problems, 27,* 210–219.

Baca Zinn, M. (1991). Family, feminism, and race in America. In J. Lorber & S. A. Farrell (Eds.), *The social construction of gender* (pp. 119–133). Newbury Park, CA: Sage.

Baca Zinn, M., & Dill, B. T. (1994). *Women of color in U.S. society*. Philadelphia: Temple University Press.

Bakhtin, M. M. (1981). *The dialogic imagination*. Austin, TX: University of Texas.

Baron, A. (1994). The making of a gendered working-class history. In A. Shapiro (Ed.), *Feminist revision history* (pp. 146–171). New Brunswick, NJ: Rutgers University Press.

Benyon, J. (1990) "A school for men": An ethnographic case study of routine violence in schooling. In S. Walker & L. Barton (Eds.), *Politics and the process of schooling* (pp. 191–217). Milton Keynes, UK: Open University Press.

Bloom, A. (1987). *The closing of the American mind.* New York: Simon and Schuster.

Bowles, S., & Gintis, H. (1976). *Schooling in capitalist America.* New York: Basic Books.

Brah, A., & Minhas, R. (1988). Structural racism or cultural difference: Schooling for Asian girls. In M. Woodhead & A. McGrath (Eds.), *Family, school and society* (pp. 215–222). London: Hodder and Stoughton.

Brantlinger, E. A. (1993). *The politics of social class in secondary school.* New York: Teachers College Press.

Brewer, R. M. (1993). Black women in poverty: Some comments on female-headed families. In A. M. Jaggar & P. S. Rothenberg (Eds.), *Feminist frameworks* (pp. 371–378). New York: McGraw-Hill.

Brittain, A., & Maynard, M. (1984). *Sexism, racism and oppression.* Oxford: Basil Blackwell.

Burawoy, M. (1991). *Ethnography unbound: Power and resistance in the modern metropolis.* Berkeley, CA: University of California Press.

Carrigan, T., Connell, R. W., & Lee, J. (1985). Towards a new sociology of masculinity. In H. Brod (Ed.), *The making of masculinities* (pp. 63–100). Boston: Allen and Unwin.

Carspecken, P. F. (1996). *Critical ethnography in educational research.* New York: Routledge.

Clark, R. M. (1983). *Family life and school achievement: Why poor black children succeed or fail.* Chicago: University of Chicago Press.

Coleman, J. S., et al. (1966). *Equality of educational opportunity.* Washington, DC: U.S. Government Printing office.

Collins, P. H. (1990). *Black feminist thought—knowledge, consciousness, and the politics of empowerment.* Boston: Unwin Hyman.

Collins, P. H. (1994). Shifting the center: Race, class, and the feminist theorizing about motherhood. In E. N. Glenn, G. Chang, & L. R. Forcey (Eds.), *Mothering—Ideology, experience, and agency* (pp. 45–65). New York: Routledge.

Collins, R. (1979). *The credential society.* New York: Academic.

Connell, R. W. (1987). *Gender and power.* Oxford: Polity Press.

Connell, R. W. (1993a). Cool guys, swots and wimps: The interplay of masculinity and education. In L. Angus (Ed.), *Education, inequality and social identity* (pp. 91–103). Bristol, PA: Falmer.

Connell, R. W. (1993b). Disruptions: Improper masculinities. In L. Weis & M. Fine (Eds.), *Beyond silenced voices* (pp. 191–208). Albany: State University of New York Press.

Connell. R. W., Ashenden, D. J., Kessler, S., & Dowsett, G. W. (1982). *Making the difference: Schools, families and social division.* Boston: Allen and Unwin.

Dill, B. T. (1988). Or mother's grief: Racial ethnic women and the maintenance of families. *Journal of Family History, 13,* 415–431.

Dill, B. T. (1989). Comments on William J. Wilson's The TRuly Disadvantaged: A limited proposal for social reform. *Journal of Socioligy and Social Welfare 16*(4), 69–75.

Dill, B. T., & Baca Zinn, M. (1990). *Race and gender: Re-visioning social relations.* Memphis, TN: Center for Research on Women.

Duneier, M. (1992). *Slim's table—Race, respectability, and masculinity.* Chicago: University of Chicago Press.

Everhart, R. B. (1983). Classroom management, student opposition and the labor process. In M. Apple & L. Weis (Eds.), *Ideology and practice in schooling* (pp. 169–192). Philadelphia: Temple University Press.

Fannon, F. (1967). *Black skins, white masks.* New York: Grove.

Farrell, E. (1994). *Self and school success: Voices and lore of inner city students.* Albany: State University of New York Press.

Femia, J. V. (1981). *Gramsci's political thought: Hegemony, consciousness and the revolutionary process.* New York: Oxford University Press.

Fine, M. (1991). *Framing dropouts.* Albany: State University of New York Press.

Fine, M. (1994). Dis-stancing and other stances: Negotiations of power inside feminist research. In A. Gitlin (Ed.), *Power and method: Political activism and educational research* (pp. 13–35). New York: Routledge.

Flax, J. (1987). Postmodernism and gender relations in feminist theory. *Signs, 12,* 621–643.

Fordham, S., & Ogbu, J. S. (1986). Black students' school success: Coping with the "burden of acting white." *The Urban Review, 18,* 176–206.

Fordham, S. (1996). *Blacked out: Dilemmas of race, identity, and success at Capital High.* Chicago: Univeristy of Chicago Press.

Frankenberg, R. (1993). *White women, race matters: The social construction of whiteness.* Minneapolis, MN: University of Minnesota Press.

Franklin, C. W. (1984). *The changing definition of masculinity.* New York: Plenum.

Franklin, C. W. (1991). The men's movement and the survival of African-American men in the '90s. *Changing Men, 21,* 20–21.

Franklin, C. W. (1992). Hey, home—yo, bro": Friendship among black men. In P. M. Nardi (Ed.), *Men's friendships* (pp. 201–214). Newbury Park, CA: Sage.

Freire, P. (1974). *Education for critical consciousness.* London: Sheed and Ward.

Freire, P. (1994). *Pedagogy of hope.* New York: Continuum.

Fuller, M. (1980). Black girls in a London comprehensive school. In R. Deem, *Schooling for women's work.* Boston: Routledge & Kegan Paul.

Gibbs, J. T.(1988). *Young, black, and male in America.* New York: Auburn House.

Gillborn, D. (1990). *"Race" ethnicity and education: Teaching and learning in multi-ethnic schools.* London: Unwin Hyman.

Gillborn, D. (1995). *Racism and anti-racism in real schools: Theory, policy, practice.* Philadelphia: Open University Press.

Gilligan, C., Lyons, N. P., & Hanmer, T. J. (1990). *Making connections—the real worlds of adolescent girls at Emma Willard School.* Cambridge, MA: Harvard University Press.

Giroux, H. (1983). Theories of reproduction and resistance in the new sociology of education. *Harvard Educational Review, 52,* 257–293.

Gitlin, A. (1994). *Power and method: Political activism and educational research.* New York: Routledge.

Glasgow, D. G. (1980). *The black underclass.* San Francisco: Jossey-Bass

Glenn, E. N. (1987). Racial, ethnic women's labor: The intersection of race, gender and class oppression. In C. Bose, R. Feldberg, & N. Sokoloff (Eds.), *Hidden aspects of women's work* (pp. 46–73). New York: Praeger.

Grant, C. (1988). The persistent significance of race in schooling. *The Elementary School Journal, 88,* 561–569.

Grant, L. (1984). Black females' "place" in desegregated classrooms. *Sociology of Education, 57*, 98–111.

Grant, L. (1992). Race and the schooling of young girls. In J. Wrigley (Ed.), *Education and gender equality* (pp. 91–113). Washington, DC: Falmer.

Grant, L. (1994). Helpers, enforcers, and go-betweens: Black females in elementary school classrooms. In M. Baca Zinn & B. T. Dill (Eds.), *Women of color in U.S. society* (pp. 43–64). Philadelphia: Temple University Press

Harding, S. (1987). *Feminism and methodology.* Bloomington, IN: Indiana University Press.

Hearn, J. (1987). *The gender of oppression.* New York: St. Martin's Press.

Hearn, J., & Collinson, D. L. (1994). Theorizing unities and differences between men and between masculinities. In H. Brod & M. Kaufman (Eds.), *Theorizing masculinities* (pp. 97–118). Newbury Park, CA: Sage.

Higginbotham, E. (1994). Black professional women: Job ceilings and employment sectors. In M. Baca Zinn & B. T. Dill (Eds.), *Women of color in U.S. society* (pp. 113–131). Philadelphia: Temple University Press.

Hirsch, E. D. (1987). *Cultural literacy.* New York: Houghton-Mifflin.

hooks, b. (1989). *Talking back: Thinking feminist, thinking black.* Boston: South End Press.

hooks, b. (1992). *Black looks—race and representation.* Boston: South End Press.

hooks, b. (1994). *Teaching to transgress.* New York: Routledge.

Hunter, A. G., & Davis, J. E. (1994). The hidden voices of black men: The meaning, structure, and complexity of manhood. *Journal of Black Studies, 25*, 20–40.

Jencks, C., et al. (1972). *Inequality.* New York: Harper and Row.

Karabel, J., & Halsey, A. H. (1977). Educational research: A review and interpretation. In J. Karabel & A. H. Halsey (Eds.), *Power and ideology in education* (pp. 1–85). New York: Oxford University Press.

Katz, M. B. (1993). *The "underclass" debate: Views from history.* Princeton, NJ: Princeton University Press.

Kessler, S., Ashenden, D. J., Connell, R. W., & Dowsett, G. W. (1985). Gender relations in secondary schooling. *Sociology of Education, 58*, 43–48.

Kimmel, M. S. (1987). *Changing men: New directions in research on men and masculinity.* Newbury Park, CA: Sage.

Kimmel, M. S., & Messner, M. A. (1992). *Men's lives.* New York: Macmillan.

Labaree, D. F. (1988). *Making of an American high school.* New Haven, CT: Yale University Press.

Ladd, J. (1994). *Out of the madness.* New York: Warner Books.

Ladson-Billings, G. (1994). *The dreamkeepers: Successful teachers of African-American children.* San Francisco: Jossey-Bass.

Langston, D. (1992). Tired of playing monopoly? In M. L. Andersen & P. H. Collins (Eds.), *Race, class and gender—an anthology* (pp. 110–120). Belmont, CA: Wadsworth.

Lareau, A. (1989). *Home advantage.* Philadelphia: Falmer.

Lather, P. (1991). *Getting smart.* New York: Routledge.

Lesko, N. (2000). *Masculinities at school.* Newbury Park, CA: Sage.

Lomotey, K. (1990). *Going to school: The African-American experience.* Albany: State University of New York Press.

Lorber, J. (1994). *Paradoxes of gender*. New Haven, CT: Yale University Press.

Mac an Ghaill, M. (1988). *Young, gifted and black*. Milton Keynes, UK: Open University Press.

Mac an Ghaill, M. (1991) Young, gifted and black: Methodological reflections of a teacher/researcher. In G. Walford (Ed.), *Doing educational research* (pp. 101–120). New York: Routledge.

Mac an Ghaill, M. (1993). Beyond the white norm: The use of qualitative methods in the study of black youths' schooling in England. In *Gender and ethnicity in schools: Ethnographic accounts* (pp. 145–165). New York: Routledge.

Mac an Ghaill, M. (1994a). The making of black English masculinities. In H. Brod & M. Kaufman (Eds.), *Theorizing masculinities* (pp. 183–199). Newbury Park, CA: Sage.

Mac an Ghaill, M. (1994b). *The making of men: Masculinities, sexualities and schooling*. Bristol, PA: Open University Press.

MacLeod, J. (1995). *Ain't no makin' it*. Boulder, CO: Westview Press.

Madhubuti, H. 1990). *Black men: Obsolete, single, dangerous?* Chicago: Third World Press.

Majors, R., & Billson, J. M. (1992). *Cool pose: The dilemmas of black manhood*. New York: Lexington Books.

Marable, M., & Mullings, L. (1994). The divided mind of black America: Race, ideology, and politics in the post-civil rights era. *Race and Class, 36*, 61-72.

Marshall, B. (1994). *Engendering modernity: Feminism, social theory and social change*. Boston: Northeastern University Press.

Massey, G. (1991). The flip side of teen mothers: A look at teen fathers. In B. P. Bowser (Ed.), *Black male adolescents: Parenting and education in community context* (pp. 117–128). Lanham, MD: University Press of America.

McCall, N. (1994). *Makes me wanna holler—A young black man in America*. New York: Random House.

McCarthy, C. (1994). After the canon: Knowledge and ideological representation in the multicultural discourse on curriculum reform. In C. McCarthy & W. Crichlow (Eds.), *Race identity and representation in education* (pp. 289–305). New York: Routledge.

McCarthy, C., & Apple, M. W. (1988). Race, class, and gender in American educational research: Toward a nonsynchronous parallelist position. In L. Weis (Ed.), *Class, race, and gender in American education* (pp. 9–39). Albany: State University of New York Press.

McLaren, P. (1989). *Life in schools: An introduction to critical pedagogy in the foundations of education*. White Plains, NY: Longman.

McNeil, L. M. (1986). *Contradictions of control: School structure and school knowledge*. Boston: Routledge & Kegan Paul.

McRobbie, A. (1991). *Feminism and youth culture: From "Jackie" to "Just Seventeen"*. Basingstoke, UK: MacMillan.

Measor, L. (1983). Gender and the sciences: Pupils' gender-based conceptions of school subjects. In M. Hammersley, & A. Hargreaves (Eds.), *Curriculum practice: Some sociological case studies* (pp. 171–191). New York: Falmer.

Messner, M. A. (1992). *Power at play—sport and the problem of masculinity*. Boston: Beacon.

Mickelson, R. A., & Smith, S. S. (1992). Education and the struggle against race, class and gender inequality. In M. L. Andersen & P. H. Collins (Eds.), *Race, class and gender—an anthology* (pp. 359–376). Belmont, CA: Wadsworth.

Mickelson, R. A., Smith, S. S., & Oliver, M. L. (1993). Breaking through the barriers: African American job candidates and the academic hiring process. In L. Weis & M. Fine (Eds.), *Beyond silenced voices* (pp. 9–24). Albany: State University of New York Press.

Mincy, R. B. (1994). *Nurturing young black males*. Washington, DC: Urban Institute Press.

Ng, R. (1994). Racism, sexism, and nation building in Canada. In C. McCarthy & W. Crichlow (Eds.), *Race identity and representation in education* (pp. 50–59). New York: Routledge.

Oakes, J. (1985). *Keeping track: How schools structure inequality*. New Haven, CT: Yale University Press.

Ogbu, J. U. (1988). Class stratification, racial stratification and schooling. In L. Weis (Ed.), *Class, race, and gender in American education*. Albany: State University of New York Press.

Ogbu, J. U. (1991). Minority coping responses and school experiences. *Journal of Psychohistory, 18*, 433–456.

Ogbu, J. U. (1992). Adaption to minority status and impact on school success. *Theory Into Practice, XXXI*, 287–295.

Oliver, W. (1988). Black males and social problems: Prevention through Afrocentric socialization. *Journal of Black Studies, 20*, 15–39.

Omi, M., & Winant, H. (1986). *Racial formation in the United States*. New York: Routledge.

Patton, J. M. (1981). The black male's struggle for an education. In L. E. Gray (Ed.), *Black men* (pp. 199–214). Beverly Hills, CA: Sage.

Peshkin, A. (1991). *The color of strangers, the color of friends*. Chicago: University of Chicago Press.

Roberts, G. W. (1994). Brother to brother—African-American modes of relating among men. *Journal of Black Studies, 24*, 379–390.

Sarup, M. (1991). *Education and the ideologies of racism*. Stoke-on-Trent, UK: Trentham Books.

Shor, I. (1992). *Empowering education*. Chicago: University of Chicago Press.

Sleeter, C. E. (1991). *Empowerment through multicultural education*. Albany: State University of New York Press.

Sleeter, C. E., & Grant, C. A. (1987). An analysis of multicultural education in the United States. *Harvard Educational Review, 57*, 421–444.

Sleeter, C. E., & Grant, C. A. (1988). A rationale for integrating race, gender and social class. In L. Weis (Ed.), *Class, race, and gender in American education* (pp. 144–160). Albany: State University of New York Press.

Smith, D. E. (1987). *The everyday world as problematic*. Boston: Northeastern University Press.

Solomon, P. (1992). *Black resistance in high school*. Albany: State University of New York Press.

Stack, C. B., & Burton, L. B. (1994). Kinscripts: Reflections on family, generation and culture. In E. N. Glenn, G. Chang, & L. R. Forcey (Eds.), *Mothering—Ideology, experience, and agency* (pp. 33–44). New York: Routledge.

Staples, B. (1994). *Parallel time: Growing up black and white*. New York: Pantheon.

Staples, R. (1973). *The black woman in America*. Chicago: Nelson-Hall.

Staples, R. (1982). *Black masculinity: The Black male's role in American society*. San Francisco: Black Scholar Press.

Staples, R. (1986). Black male sexuality. *Changing Men, 17*, 3–5.

Staples, R. (1987). Black male genocide: A final solution to the race problem in America. *Black Scholar, 18*, 2–11.

Stern, L. (1990). Conceptions of separation and connection in female adolescents. In C. Gilligan, N. P. Lyons, & T. J. Hanmer (Eds), *Making connections—The real worlds of adolescent girls at Emma Willard School* (pp. 73–87). Cambridge, MA: Harvard University Press.

Taylor, R. T. (1991). Poverty and adolescent black males: The subculture of disengagement. In P. B. Edleman & J. A. Ladner (Eds.), *Adolescence and poverty: Challenge for the 1990s* (pp. 139–162). Lanham, MD: Center for National Policy Press.

The black man is in terrible trouble. Whose problem is that? (1994, December 4). *New York Times*.

Thorne, B. (1993). *Gender play: Girls and boys in school*. New Brunswick, NJ: Rutgers University Press.

Torres, C. A. (1998). Interview with Michael Apple. In *Education, power, and personal biography: Dialogues with critical educators* (pp. 21–44). New York: Routledge.

Troyna, B., & Hatcher, R. (1992). *Racism in children's lives—a study of mainly-white primary schools*. London: Routledge.

Ward, J. V. (1990). Racial identity formation and transformation. In C. Gilligan, N. P. Lyons, & T. J. Hanmer (Eds.), *Making connections—the real worlds of adolescent girls at Emma Willard School* (pp. 215–232). Cambridge, MA: Harvard University Press.

Weiler, K. (1988). *Women teaching for change: Gender, class and power*. South Hadley, MA: Bergin and Garvey.

Weis, L. (1985). *Between two worlds*. Boston: Routledge & Kegan Paul.

Weis, L. (1988). *Class, race, and gender in American education*. Albany: State University of New York Press.

Weis. L. (1990). *Working class without work*. New York: Routledge.

West, C. (1993a). *Keeping faith*. New York: Routledge.

West, C. (1993b). *Prophetic reflections: Notes on race and power in America*. Monroe, ME: Common Courage Press.

West, C. (1993c). *Race matters*. Boston: Beacon.

West, C., & Zimmerman, D. H. (1991). Doing gender. In J. Lorber & S. A. Farrell (Eds.), *The social construction of gender* (pp. 13–37). Newbury Park, CA: Sage.

Westwood, S. (1990). Racism, black masculinity and the politics of space. In J. Hearn & D. Morgan (Eds.), *Men, masculinities and social theory* (pp. 55–71). Cambridge, MA: Unwin Hyman.

Willis, P. (1977). *Learning to labor*. New York: Columbia University Press.

Wilson, W. J. (1987). *The TRuly disadvantaged: The inner city, the underclass and social policy*. Chicago: University of Chicago Press.

Winant, H. (1994). *Racial conditions—politics, theory, comparisons*. Minneapolis: University of Minnesota Press.

Woods, D. (1978). *Biko*. New York: Henry Holt.

Author Index

Subject Index